PRINCES OF MONACO

1 Prince Rainier and Princess Grace with their children Prince
Albert and Princess Caroline.

PRINCES

OF

MONACO

The Remarkable History of the
Grimaldi Family

by

FRANÇOISE DE BERNARDY

Translated from the French by
LEN ORTZEN

ARTHUR BARKER LIMITED
20 NEW BOND STREET LONDON WI

MADE AND PRINTED IN GREAT BRITAIN BY
MORRISON AND GIBB LTD., LONDON AND EDINBURGH
27/5151

CONTENTS

ILLUSTRATIONS

PREFACE

Monaco io sono
Un scoglio
Del mio non ho
Quello d'altrui non toglio
Pur viver voglio.

Monaco I be
A rock in the sea
Nothing have I
Though from others I take not
Yet live would I.

FOLKLORE HAS SUMMED UP in five lines the problem that one of the smallest independent States in the world has triumphantly resolved throughout seven and a half centuries. But what the old jingle omits is that the Rock of Monaco juts out into the Mediterranean and protects a good safe harbour; and that, standing where the Alps come down to the sea, it guards the road between France and Italy. And this enchanting site has a good, equable climate, with the purest light in the world.

For many years Monaco lived from its harbour and the sea-tribute, and then from its fortress, a key-point angled for by the great Powers. Later, in a more ordered Europe, when the military importance of both harbour and fortress had disappeared, another rock, to the east of the harbour, provided prosperity and a greater, more brilliant future for the Principality.

Nature had prepared the setting for so much ingenuity and skill; but it was a race of bold and hardy men that steered the fortunes of the rocky territory, for thirty generations—the Grimaldis, Princes of Monaco.

PART ONE

THE SEIGNEURS OF MONACO
(1297–1662)

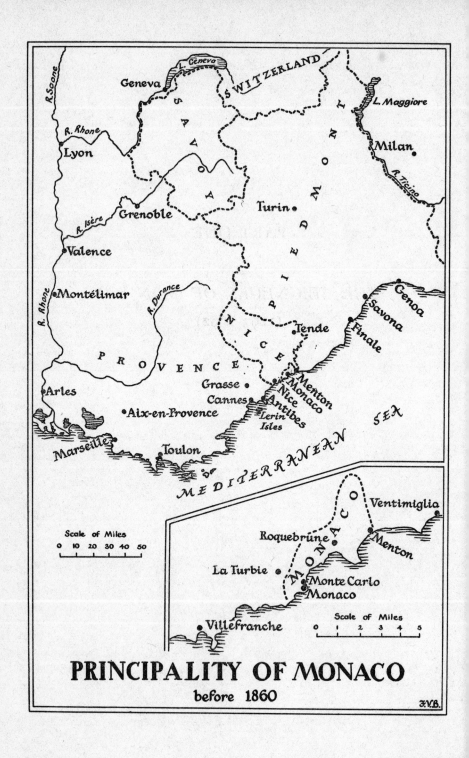

PRINCIPALITY OF MONACO
before 1860

CHAPTER I

THE GENOESE PERIOD (1297–1494)

A FINE, CALM JANUARY DAY by the Mediterranean was drawing to a close. Inside the castle of Monaco—a fortress with four towers and a thirty-seven-sided circumference of wall built eighty years earlier by Foulques de Castello—no ruffle of uneasiness disturbed the drowsy garrison of Genoese soldiers. Yet not long since, at the end of 1295, fighting had again broken out in Genoa between the Guelphs and the Ghibellines—the former, the party for the Pope, the other for the Holy Roman Emperor—and the defeated Guelphs had fled to take refuge in Provence. Charles II of Anjou, King of Naples and Count of Provence, although a supporter of the Guelphs because he owed allegiance to the Pope, favoured the Ghibellines when they were in the ascendancy. He had unavailingly ordered his Seneschal in Provence to disarm the Genoese Guelphs taking refuge there, among whom were the turbulent and astute Grimaldis. But these had found help and support at Nice and at La Turbie, just inland from Monaco, and had started to attack their enemies again by sea and by land too. . . .

Twilight had fallen and the dusk was now thickening around the fortress; the fires had burned out. Only a few men, half asleep, were on guard when someone knocked on the postern gate. It was a friar, a Franciscan, asking hospitality for the night. The soldiers let him in, paying no attention to the fact that his shod feet were in contradiction with his garb. Once inside, the man drew a sword from under his gown, killed the heavy-eyed soldiers and called to his waiting companions pressed silently along the castle wall.

And so, on January 8th, 1297, François Grimaldi, nicknamed the Spiteful, captured Monaco.

Although François the Spiteful is the first Grimaldi to be associated with Monaco, the head of the clan at that time was a certain
Rainier, his uncle after a fashion. These *Albergo dei Grimaldi*
were an eminent family. Made wealthy by sea-trading, its members
were often called upon to fill the highest posts in the Genoese
Republic. In times of peace from internal strife, Grimaldis were
Consuls or Ambassadors of the Republic; but they were always,
first and foremost, sailors.

Their first known ancestor, Otto Canella, was a Consul of
Genoa in 1133. When he died ten years later he left several sons;
the youngest, Grimaldo, who on three occasions between 1162
and 1184 was entrusted with consular missions, to the German
Emperor, Frederick I, to the Sultan of Morocco, and to the
Emperor of Constantinople, gave his name to the family. His
son Oberto also became prominent in the affairs of the Genoese
Republic, and Oberto's four sons were the founders of the chief
branches of the Grimaldis. It was the eldest of these, another
Grimaldo, who was Rainier's grandfather and the great-grandfather of François the Spiteful.

The Grimaldis and the Genoese Guelphs were unable to hold
Monaco for long, after François the Spiteful's seizure of the
fortress in 1297. By 1301 they were forced to abandon it to
the Seneschal of Provence, who restored it to Genoa where the
Ghibellines were still in power. One hundred and twenty years
were to pass, the space of three generations, before the Grimaldis
definitely recovered possession of the Rock, through the great-
grandsons of Rainier.

A portrait of this Rainier Grimaldi, who was born in 1267,
shows him in a coat of mail covered by a pointed doublet, and
wearing a rounded helmet. He has a long face with regular
features and fine dark eyes. He looks elegant, a man of breeding,
and very Italian.

A bold sailor too, he commanded ships in the service of
Charles II of Anjou and won distinction, although receiving
little reward. But word of his valour as a sea-captain must have
been given by Charles of Anjou to his nephew, the King of
France, Philip IV the Fair; for when the latter decided to intensify
his struggles against England and Flanders he called on the

services of Rainier Grimaldi, whom the loss of Monaco had left free for other enterprises.

The ancient quarrels over the English possessions in France were breaking out again; Philip IV had attempted to isolate Edward I by allying himself with the Scots, and his enemy had riposted by a military alliance with the rich weavers of Flanders, the chief buyers of English wool. This had caused the French Channel ports to lose almost all their sea-trade to the English and Flemish. A local incident, a fight between English and Norman seamen, sparked off hostilities.

In 1302 the Flemish militia heavily defeated the chivalry of France at Courtrai, at the Battle of the Golden Spurs, so called because 2,000 of them were lost by the French knights, according to some accounts. To avenge this disaster, and if possible to crush the Flemish fleet, Philip the Fair assembled a large sea-force and gave the command of it to Rainier Grimaldi. The Genoese had sixteen galleys with him, to which the King added twenty French ships, heavily built and poorly armed however. Grimaldi tried them out by attacking English ships, easier prey than Flemish, but not until the spring of 1304 was he able to launch a real offensive.

On July 14th, the French army supported by five Genoese galleys captured Gravelines. But Philip's ally, the Count of Holland and Hainaut, was besieged in Zierikzee, on one of the Zeeland islands, by 15,000 Flemings who were, moreover, expecting English reinforcements. It was urgent to get there first. Rainier set sail with a fleet of eleven galleys, eight Galician ships, and thirty Norman. At the mouth of the Meuse he landed the 10,000 men that William of Hainaut had raised to relieve his besieged father, and Rainier finally arrived off Zeeland in August.

He battled his way up the estuary of the Escaut, but it was obviously going to be a tough fight to take the sea-wall protecting Zierikzee, which gave cover to the besieging Flemish forces. He drew up his fleet in four lines of battle. Keeping the eleven Genoese galleys in reserve, he drove the first three lines of ships aground to form one great platform or landing-stage. There it was a matter of victory or death, as Rainier had ordered all the lifeboats to be removed. The Flemings sent down fireships, the wind turned them back, and then the ebb tide refloated the grounded ships. Towards midnight the French set two of their ships alight, and by the blaze Rainier saw that the Flemings were weakening. If he threw in his reserves, the enemy would be put to flight. Quickly, he alerted his Genoese. 'Launched like horses at the gallop, swept forward by the oars and lashed by the flood-tide, the galleys surged on.'

The enemy was routed, Courtrai avenged. Guy of Namur, the heir to the Flemish kingdom, was among the prisoners taken.

Without losing a moment, Rainier landed his victorious troops at Boulogne and hurried to the aid of the French king besieging Lille. A few days later the victory at Mons-en-Puelle was followed by the Peace of Athies.

The chief artisan of these successes had been Rainier Grimaldi. The only man of his race to command a French fleet and army in battle, he had led them to victory by his skill as a sailor, his courage as a fighter.

Philip the Fair showered honours and favours upon him. Rainier Grimaldi, Seigneur of Villeneuve in Normandy, and of Cagnes in Provence, Grand Admiral of France, died in 1314, the same year as the king he had served so brilliantly.

There came a lull in the wars between England and France; but the conflict between the Guelphs and Ghibellines in Genoa broke out again, the former gaining power in 1317 and thus recovering Monaco. They held it for ten years, then another siege caused the Rock to fall again into the hands of the Ghibellines, until the two parties became reconciled in 1331 through the intervention of King Robert of Naples, and the Ghibellines were allowed to return to Genoa. This brought Charles Grimaldi, Rainier's son and a loyal follower of King Robert, back to Monaco. He retained possession until his death in 1357. It was a peaceful possession, and enabled him to make the Rock the sea-base and fortress of the Guelphs; and enabled him, too, to take service under the Valois King of France, Philip VI, whose throne was being disputed by Edward III, a grandson on his mother's side of Philip the Fair.

On February 12th, 1338, Charles Grimaldi undertook to serve Philip VI with twenty-one armed ships. This force of over 8,000 Genoese should have sailed on May 1st, but it did not in fact leave the Gulf of Genoa until July 25th, 1338—too late to take part in the fighting that year. It seems likely that some under-hand business occurred, as the French naval historian, La Roncière, has written, and that English gold outweighed the agreement made with the French King.

However, during two successive autumn campaigns the Franco-Genoese sea-forces[1] held the mastery of the English Channel and ravaged the south coast. Southampton was twice captured and set on fire; unfortunate fishermen were taken prisoner and tortured. This plundering and cruelty was in part responsible for the fierceness of the siege and taking of Calais, eight years afterwards, which had been the lair of the Genoese. The skirmishes along the south coast had little military value either; it would have been more to the point to attempt an invasion of England while her fleet was detained in Flemish waters. In 1340 the French fleet was destroyed at the Battle of the Ecluse, and Edward III was able to prepare his invasion of France without fear of threat by sea.

Charles Grimaldi had not taken part in the Battle of the Ecluse. At the end of 1339 he was sent back to the Mediterranean, with Doria, to protect the French merchant shipping against pirates and in general to police the sea on behalf of the French King. What a peculiar idea of Philip's it was, to set wolves to guard sheep. . . . But that did not last long, and at the end of the winter of 1340–41 the King recalled his sea-captain. Charles Grimaldi showed up again in Normandy on March 1st, 1341, having passed through the Straits of Gibraltar in the worst of winter, a fine feat of seamanship and worthy of a son of Rainier, Grand Admiral of France.

For two whole years, from 1341 to 1343, Charles Grimaldi was fighting in Brittany, where French and English forces were sparring with each other prior to the decisive battle at Crécy. But the Genoese had not forgotten Monaco. During his absences the Rock had been entrusted to two relatives, Antoine and Gabriel Grimaldi, who called themselves seigneurs of Monaco too. With

---

[1] In addition to the ships and men of Charles Grimaldi, Philip VI had hired those of the Genoese Ghibelline, Antoine (Ayton) Doria. The hostile compatriots had sailed on different courses to reach the English Channel, and had been allotted different bases, Doria using Harfleur, Grimaldi using Calais.

a rigour that led to more than one complaint, they applied what was called the *droit de mer*, or sea-tribute, a levy of two per cent. on all goods carried by sea and passing within sight of the rocky fortress. Charles was looking after his personal interests as well as the family interests. Made wealthy by his subsidies from the French, in 1341 he purchased land at Monaco, Roquebrune, La Turbie, Eze, etc., owned by a Guelph named Spinola. These were to become the nucleus of the private domains of the princes of Monaco. Charles Grimaldi also acquired, in 1346, the seigniory of Menton and land at Roquebrune and Ventimiglia; and finally, in 1355, the seigneurial rights over Roquebrune held by the Count of Tende. Beside the private property, Monaco, Menton and Roquebrune were now closely united and the territory of the Grimaldis was taking shape.

Before these last transactions were effected—and perhaps to facilitate them—Charles Grimaldi had responded for a third time to a call from Philip VI, who wanted to use his military services again in the war with Edward III.

Though as skilful a sailor as his father, Charles Grimaldi was without the dashing valour which had taken Rainier to the head of the assault at Zierikzee. The ambition of the seigneur of Monaco was too keen and strong for his support of others not to be calculated, as was proved during 1346.

Towards the end of 1345 Philip VI began assembling 'a fine, large sea-force,' and sent a confidential messenger to Charles Grimaldi. The latter replied, in a letter from Monaco dated December 27th, that he would aid the King in his desires 'by God's help, with all that was in his power'—which meant, in effect, the promise of thirty-three ships and 7,000 Genoese crossbowmen.

The campaign of 1346 was due to open on April 16th, after Easter, but—to quote La Roncière, again judging the seigneur of Monaco severely—'they had to wait for the ships from Monaco, and waited four months, while the English forces had already put to sea.' Slackness or treachery? that historian asks. In any case, after having played truant and called in at the Balearics in response to the King of Majorca, Grimaldi had still not got beyond the mouth of the Tagus by July 5th. He dallied further to ravage the islands of Ré and Ouessant off the west coast of France, and it was mid-August when he at last sailed up the Seine to reach Rouen. When one considers that the galleys would be disarmed when the campaigning season ended, by traditional respect for the Church, on the eve of All Saints, October 31st, it becomes plain that the services of the seigneur of Monaco were shrewdly limited.

Yet the presence of the Genoese crossbowmen, hastily landed at Rouen, could well have thrown the balance in favour of the French forces at Crécy. But if Grimaldi perhaps lacked dash, Philip VI certainly lacked judgment. On August 26th, the King caught up with the retreating English army. It would have been wise to wait until the morrow, to let the foot soldiers have some rest, for they were tired out after a long forced march through the rain, which had moreover made the bows of the Genoese slack. But the King would have none of it, gave the order to attack there and then, and the disastrous defeat for the French followed.

Charles Grimaldi had not taken part in the battle, but had stayed with his ships at Rouen. The evening after Crécy, Philip VI ordered him to get them ready for sea again. It was a fortunate decision, for the English set siege to Calais on September 4th. Thirteen days later, Grimaldi at last made a fight, boarding and capturing twenty-five of the blockading ships. But it was a short-lived success, as six weeks afterwards the campaigning season came to an end.

Was Philip VI disappointed with the cautious nature of Grimaldi's contribution? Only the name of Doria is mentioned the following year.

Back on his Rock, where a township was growing in the shadow of the fortress, Grimaldi spent the last years of his life, as mentioned above, increasing the private domains and adding to the seigneurial possessions; hiring out, at the same time, the galleys of Monaco to the Knights Hospitaller of Rhodes, or to Jeanne, Queen of Naples, or again to the King of Majorca. He attended to administrative matters too, empowering the township of Monaco to have councillors and consuls, and allowing it tax privileges which were so popular and were later remembered with

such envy that, a century afterwards, the inhabitants petitioned
to have them restored 'as in the time of Charles Grimaldi.'

In short, the seigneur of Monaco had become in less than thirty
years the richest of the minor princes along the Riviera; and, it
would seem, one of the more securely established.

And yet a few months were enough for the whole edifice to
collapse. The Genoese Republic had never renounced its claims
to the Rock. It seized its opportunity when the French defeat
at Poitiers (where Charles's son, Rainier, had gone with 4,000
archers) deprived Grimaldi of any French support or protection;
when the Queen of Naples was unable, either, to send help to
her Monaco ally because her lieutenants in Provence were
occupied with a revolt in her fief of Les Baux. Twenty Genoese
galleys and 4,000 troops attacked Monaco by land and by sea.
Charles Grimaldi died in that spring of 1357, before the collapse
of all he had built up. After an energetic resistance the Grimaldis
capitulated on August 15th, receiving an indemnity of 20,000
florins for the fortifications added during the previous twenty-six
years. And so Rainier II left the Rock, never to set foot on it again.

The death of this second Rainier in 1407 marks the end of the
warring and sea-adventuring period of the Grimaldis of Monaco.
Almost continuously in the service of the lilies of France during
that time, the first three Grimaldis had used their Mediterranean
possessions as armed bases from which they set off on distant
expeditions that brought them renown and riches. In addition,
there were the proceeds of sea-excursions against the Catalans,
the Pisans and Venetians, hereditary enemies of Genoa as of
Naples; and, finally, the sea-tribute profited the ever-increasing
population that clung to the Rock.

During the following period, after a reign of transition, the
Grimaldis fell back on themselves more, as will be seen, and
looked to their title of seigneur of Monaco to provide the main
support of their new fortune. Maintaining the independence of
their seigniory became the major concern of their policy, and
reinforcing it the aim of their negotiations, their treaties and
alliances. After the heroic phase came the diplomatic.

The capture of Monaco by François the Spiteful in 1297, and

the return of Charles Grimaldi to the Rock in 1331, are precise, historical facts. But less clear is the manner in which the three sons of Rainier II, Ambroise, Antoine, and Jean, obtained from Queen Yolande of Aragón, the widow of Louis II of Anjou and Count of Provence, the restitution of Monaco after its conquest from the Genoese by the Angevins; the exact date of the Grimaldis' petition is not known, nor anything of the negotiations. In March, 1419, a pay account for the garrison at Monaco was supplied to the exchequer of Provence; but then on June 5th following, in the *chambre du Parement* at the castle of Monaco, the Grimaldi brothers conducted a ceremony enfeoffing land on the Cap d'Ail, and in the deed they were given the title of seigneurs of Monaco.

What was the aspect of the citadel of Monaco now that the Grimaldis had recovered their Rock—and recovered it for good? There were three main defence works: the old castle, the new one, and the fortified harbour.

The old castle, whose boundary walls had been built by Foulques de Castello in 1215, as already stated, was the main fortress. It dominated and commanded the gorge on the land side of the Rock, a gorge that still separates the little peninsula from the Tête-de-Chien mountain. But once across the gorge the rocky plateau could be easily taken, and so Castello's castle had been flanked by two towers joined by a high wall, the Albanaise tower and the Serravalle tower. The main lodge of the castle contained the ceremonial chamber, or *chambre du Parement*; though there was another building within the walls, called the small palace, or Il Parasetto.

The new castle had been begun during the thirteenth century, on the east side, above the place where ships accosted; but even with this supplementary defence, the weak point of the stronghold had still not been completely remedied.

Charles Grimaldi had erected a stretch of palings with wooden towers along the shore where ships could anchor in deep water, which constituted the harbour at that time. These palings went from the steep castle entrance, itself walled and flanked by towers, to the head of the peninsula, commanding access to the harbour, where there was a final fortification called the Spur.

. . . . .

A rule of the Grimaldis had always been to keep family inherit-
ances intact, so when the three sons of Rainier II regained possession of Monaco they did not think of establishing any other
régime than one of co-partnership or co-seigniory. Each brother
in turn governed and commanded the citadel for one year;
during this period of office he had absolute authority, and
neither of his two brothers could interfere in any way.

Two Florentine ambassadors learnt this to their cost. They
came to complain about Jean Grimaldi harrying ships of their
Republic that refused to pay sea-tribute to Monaco.

Michel Pagnini and Nicolo Calvanesi landed at Monaco on
this mission one fine spring day in 1421. They found only
Ambroise and Antoine, who declared they had no authority as
the citadel was being governed that year by their brother Jean,
then away at sea. The Florentines stayed on, waiting patiently.
Jean showed up eventually, but after a fruitless conference he
set sail again in the direction of Menton. The Florentines followed
him; they were about to board the galley of the seigneur of
Monaco when he had the ladder hauled in and steered for his
Rock. The ambassadors understood, and returned home.

Venturesome and often abrupt, endowed more for action than
for diplomacy, such does Jean Grimaldi appear by the light of
this incident. The youngest of the three sons of Rainier II, he
alone concerns this history, and on two counts: after 1427 he was
in sole charge of Monaco; and he was the only one to found a
family, whose descendants became Princes of Monaco. Moreover,
through his marriage to Pomelline Fregoso he was to become
involved for many years in the risky Genoese policy of his
cousin, the Doge Thomas Fregoso. Pomelline, a strong-minded
woman in a Biblical sense, boldly partnered her husband in his
enterprises, and then after his death pursued her own ambitions.

The Doge Fregoso had been forced to flee from Genoa when
the Duke of Milan, Philippe-Marie Visconti, obtained power in
the Republic and appointed a puppet government. Fregoso had
then formed a League with the Florentines, the Venetians, and
the Duke of Savoy (also Count of Nice, since 1388). The seigneur
of Monaco signed a treaty of alliance with them, on August 5th,
1424, which bound him to support their friends and to wage war

on their enemies. The League met with nothing but disaster. Before long, Milanese troops advanced along the Riviera; Ventimiglia fell to them, Menton and Roquebrune followed, and finally Monaco fell too. On October 6th, 1428, Jean Grimaldi relinquished the Rock to the Duke of Milan for 12,500 Genoese *livres*.

Visconti had promised the defeated seigneur that he would be received at the court of Milan with all due honour and respect for his rank, so Jean Grimaldi did not hesitate to put himself at the service of the Duke. Perhaps he hoped in this way to have his lost fief restored to him, with the Duke as his liege lord.

War broke out again between Milan and the allied Republics of Venice and Florence. Jean Grimaldi sprightly changed sides —a not surprising act in an Italy of the *condottiere*, the professional soldier who belonged to no country—and he was given command of the Milanese forces opposing the Venetian fleet which had succeeded in sailing up the Po as far as Cremona. By a clever manœuvre, Grimaldi cut the Venetian ships off from the north bank and the support of their army commanded by Carmagnola. Then, embarking some of the Milanese heavy infantry on his improvised flotilla, he launched an attack at dawn on May 23rd, 1431. The Venetian ships, built for sea-going, had difficulty in manœuvring in the river. They were boarded and captured by Milanese cuirassiers and Genoese sailors. This brilliant victory of Grimaldi's cost the Venetian Republic 2,500 killed and 8,000 prisoners, the loss of twenty-eight of the thirty-seven galleys, and more than forty troop-transports.

The Duke of Milan had every reason to show gratitude towards the dispossessed man who had served him so well. And when, in the autumn of 1435, another revolt in Genoa brought about the downfall of the puppet government and the return of Thomas Fregoso, the Duke decided to restore Monaco to Grimaldi, merely retaining his overlordship—which was soon to lapse under pressure of events.

One would have thought that Jean Grimaldi, now well past fifty, would have been satisfied at getting back his fief and remained there contentedly. But the adventurous spirit of the early Grimaldis pulsed in his veins. Perhaps, too, an instinct warned him that he would be the last of his race to be free to scour the Mediterranean—part of whose waters were to be closed less than twenty years later by the fall of Constantinople. Anyway, two years after his return to the family castle, Jean Grimaldi left Monaco in the hands of his wife, Pomelline, who was as capable as she was domineering, and accompanied Nicod de Menthon, the governor of Nice (with whom, however, he was on poor terms) on a queer, adventurous mission.

The Council of Basle had been trying, since 1431, to bring an end to the Great Schism and to promote radical reforms within the Church; but the Council had split on the question of whether its œcumenical authority was higher than that of the Pope, then Eugene IV. The opposing factions had both tried to gain an advantage by bringing the Greek Orthodox Church back to Rome, and each was conducting interminable negotiations with the Byzantine Emperor, Jean Paléologus, and the Greek Patriarch. The Pope and his supporters wanted the Synod for the reconciliation of the two Churches to be held at Florence or Ferrara; the opposing side wanted it held in Avignon, which was offering 70,000 gold florins for the privilege.

The Pope's opponents in the Council signed an agreement with Nicod de Menthon on November 4th, 1436, whereby the latter, in consideration of the sum of 30,000 ducats, would hold in readiness four galleys armed with 300 archers to go to Constantinople and bring back the Emperor and the Greek Church dignitaries. Almost another year passed before Nicod de Menthon, and with him Jean Grimaldi, received orders to leave. At last, on September 27th, 1437, the ships set sail.

But the Pope, having learnt their departure was imminent, had issued a Bull on September 18th proclaiming the holding of the Greco-Latin Synod at Ferrara, and had sent his nephew to Constantinople with galleys placed at his disposal by Venice, the Pope's birthplace. So when Menthon and Grimaldi arrived in the Bosphorus, having narrowly escaped capture by Provencal pirates drawn by the prospect of the 70,000 florins, they found they had been forestalled. The Emperor sent a courteous welcome, and on October 3rd, 1437, watched by the joyful Greek population, the galleys from the Riviera entered port, banners fluttering in the breeze and the standard of the Roman Church flying astern.

But it was an empty demonstration, for Jean Paléologus had already accepted the Pope's invitation.

Menthon and Grimaldi sailed away from the Golden Horn on November 1st. They encountered rough weather and were forced to seek shelter in the island of Chios, whose Genoese governor held them to ransom. After weeks of negotiation they were finally set free, and on December 15th Jean Grimaldi dropped anchor in the harbour of Monaco.

But it was impossible for him to stay put for long. The seigneur of Monaco obtained a safe-conduct almost at once and set off for Lombardy at the beginning of January, 1438. True, he was going to fetch his son, Catalan—to bring him back from a semi-captivity, perhaps, in which he was held by the Duke of Milan. In spite of the safe-conduct it was an imprudent journey to make, for Pomelline had concluded a treaty of alliance the previous July with the Republic of Genoa, which was once again governed by her cousin, Thomas Fregoso, the sworn enemy of Visconti.[1] Grimaldi paid for his carelessness—and not for the last time— by two years of trial and trouble.

The Duke of Milan had the two Grimaldis, father and son, thrown into prison. At the end of 1438 the Duke of Savoy took over the prisoners, hoping that with them in his power he could get Monaco ceded to him. Jean was taken under guard to La Turbie—his son being kept behind at Pignerol—as a means of trying to break down Pomelline's resistance. He, on his part, directed his wife not to give way to the demands of Savoy, even if he was put to death below the castle walls; and she greeted the Duke's envoys in such a manner and with so great a show of armed force that they hurriedly beat a retreat and went back over the mountains with their intractable prisoner. The two Grimaldis were held for another eighteen months, in the castle of Moncalieri, before being set free in September, 1440—on condition that they paid the costs of their detention, and without being any wiser over the reason for their release than they had been for their arrest.

[1] This was the first time a formal, written treaty had been made between Genoa and the Grimaldis. The Republic thus in fact disowned its rights over Monaco, which in any case had never been recognized by the Grimaldis.

During the next ten years, grown wiser with age or through imprisonment, Jean Grimaldi hardly ever left his Rock and its neighbourhood. Few months passed without his being uneasy for the fate of his stronghold, liable as he was to attack by agents of Savoy based in Nice, to the consequences of revolts in Genoa, and to the crafty policies of the Duke of Milan. Tired of so many difficulties, he ended by renouncing an independence which suddenly seemed too costly, for his only real resource—the sea-tribute—was constantly disputed. On December 19th, 1448, the seigneur of Monaco ceded the suzerainty of half Menton and the whole of Roquebrune to the Duke of Savoy against a perpetual annuity of 200 florins to be provided from the salt-tax in Nice.[1] Fear of trouble with Genoa had held back the Duke from accepting the suzerainty of Monaco as well. Jean Grimaldi offered this to the French Dauphin, the future Louis XI, who was negotiating with one of the Genoese parties for his recognition as overlord of that Republic.

Jean Grimaldi's negotiations with the Dauphin were still continuing when one more adventurous episode occurred in his tumultuous life, and almost at the end of it.

In the autumn of 1450 the seigneur of Monaco and his wife decided to go to Rome for the Jubilee. They expected to be warmly received by Pope Nicholas V, to whom the new Doge of Genoa, their son-in-law, Pierre Fregoso, had specially recommended them. In fact, as soon as Jean Grimaldi arrived in Rome he was thrown into prison. He had forgotten, in his often careless way, that a few weeks earlier his son, Catalan, had seized a ship carrying wine from Languedoc for Cardinal Pierre d'Aquilée. The greedy Roman prelate was one to bear grudges. Pierre Fregoso had to intervene to appease him. The seigneur of Monaco was set free at the end of December, 1450, and got back to his Rock soon afterwards.

He at once reopened his negotiations with the Dauphin. In the summer of 1451 he agreed to cede Monaco to France for 12,000 gold crowns—almost the same value as the amount the Duke of Milan had paid in 1428. Until the money was received,

[1] The almost continual default of this payment constituted the basis of refusal by the seigneurs of Monaco and Menton, three generations later, to recognize the suzerainty of the Dukes of Savoy.

Jean Grimaldi was to retain command of the stronghold and to fly the Dauphin's standard from his castle alongside his own. But the contract had still not been signed when Jean Grimaldi died, on May 8th, 1454.

On April 3rd, feeling his end approaching, Jean Grimaldi dictated his will and testament in the great room of the old castle; he took every precaution to ensure that Monaco should always remain in the possession of the Grimaldi family, for he had lost hope of concluding the deal with the Dauphin. There was reason for him to be concerned about the continuation of his line. His son had only one child, a young girl named Claudine, from the unhappy marriage with Blanche del Caretto, a daughter of the marquis of Finale. So it seemed likely that the Grimaldis of Monaco would die out; either the line would end with Claudine, or if she died young the inheritance would go to Bartholomée Grimaldi, the wife of Pierre Fregoso, or their children.

Jean Grimaldi made known his desire to be buried beside his parents and brothers in the church of St Michael at Menton; and then, after leaving some furniture to his wife, Pomelline, and also a house at Menton and some land above the harbour of Monaco but attached to La Turbie, he made his son Catalan his sole heir, and then Catalan's male children in order of birth. If there should be no male issue, girls would succeed on condition that their husbands and issue assumed the name and arms of Grimaldi; should no child of Catalan's survive him, the succession would go to his sister Bartholomée and her issue on the same condition. And in the final resort, the nearest relatives with the name of Grimaldi were to inherit, the Grimaldis of Antibes. It was this testament made by Jean Grimaldi, substantiated later by that of his son Catalan and then by those of Lambert and Claudine, which regulated the succession to Monaco throughout the next five centuries—down to the present day, in fact.

Catalan only survived his father by three years. Completely under the domination of his mother, Pomelline, and his brother-in-law, Fregoso, he tied Monaco to the foreign policies of Genoa, and so suffered repercussions from the Republic's struggles with Alphonso V, King of Aragón. On the other hand, when the

Duke of Calabria, acting for Charles VII, signed an alliance with the Genoese government on May 24th, 1456, the French King then guaranteed Catalan and his possessions against any aggression and formally acknowledged Monaco's right to sea-tribute.

Catalan did not live long enough to see the outcome of this French policy. He became very ill at the end of 1456, and died in July, 1457, not quite thirty-five.

As soon as he had felt his illness might be fatal, Catalan had in his turn made his testament, on January 4th, 1457, in the small palace within the old castle walls. A remarkable clause, which was indicative of the hold that the strong-minded mother had over the weak son, made Pomelline sole successor; and, after her, Claudine and then Bartholomée Fregoso on the same conditions as laid down by Jean Grimaldi. Catalan also designated a husband for Claudine, who was then six years old. He was Lambert Grimaldi of Antibes, co-seigneur of Menton, and Catalan's nearest male relative. But Catalan appointed Pomelline the child's guardian until her marriage, or if Pomelline died before then her place as guardian was to be taken by Pierre Fregoso. In short, though Catalan dared not contravene his father's testament, he at least gave an inordinate amount of power to his mother, and thereby created obvious difficulties for the future husband of Claudine.

Fortunately, although Claudine was of tender age, this husband-designate was no stripling. In 1457 Lambert Grimaldi was not far off forty. He was a younger son of a prominent family, and was possibly intended for the church at one time; he had studied hard at the University of Pavia—where his brother, Jean-André (later ambassador of Pope Sixtus IV in Denmark and in France), had read theology.

Though Lambert Grimaldi showed himself to be a vigorous military leader when occasion demanded—but never a sailor—he was essentially a studious man, calm and earnest, preferring a secluded life. Well-balanced and pious, he showed much prudence and resolution throughout the forty years of his rule. His keen sense of awareness often enabled him to anticipate and get on top of events. Though less spectacular than the hotheaded

Jean, shrewd Charles, or grand Rainier, he often displayed greater wisdom, and by his cleverness and tractability he completed the work of Claudine's forbears. Through his efforts, the *de facto* independence and sovereignty of Monaco came to be lawfully recognized by leading Powers—Savoy, France, Aragón.

Lambert found help and support for this prudent task among his own family. From his brothers to begin with; Jean-André, a shrewd diplomat who became Bishop of Grasse, and Louis, a brave soldier and a Knight of St John of Jerusalem. Other Grimaldis, of Genoa, Milan, and in Provence, aided the seigneur of Monaco 'as one man'—as the Duchess of Milan, Bonne de Savoie, was reputed to have said.

But first, as might have been expected, trouble soon arose between Lambert and Pomelline. Jean Grimaldi's widow had no thought of withdrawing to the house in Menton that he had wisely left to her, but showed every intention of remaining at Monaco and exercising the same powers as when her son was alive.

However, Catalan's testament lacked some validity by endeavouring to restrict Lambert; and by precluding the natural heiress in favour of her grandmother, a woman with no Grimaldi blood, it plainly violated the testament of Jean Grimaldi. Lambert, therefore, had a good case for asserting his rights, and was upheld by the inhabitants of each seigniory. On October 20th, 1457, barely four months after Catalan's death, an agreement was made that upset his clever dispositions. By this, Pomelline retained the administration of the seigneurial domains and their revenues 'just as in Catalan's time,' and in return undertook to treat Lambert as an adopted son and to share authority and command with him. She also promised to ratify the marriage clause and to ensure that the wedding between Claudine and this adopted son took place.

The ambitious woman had little intention of keeping such fine promises. Abetted by her son-in-law, Fregoso, and by Pierre Grimaldi, the seigneur of Beuil—to whom she promised the hand, and the dowry, of Claudine for his grandson, Georges—she plotted to have Lambert assassinated, in March, 1458. But, warned in time, Lambert escaped the hands of the hired assassins who landed in Monaco harbour; and, gathering supporters from

Menton and Roquebrune, he stormed into the castle of Monaco. He had himself recognized seigneur, by right of conquest and as controller of Claudine's entitlements, and received the oath of loyalty from the inhabitants of the three seigniories. Pomelline was banished to her house in Menton. Some years later, Lambert was to pay dearly for his sufferance.

For twenty years, until a treaty of alliance was concluded with Milan and an entente reached with Savoy, Lambert Grimaldi had to struggle against a crowd of enemies—the neighbouring seigneurs of Beuil and of Tende, the Bishop of Ventimiglia, and agents of Savoy—and he suffered from the effects of French policy when Louis XI abandoned the Genoese Republic to the Duke of Milan, François Sforza, in 1463. Then, although his marriage to Claudine took place in Ventimiglia in July, 1465, the following year Pomelline returned to the attack once more by raising Menton against her grandchildren. The revolt was soon put down; but two years later its exiled leaders captured the town by a surprise attack and called in Milanese troops. Nearly ten years were to pass before Lambert recovered Menton.

These were difficult times for the seigneur of Monaco, and only his prudence in remaining behind his castle walls as much as possible enabled him to avoid periods of captivity such as Jean Grimaldi had so carelessly risked; nevertheless, these years brought happiness to his private life. He and Claudine soon became a united couple, in spite of the thirty or so years separating them, and they had many children—fourteen in fact—the last being born almost at the end of Lambert's life. He also had the satisfaction of receiving letters patent from Louis XI, dated Bordeaux, 1462, that formally recognized Monaco's right to sea-tribute. They were, then, constructive as well as difficult years, and during them Lambert laid the foundations of the prosperity that flourished on the Rock in the last seventeen years of his rule.

The year 1477 marked a definite turn for Lambert: his patient tenacity at last brought its rewards.

At the end of 1476 Galéas-Marie Sforza was assassinated; and on March 16th following, Genoa rose against the Milanese, thus giving the signal for revolt to all the seigneurs along the Riviera.

2   Jean II, Seigneur of Monaco, 1494–1505.   *Portrait by Ambrogio de Predis.*

3   Prince Honoré II of Monaco, 1597–1662.   *Portrait by Philippe de Champaigne.*

4 Prince Antoine I of Monaco, 1661–1731. *Portrait by
Hyacinthe Rigaud.*

CHAPTER II

THE SWING FROM FRANCE TO SPAIN
(1494–1604)

JUST UNDER TWO CENTURIES the Grimaldis had made their hold
Monaco secure enough, and its autonomy assured, for neither
be seriously challenged again. But, faithfully reflecting the
lowing period when learning and the arts flourished while
s of the greatest cruelty were perpetrated, when Italian princes
soned each other, the English King had his wives beheaded,
French leaders waged civil war, and the Spanish Inquisition
rnt its prisoners at the stake, four seigneurs of Monaco were
die violently—while their little realm enjoyed a period of
accustomed calm, after enduring a final siege by Genoese forces.
At the same time the characteristics of the Grimaldis seem to
ve undergone a change. The Genoese ruggedness of Lambert
d already been tempered by gentle Provence; the Grimaldis no
ger scoured the seas. Those who followed after Lambert were
l soldiers, and courageous ones, but their main preoccupation
s to keep what they had, and for that they preferred the
lomat's pen to the warrior's sword. The sustained efforts
r two centuries had worn out the pioneering spirit of the
imaldis, as the tragic happenings of the early sixteenth century
re to do further; their heirs then led comparatively quiet lives,
hdrawn from outer contact, while the heavy patronizing hand
Spain extended over their Rock. It seems a somewhat dim and
omy period, yet inward strength was being gathered for a
h surge of vigour.

ean II Grimaldi, the successor to steady Lambert, was an
lligent and energetic young man of twenty-six, but with a
less and violent nature. His difficult character and rash under-
ings are reminiscent of his great-grandfather, the first Jean.
, supported by his wife, Antoinette de Savoie, and his mother,

On the 18th Lambert laid siege to Menton, helped in this by the
authorities governing the territory of Nice for Savoy, and after
nine days the town fell to him.

In return for the aid given by Savoy, Lambert had agreed to
acknowledge the suzerainty of the Duke over the five-twelfths
of Menton that he possessed in his own right. The feudal ceremony took place on April 21st; and so almost the whole of
Menton came under the domination of the House of Savoy, Jean
Grimaldi having enfeoffed his half in 1448, as previously mentioned. But such feudal links had a two-way pull: although later
Grimaldis were often to feel offended by this vassalage, at the
time it prevented any attempt by the Sforzas to retake Menton.

Having settled the question of Menton satisfactorily, Lambert
had then to calm the anger of Milan. This piece of diplomacy
was his master-stroke. Unable and in any case unwilling to
make concessions regarding Menton, the seigneur of Monaco
offered the Duchess of Milan certain advantages regarding the
Rock, but so formulated that its independence was once again
confirmed. A treaty of alliance was signed on July 14th, 1477.
It was valid for five years only, and was accompanied by an oath
of loyalty to the Duchess-Regent that Lambert gave, not as
seigneur of Monaco, but as a citizen of Genoa.

In less than six months of clever campaigning, Lambert had
therefore recovered Menton and established useful relations with
Savoy, by accepting the suzerainty of the Duchy, and had also
gained the favours of Milan with a treaty so skilfully worded
that it formally recognized the independence of Monaco.

Two years later Milan abandoned Genoa, where the revolt of
1477 had only been temporarily suppressed. Lambert then began
to look towards the French Court, to the monarch who, in 1481,
inherited the title of Count of Provence from the line of Angevin
kings of Naples whom the Grimaldis of Antibes and of Monaco
had served so constantly.

Before his relations with France had fully developed and led to
the signing of a treaty, Lambert—nearly seventy and with sons
almost of age—decided to have his situation properly legalized
regarding the seigniories that had been tacitly assigned to him
and that he had controlled for the past twenty-six years.

An act was drawn up by a lawyer of Nice, Pierre Nitard, on August 14th, 1483, whereby Claudine made over to her husband, fully and entirely, her seigniories of Monaco, Menton, and Roquebrune, but with the proviso that he must not part with them other than to the children of the marriage, and in order of birth.[1]

Negotiations for the treaty with France were held up by the death of Louis XI in 1483 and the subsequent revolts against the regency of Anne de Beaujeu; but during this time a marriage was arranged that drew the Grimaldis closer to the Valois Court. At the end of 1486, Lambert's eldest son, Jean, went to Tours to marry Antoinette de Savoie, a natural daughter of Philippe, Count of Bresse and governor of the Dauphiné. She had been brought up by her aunt Charlotte, Louis XI's wife, in company with her cousin, Anne de Beaujeu. The wedding took place early in 1487.

In the same year, Jean-André Grimaldi, Bishop of Grasse, whom Pope Sixtus IV had sent with holy relics to the dying Louis XI, was appointed by the new Pope, Innocent VIII, to help and advise the young French King, Charles VIII, during this troubled period of his reign. The Bishop's influence at the French Court was soon felt at Monaco. On March 2nd, 1488, Lambert was made a Chamberlain of Charles VIII; and less than a year later he received letters patent granting him royal protection and safe-conduct. The month following, on March 20th, 1489, the Duke of Savoy sent him similar letters. Although the Duke recalled that he had rights of suzerainty over Menton and Roquebrune, he affirmed the complete independence of Monaco, 'which acknowledges no overlord.'

A final success concluded Lambert's life-work. An agreement had been made between Genoa and Ferdinand V of Aragón and Castille concerning the marauding pirates in the Mediterranean, and Lambert consented to be party to it if the Spanish monarch signed a separate treaty of alliance with him. This first diplomatic act between Monaco and Spain was concluded at Valladolid on February 19th, 1494.

[1] In his testament dated October 30th, 1487, Lambert confirmed the order of inheritance decreed by Jean and Catalan. His eldest son, Jean, would succeed to the three seigniories. In the event of Jean's death without male issue, the other sons and their children would succeed, with the exception of those who had entered the Church. Should only females survive, they would have to marry a Grimaldi in order to inherit.

Hardly had Lambert learnt of its completion Menton, on March 15th, 1494. During the thirt his administration he had always put his trust i his shrewd diplomacy. He summarized this t phrase which was to become the device of the Ho *Deo juvante*—With God's help.

Claudine, and responsive to the guidance of his father-in-law, Philippe de Bresse (who became Duke of Savoy in 1496), it seemed likely that the new seigneur of Monaco would govern wisely and consolidate the work of his father by following in the wake of France.

The first years were in fact auspicious. When Charles VIII was forced to withdraw from Italy after his Neapolitan expedition, the seigneur of Monaco protected the retreat of the French army along the Riviera. This loyal action brought Jean honours and reward—the appointment of Captain-general of the Riviera, and the confirmation of Monaco's right to sea-tribute.

It also earned him the animosity of Ludovic Sforza who was then in league against the French King; and, like any good Renaissance prince, the Duke of Milan tried to have the young seigneur of Monaco assassinated. The accession of Louis XII and the fall from power of Sforza eliminated all danger from that direction. At the end of 1500 Jean received fresh favours from the French King, now also seigneur of Genoa and Duke of Milan, when he was appointed governor of Ventimiglia and had the right to sea-tribute confirmed once more.

But then the tide began to turn. Philippe de Bresse had died in 1497, and Jean's wife, Antoinette, passed away in 1500, leaving him only a young daughter, Marie. Deprived of their steadying influence, Jean gave way increasingly to his wild impulses. Justifiable complaints were soon made about his conduct of affairs at Ventimiglia, and he was soon engaged in a risky quarrel with Savoy, trying to disclaim the suzerainty of the young Duke on the grounds of the non-payment of the annuity of 200 florins promised to Jean I in 1448. Louis XII liked the seigneur of Monaco and his wild ways, and gave consent to the breaking-off of the feudal link; and Jean, with an escort of twenty-five gentlemen-at-arms dressed in grey damask, was in the French King's train when he made ceremonial entry into Genoa in 1502.

Nevertheless, the arrogance of Lambert's successor increased, and with it his difficulties at Ventimiglia and in Provence. 'See here,' he replied roughly to a trader from Marseille, Raphael Rostan, who had come to Monaco to complain about the sea-tribute, 'I'm not dependent on France, nor on Genoa, nor any other

State, Spain no more than the rest. Whoever wants to be friends with me, I'll be friends with him, otherwise I keep to myself.'

It was very likely the violent temper of Jean II that provoked his murder. Early in October, 1505, he was staying at Menton, in the chateau he had extended and made into a luxurious residence. His mother, Claudine, was there too, and Lucien Grimaldi, his younger brother and legal heir by Lambert's testament. What scene took place between them towards midnight on October 10th? It was never known with any certainty, but it ended in Lucien Grimaldi stabbing his brother with a dagger and killing him.

The murder of the seigneur could result in the confiscation of Roquebrune and Menton by Savoy, so Lucien Grimaldi sent his cousin, Peyron Grimaldi, to the Duke on October 15th with promises that homage would be made and with an account of the death of Jean II. 'And you will begin by informing him of the death of my brother, the seigneur of Monigues (Monaco),' read the cousin's instructions. 'And when the said Duke and Madame his wife desire to know the truth of his passing, you will tell them the truth, that when I remonstrated with him over the great wrong he was doing his brothers and sisters by planning dishonourably to sell this stronghold of Monigues to the Venetians, he did taunt me and struck at me with a knife, thereon in my defence I did draw my dagger upon him and so killed him.'

What reliance can be placed on this account, the only version of the tragic event that has come down to us, written not merely by the murderer but also the beneficiary of the crime?

It is difficult to believe that Jean had actually considered selling Monaco to the Venetians—no mention of such a project has ever come to light—but on the other hand it is quite possible to imagine a sudden quarrel breaking out between the two brothers, a quarrel that became more bitter the longer it went on. From what is known of their characters, Lucien's account then becomes plausible—that he, who was always restrained, kept his temper, but Jean was carried away by one of his insane rages.[1]

[1] Louis, the second son of Lambert and Claudine, was insane, and had been disinherited by his parents because of this.

36

Lucien's version is supported by the subsequent attitude of his family towards him. Although Claudine (who, according to tradition, was present at the murder) retained her affection for her first-born, and in her will asked to be buried in the church of St Nicholas at Menton beside 'her well-beloved son, Jean Grimaldi,' she made no objection to Lucien inheriting the three seigniories—for she could have revoked the deed making them over to Lambert, and reclaimed her rights. Moreover, she always showed a fondness for Lucien. In this she was followed by all the family, who never hesitated to back up Lucien and assist him whenever necessary.

At first, Lucien appeared to have no need of support. He was accepted in the three seigniories without any difficulty; and the Court of Savoy showed itself agreeably disposed towards him, perhaps satisfied at having a docile vassal at Monaco again. He was soon allowed to do homage for Menton and Roquebrune. His first disappointment came from France. Louis XII, as mentioned earlier, had always shown a liking for Jean II and had conferred favours upon him. Although the murdered man's brother-in-law, René de Savoie, Count of Tende, pleaded Lucien's cause, and was supported by Lucien's brother, Augustin, who had just been appointed Bishop of Grasse, the French King refused in no uncertain terms, on February 1st, 1506, to allow the new seigneur of Monaco to retain the command of Ventimiglia.

But political necessity soon caused the King to forget his antipathy, and Lucien the obduracy of the other. A popular revolt broke out in Genoa and, although no attack was made on the French there, the nobility was forced to flee. Among the more detested was the Grimaldi family. To seize the Rock of Monaco that had been outside Genoese suzerainty for many years seemed to the revolutionary government an undertaking that would satisfy its pride and its spite, as well as delivering Genoese sea-trade of a costly impediment.

As soon as Lucien received news of the revolt he realized its menace to him, and on July 21st, 1506, he sent Peyron Grimaldi to Louis XII with the mission of reminding the King of the loyalty of the seigneurs of Monaco to the French crown, asking for the King's protection, and requesting him to make known his wishes to Lucien, who 'would carry them out with every means in his small power.' Louis XII could not fail to realize either that the Genoese people, in revolt against their nobles now, would turn against the French next. So Lucien found himself back in the royal favour, and on November 28th, 1506, he was made a Chamberlain to the King, on the eve of a siege which was to be the longest in Monaco's history, and the last.

The Genoese had raised an impressive force—between twelve and fourteen thousand, composed of professional soldiers and armed peasants, and supported by artillery consisting of two heavy guns called 'Buffalo' and 'Lizard,' twenty-two medium guns and a number of smaller ones. This horde, encamped at Ventimiglia, was commanded by a couple of *condottieri*, Tarlatino Tarlatini and Gambacorta. But the revolutionary government did not have complete confidence in them, and four commissars—precursors of those in other revolutionary forces—were in charge of all material matters concerning the army. There was also a military engineer, Ambrosio Joardo, to direct the siege.

The invading army advanced from Ventimiglia on December 6th. It entered Menton without a fight, Roquebrune was taken and set on fire. The same evening the army reached the Spélugues (on which Monte Carlo stands today) and set up its camp. A herald called upon the fortress to surrender. Lucien refused, and a price of 3,000 gold crowns was set on his head. These preliminaries over, the siege began.

The garrison was small in number, being about six hundred; but they were well armed, and were soldiers prepared to fight for their seigneur and their homeland. Lucien had assembled a considerable amount of artillery—more than 300 cannon—and laid in a large stock of food. The ramparts built by Charles Grimaldi had all been strengthened. And, before long, the French governor of Savona, Yves d'Allègre, sent a force of six or seven hundred men to La Turbie, and this was able to maintain contact with the besieged most of the time, and to keep them supplied.

During the first few weeks the Genoese commanders, Tarlatini and Gambacorta, made little attempt to press the siege.

No doubt they thought this isolated fortress would fall to them easily enough, like a ripe fruit; and, as cautious *condottieri*, they considered there was no point in getting their men killed unnecessarily, in ruining their stock-in-trade. But Genoa became impatient, and at the end of January, 1507, the commanders had the heavy guns brought up, fired them day and night, and battered down eighty yards of the ramparts. The Monaco garrison prepared for the expected assault, but it did not come. Tarlatini and Gambacorta were weighing their money.

Genoa grew more impatient. The siege guns increased their destructive work. At the beginning of March the garrison's situation worsened. The enemy concentrated its guns on the west walls of the old castle, where—as explained earlier—the two towers, Albanaise and Serravalle, guarded the tongue of land joining the Rock to the slopes of the Tête-de-Chien mountain; this was the weak point of the fortress, its Achilles' heel. The walls crumbled and the gaps increased dangerously. Lucien had a defensive earthwork made behind the breach, and there he stood to meet the attack, positioning his remaining men as best he could.

On March 19th, 1507, harried by threatening orders from Genoa, and urged on by news of the approach of a French relief force commanded by the governor of Savona in person, the Genoese generals decided to launch an assault. Clambering up the escarpment under a rain of boiling oil, burning sulphur, and hot pitch, and a hail of arrows and of shot from arquebuses, the attackers succeeded in reaching the breach; for five hours a hand-to-hand struggle went on.

In the front rank of the defenders were Lucien Grimaldi, his brother Charles, his cousin Barthélemy, and the Frenchmen Arigois and Sainte-Colombe. Eventually, the attackers were forced to withdraw. Discouraged, and alarmed by the approach of Yves d'Allègre and his force, the Genoese began to enship their artillery, including the 'Buffalo' and 'Lizard,' the same night. The following night they burnt their huts, and on March 22nd began to retreat towards Ventimiglia. The Monaco garrison pursued them, recaptured Roquebrune and Menton, and joined up with the French force marching to their relief.

Lucien and his Rock had been in great danger. Never had the

Grimaldi sovereignty over it been put to such a severe test. The cool courage and determination of the seigneur and his family had preserved the inheritance; but the castle and domain had been badly damaged. (Repairs were still going on nearly a century later.) Another consequence was that the Grimaldi family, left prosperous by Lambert, was now impoverished, almost ruined. They had retained their territorial independence, but their financial independence was threatened.

Leaving his brother Augustin in command at Monaco, Lucien accompanied the French army to Genoa and attended Louis XII's entry into the city when it again capitulated. The siege of Monaco had, to be sure, brought the heroic defender into the limelight, and the French King warmly congratulated him. Yet was it altogether wise for attention to be thus drawn to the seigneur and his Rock?

Louis XII was thin and had a slight stoop, his face was bony with a long nose; he could not be called handsome, but he was elegant and refined. He had an Italian grandmother, a Visconti, and his mother was from the Rhineland, but he was distinctly French—as though his birth and childhood in Touraine, the garden of France, had had more effect than his heredity. In his youth he had been adventurous and lighthearted, but had grown wiser with the years although never becoming shrewd politically. Lucien Grimaldi, thin-lipped and with a slightly upturned nose, heavily built, thick dark hair falling over a neck like a bull's, was a wily Italian, headstrong and determined and no doubt more cunning because of his weak position. Ambitious, too, as any younger son whose future has for a long time seemed limited. With such differences, personal relations between the two men could not be expected to remove an antipathy. And then there was a ghostly figure between them—a spirited young man escorted by gentlemen in grey damask.

Diplomacy might have overcome personal feelings, but during the last few months Louis XII's counsellors had noted the importance of Monaco, of its harbour and fortress, in assuring the security of communications between Genoa and Provence. And, besides, its right to sea-tribute was decidedly expensive for others. In short, Lucien felt the atmosphere around him getting heavy, and near the end of the French King's stay in Genoa he thought it wise to ask for letters of safe-conduct for himself and his family. He was granted them on May 11th, 1507, three days before Louis XII left for Milan.

What were they worth? Past episodes in his family's history ought to have taught the seigneur of Monaco that they had no great value, and that the wisest thing was to return to his Rock. But throughout his life this spry, knowing man gave way at times to inexplicable rash urges. Sixteen years later one was to cost him his life. This time, it was only his freedom. Like Jean I in 1438, Lucien cast himself into the lion's mouth.

Having followed the French King to Milan—the reason is not known, perhaps it was in the hope of obtaining the subsidies promised him during the siege—Lucien at once met with the most pressing and threatening demands that he should sell Monaco, or at least acknowledge the King's suzerainty over it. With a quiet courage he pointed out that he was unable to relinquish rights which were entrusted to him only during his lifetime; and at the end of May, only a fortnight or so after receiving the letters of safe-conduct, Lucien found himself imprisoned in the castle at Milan, the same castle where his ancestor had been held captive seventy years previously.

Lucien was kept prisoner there for a whole year. Meanwhile, his brother Augustin steadily and tactfully negotiated for his release. By so doing, the Bishop of Grasse also spared Monaco another siege, by the French this time, and one which it could not have stood up to in its half-dismantled state. Eventually, in May, 1508, the seigneur of Monaco was set free against a ransom of 4,000 gold crowns and the undertaking to join the King in France.

On August 14th, 1508, before going off to what might be a semi-captivity, Lucien—more wary this time—disclaimed before a lawyer any transaction that might be extorted from him. Seven months passed before he got back to Monaco, in March, 1509, not quite the victor of an unequal struggle but at least almost unharmed.

The terms he had obtained were indeed much better than had been expected. The French King desisted from seizing the Rock, he even waived his demand for the suzerainty and homage. He was satisfied with an oath whereby Lucien, as seigneur, swore perpetual loyalty to the French crown, to be a friend to its allies, and a foe to its enemies. It was similar to the treaty of alliance that Lambert had made with the Duke of Milan in 1477, but was worded to be perpetually valid. On one particular point, however, Lucien had been obliged to give way: any protest by subjects of the French King against the paying of sea-tribute to Monaco would be examined and a decision given by the French Chancery. This was certainly a severe restriction of the sovereign rights of the seigneur of Monaco; nevertheless the principle was untouched, only its practice was subject to an interference that Lucien hoped to see disappear.

What could have been his feelings when back in his castle after two years of constraint, of almost harsh treatment at times? No document of the period supplies an answer, and Lucien had enough self-control not to display his grudges. But without delay he set about finding other support than from an indifferent Savoy or from a dangerous France. So it was that in the spring of 1511 Nicolas Machiavel arrived at Monaco to sign a commercial treaty with Lucien on behalf of the Florentine merchant-princes. A few months later, on October 6th, Ferdinand, King of Spain and of Naples, granted privileges to Lucien and his subjects permitting them to reside and trade in all the King's dominions. It was a valuable concession, and a significant one, too; for war had just been declared between the Spanish and the French, and this agreement was the equivalent of recognition of Monaco's neutrality. A foe to his enemies, Lucien had sworn to the French King; but what had been the value of the letters of safe-conduct in May, 1507?

There were no delusions about Lucien at the French Court, and efforts were made to assure the alliance of this seigneur whom unjust coercion had estranged. In response to a petition by Lucien, based on the fact that 'the seigniory of Monigues is held by the grace of God and the power of the sword alone,' and that its seigneurs had never owed allegiance 'to any sovereign king or prince, save God,' Louis XII granted letters patent dated February 20th, 1512, that declared the convention of March, 1509, to be null and void, recognized Monaco's right to sea-tribute and abolished the right of appeal to the French Chancery.

In return, Lucien had once again to make a friendly and perpetual alliance with the King of France. The latter, though, granted the seigneur of Monaco a pension of 500 *livres*, and agreed to maintain 200 *mortes-payes* (soldiers paid whether fighting or not) to garrison the Rock.[1]

Having gained this diplomatic victory and completely re-established his rights, Lucien became indifferent to the wars in Italy, and for the next ten years showed no ambition or interest outside his fiefs, and remained absorbed in his private affairs and the administration of his territories.

In 1514 two things happened of importance for the future of the Grimaldi dynasty. On May 23rd, Claudine made her last will and testament.[2] She named Lucien Grimaldi her sole heir, and went on to recall how, by his courage, prudence, and foresight, he had withstood the siege by the Genoese; and how, through his great qualities and skill, he had afterwards avoided, with God's help, the traps laid for him by his enemies. It would seem that Claudine, who had been present at the tragic happenings on the night of October 10th, 1505, wished in this way to record a solemn plea on behalf of the murderer; that, feeling her last hours approaching, she wanted to dispel the odious suspicions cast upon him which had injured his cause with Louis XII.

Claudine then stipulated, breaking faith with the accepted principle of succession, that Augustin was to become seigneur for life after his brother Lucien, even if the latter left male children. Her intention was to reward the Bishop of Grasse for all his endeavours. Perhaps, too, remembering the strife during her own minority, she wanted to spare Monaco the dangers of a regency.

If no male heirs of Lucien survived, his daughters were to succeed; next in line came Marie Grimaldi, Jean II's daughter, and then the daughters of Claudine and Lambert on condition—

[1] These letters patent were confirmed by François I on August 12th, 1515.

[2] Claudine had made a previous will dated August 20th, 1510, identical in essentials. But since that time she had lost two of her sons: Lambert, who had died at Blois in September, 1510, aged 18; and Charles, the valiant fighter with Lucien in the breach during the siege, who died in Rome a couple of years after young Lambert.

as already expressed in the testament of Jean I—that should any of their issue inherit they were to take the name and arms of Grimaldi.

Finally, Claudine forbade her descendants ever to transfer Monaco to any other Power, by cession or exchange or by any manner whatsoever; and if any future seigneur paid homage or took any oath of allegiance in the name of the fief, or placed it under any kind of servitude, the very act would lose him the inheritance and make him unfit to rule.

Claudine thus definitely established the rights and conditions of succession. Towards the end of 1515 she died at her house in Menton. But a few months after she had made her will, Lucien married Jeanne de Pontevès, on September 25th. And it was from this marriage that the seigneurs of Monaco were to descend, in the male line, for the next two hundred years and more.

While these family matters were being resolved, Lucien was also busy with the public administration. At a time when the major Powers were fighting in Italy, the seigneur of Monaco was giving much thought to the procedures of meting out justice in his territories, and was aiming at instituting a civil and penal code permitting cases to be dealt with more quickly and making the penalties less harsh. His Statutes of Menton, promulgated on May 27th, 1516, were the result of several years of study, and contained a number of innovations that testified to his progressive outlook.

The war between France and Spain broke out afresh at the end of 1521, and this time Lucien was unable to remain unaffected by it. However, his financial situation was precarious, to say the least. To the crippling cost of the siege and its damage had been added the provisions to be made for Marie Grimaldi's dowry—in 1515 she had been married to Jean de La Rovère—and for the generous legacies made by Claudine. The pension granted by the French was not always forthcoming, and the subsidy for the maintenance of the garrison had not been paid. But the capture of Genoa by the Imperial forces at the end of May, 1522, meant that the little ally of the French King was directly menaced in his isolated position on the Riviera. For once,

Lucien, who had so often shown qualities of self-control, seemed to give way to panic; he opened double negotiations, through his brother Augustin and through the Grimaldis of Genoa.[1] Ignoring what had been expressly forbidden in his mother's testament, the seigneur of Monaco offered to sell his Rock to François I or to exchange it for other territory. He had a similar offer made to the Republic of Genoa and to the Emperor Charles V. But each of these negotiations dragged on.

What would have been the final outcome? Any speculation is fruitless, for fate intervened before Lucien had to make a decision.

In June, 1522, soon after the occupation of Genoa by Imperial troops, a number of Genoese took refuge in Monaco. Among them was André Doria, a brilliant sea-captain with great ambitions who was ready to sell his services to the highest bidder. He was hesitating between the Valois King and the Hapsburg Emperor, and in order to maintain his freedom of choice and also the worth of his offer he had sailed into the harbour of Monaco with the four Genoese ships he commanded.

Doria was warmly welcomed by Lucien, and stayed for many months. While the seigneur was pursuing negotiations with François I and with Charles V, Doria was also negotiating with them; and was the first to conclude a deal, by accepting the offer from the French King.

During his stay at Monaco, Doria often met a young relative, Barthélemy Doria, seigneur of Dolceaqua, who was the son of Françoise Grimaldi, the eldest of Lucien's sisters. Barthélemy, who had ruined his health by loose living, had a weak and spiteful character. Although treated as an elder son at Monaco, he was greatly annoyed with Lucien, the executor of Françoise's will, for delaying (which the will directed) to put him in possession of his inheritance.

Doria was easily able to gain a strong influence over this

[1] The Genoa branch of the Grimaldis had always taken a great interest in the fortunes of Monaco, and frequently aided negotiations concerning the fortress. Its seigneurs, for their part, were grateful for this family support, which dated from the time when the Guelphs of Genoa had seized the fortress, and in their wills always ensured that the heritage should go to a Grimaldi. The influence of members of the Genoa branch in the affairs of Monaco was to increase during the sixteenth century; an influence altogether favourable to Spain, as the head of the branch, Ansaldo Grimaldi, was one of the bankers to the Emperor Charles V.

weakling, and a plot was formed between them to seize control of Monaco.

André Doria's motive is obvious. By capturing the Rock he would become master of an excellent and easily defensible sea-base, and be independent. For a seaman ready to make a deal with either France or Spain, and to change sides if offered more (as in fact he did a few years later), the temptation was irresistible. What drove Barthélemy is less clear. Malice, ambition, the desire to further the Dorias at the expense of the Grimaldis, the pressure on him of a stronger will, all contributed no doubt; enough, anyway, to lead this unbalanced creature to commit a crime.

The conspirators' plan depended entirely on the crews of Doria's ships taking and holding the fortress, so the date for putting it into effect could only be decided when the absent ships arrived back and were off Monaco. At the beginning of August, 1523, Doria was at the French Court, then at Lyon, and from there wrote to Barthélemy that 'the time had come to start on the project he knew about. . . .'

Barthélemy went to see his uncle and spun a tale about intending to go and join the French forces at Lyon, and asked Lucien to lodge at the castle a score of men, dependents of his, who had been banished from San Remo for a street affray, and who were going to Lyon with him. Lucien, with that surprising rashness which once before in Milan had cost him a year's liberty, agreed to give the men temporary shelter.

Having got his hirelings inside the walls, Barthélemy returned to Dolceaqua until August 22nd. Very early that day he left for Ventimiglia and there went aboard a brigantine come from Monaco to fetch him. Lucien was about to go to Mass when his nephew arrived. The young man declined to accompany him; and people present at the meal later in the morning were struck by his nervous manner.

It was now the middle of the day, and the favourable moment had come. Barthélemy knew the daily round of the people of Monaco and at the castle; most of them were either out at sea or in the fields. On the pretext of getting his uncle to write some letters of introduction to take to the French Court, Barthélemy led him along to a room at the end of the gallery on the first floor overlooking the sea; at the same time the major-domo was sent off with fourteen men to welcome the ships of André Doria, which had been sighted off the Cap d'Ail. Left alone with the conspirators, Lucien was set on and done to death. Forty-two dagger wounds, most of them mortal, were found on his body.

The first part of the plot had succeeded—the easiest part, as the seigneur of Monaco did not distrust his nephew. It now remained to signal to the ships, for the crews to land and be let through the gates. But Barthélemy's feeble mind then became completely confused. He had forgotten to send his men to occupy the loggia above the gallery, which led to the tower from which the signal was to be given; and a few of the castle retainers were holding the loggia, and so preventing access to the tower. The signal was given from another point, but was either not seen or was misunderstood; and the necessary diversion did not take place. Meanwhile the people had returned from their occupations; drawn by the shouts of the men in the loggia, they forced an entrance to the main courtyard, and discovered Lucien's corpse.

The plot had failed, and the assassins thought only of escaping with their lives. They had the murdered man's wife and children in their hands, and they threatened to kill them if they were not allowed free passage from the castle. The people of Monaco were obliged to let Barthélemy and his men get away to La Turbie.

Rarely can a conspiracy so cunningly laid have more wretchedly miscarried. Yet this odious crime affected the future of Monaco for the next hundred years.

It has often been said that truth is stranger than fiction. Who would have thought that on the very day Barthélemy assassinated his uncle, waited in vain for Doria's seamen to show up, and then fled to La Turbie, my lord Bishop of Grasse would suddenly decide to go to Monaco? And yet, after a peaceful sail on the calm blue waters of the Mediterranean in August, having met Doria's small fleet without being recognized, Augustin Grimaldi landed at the foot of the Rock just as the people of Monaco were beginning to discuss the terrible events. . . . The seigneur is dead, long live the seigneur! they could then have shouted.

By Claudine's testament, it will be remembered, Augustin was first in line to succeed, before Lucien's sons. But his was only a life-interest, as he made public. The people of the three towns took the oath of loyalty to him, but also to his two nephews, François and Charles-Honoré.[1]

What was this man like, who was now burdened with a heavy and unexpected task by his brother's death?

Augustin Grimaldi was forty at this time. He had been very intimate with Lucien—there was little more than a year's difference between them—and had helped him zealously since the tragic night of October 10th, and had shown himself to be a shrewd and hardy diplomat during the two difficult years after 1507. The peaceful period that had followed for Monaco had enabled him to concentrate on his proper sphere. He had begun to improve the buildings of the abbey on the Lérin islands just off the coast, and had ably administered his diocese, rarely leaving it except for journeys to Rome and to make a pilgrimage to the Holy Land. Pious, scholarly and cultured, he had attracted attention at the Concile of Latran in 1517, where he had met Cardinal Jules de Médici, later Pope Clement VII.

But although distinguished by his moral and intellectual qualities, Augustin Grimaldi lacked the force of character that Lambert and Lucien had always shown. He had a gentle, retiring nature, and little resolution; his policy was often to seem intricate when it was really only hesitant and susceptible to outside influences. Like all weak-willed people, he mistook obstinacy for firmness, and the former sometimes reached the point of obsession.

During the first year of his rule, influences and obsession combined to lead him to reverse the alliances of Monaco. The influences were those of the Grimaldis of Genoa, who were all for Spain; of the Duke of Bourbon, who had turned traitor and gone over to the Emperor Charles V; and of Pope Clement VII, whose hostility to François I was notorious.[2] The obsession was

[1] François died soon afterwards. But Charles-Honoré, later Honoré I, received the same oath of loyalty on three future occasions.

[2] In February, 1524, soon after his election, the Pope sent a Bull to the Seigneur-Bishop granting certain dispensations and adding that in temporal matters 'the seigniory of Monaco knew no overlord.'

to avenge his brother and have the murderer's possessions as forfeit.

Both François I and the Duke of Savoy were willing for Barthélemy to be punished, and issued orders to that effect. But the protection of André Doria, himself supported by Louise de Savoie, was apparently sufficiently powerful to prevent either the royal or the ducal orders from being carried out. Much to Augustin's indignation, Barthélemy remained unmolested at the French army headquarters in Italy.[1]

In odd contrast to this lack of justice was the support given from Genoa to enable Augustin to capture the assassin's possessions—the fiefs of Dolceaqua, Apricale, Isolabona, and Perinaldo, whose inhabitants came to take the oath of loyalty to the seigneur of Monaco on November 3rd, 1523. By Genoa is meant not only the Grimaldis, Ansaldo and Nicolas, but the Duke of Bourbon too, who was there at the head of an Imperial army and preparing his invasion of Provence. . . . As a means of drawing Augustin into the Imperial alliance they held out to him the glittering prospect of having these recent conquests consolidated by the assent of the Emperor Charles V.

During the early part of 1524 Augustin remained confused and undecided. Although the French under Bonnivet were defeated in March, he continued to waver, sending Leonard Grimaldi to Spain as his plenipotentiary while still keeping open his negotiations with France. Then an event occurred which caused this hesitant man to make up his mind: André Doria's ships, flying the French flag, came and bombarded Menton for two hours (Augustin narrowly escaped being struck by a cannonball), and the seigneur was unable to obtain amends for the affront. It was too much to stand. He gave permission for the Duke of Bourbon to use Monaco as a supply base for the invasion of Provence, and at the same time he sent instructions for his envoy in Spain to sign a treaty.

On June 7th, 1524, at Burgos, Leonard Grimaldi signed the convention by which the seigneur of Monaco became a vassal of the Emperor Charles V. In return, the latter undertook to protect

---

[1] Barthélemy Doria met his death in 1525 or 1526 while attacking the castle of Penna, which was then in Augustin's charge.

his vassal, and to maintain and pay 200 soldiers to garrison Monaco in time of war. The Emperor also promised to compensate Augustin for the certain loss of his church benefices in France, and especially to invest him with the seigniory of Dolceaqua.

By this agreement the seigneur of Monaco broke the long allegiance of the Grimaldis to the lilies of France; but this date, June 7th, 1524, had yet another significance, for it was the day that cannons brought from Naples were landed at Monaco. A fresh page had opened in the history of the Rock. For more than two hundred years the strength of the Grimaldis had resided in their harbour and their fighting ships. But the presence of the fleets of two great rival Powers, France and Spain, who were struggling over Italy, put an end to the importance of the few Monaco ships (the last of this small navy disappeared in 1569). If the seigneur of the Rock were to survive as such, and not be absorbed as Provence had been by France, as Naples and Genoa had just been by Spain, he had to base his strength on some new argument.

The cannons were set in position, and the fortress became a key position on the road to Italy, barring the way to the armies advancing towards or retreating from the peninsula. Henceforth, the sea was to matter little for the descendants of Grand Admiral Rainier, and three and a half centuries were to pass before another sailor appeared among them. Instead, the Rock and its ramparts became their sanctuary; they felt assured only within their walls, and for many years did not, dared not, go far beyond them.

When Augustin learnt the exact terms of the treaty with Spain he was greatly surprised. The formal abandon of his complete independence shocked him; the clause agreeing to pay for the garrison only in wartime worried him; and the order he received to pay homage to the Emperor without delay, and to be invested with the fiefs, displeased him. In short, he began to regret his decision. However, he dare not break the treaty. How could he, with Imperial forces in the town and the Neapolitan fleet in the harbour? The unhappy seigneur could only protest to the over-greedy protector.

The Emperor accepted his objections with a good grace, and wrote to him from Valladolid in September, 1524, that he was sending an envoy to revise the treaty 'in such manner to make you well content.' Possibly the fact that the Imperial army had been defeated in front of Marseille and was in full retreat back to Lombardy, while the Neapolitan fleet was taking its artillery aboard and preparing to sail, is sufficient explanation of the Emperor's complaisance.

In any case, at Tordesillas on November 5th, the Emperor ratified the Burgos treaty but deleted the clause making Augustin his vassal, and instead formally acknowledged the independence of Monaco. In addition, he granted Augustin a pension of 2,000 crowns from the revenues of his Kingdom of Naples, with the authorization to claim duty-free wheat up to that value in order to make sure of the pension.

Five months went by before Augustin decided in his turn to ratify the treaty. This he did on April 10th, 1525, six weeks after the French defeat at Pavia. Still under the influence of the Duke of Bourbon, he no doubt thought himself definitely on the winning side.

The terms of the new alliance were not so favourable to Monaco as those obtained in the past from France, for the subsidies were now payable only in time of war. Once Augustin's desire for vengeance had been appeased by obtaining possession of Dolceaqua and by the death of Barthélemy, it was essential for Spain to keep punctually to the commitments of the treaty if Augustin was not to regret a decision which was contrary to his instincts and upbringing, to his father's advice in the past, and to his own interests. But it soon became apparent that regular payments by the Spaniards were even more hypothetical than those by the French had been; and Augustin's financial situation was rapidly becoming acute, what with the worth of the sea-tribute reduced to nothing by the war, and with his seigniory impoverished ever since the siege. When the League of Cognac was formed in May, 1526, and France, Venice, Milan, Florence, and the Pope, joined forces against the Emperor Charles V, the perils of war were added to Augustin's financial worries.

The Emperor sent his little ally letters of safe-conduct and protection, but the subsidies remained unpaid, and the negligence or bad faith of Spanish agents in Sicily and Naples held up the shipments of wheat. Augustin and his Rock were threatened by land by French-dominated Savoy, and by sea by André Doria, now governing Savona. The death of the Duke of Bourbon at the sack of Rome in May, 1527, followed by the recapture of Genoa by the French, and of Dolceaqua by Doria, shook Augustin and made him lose heart. He opened negotiations with Lautrec, the French army commander, for a return of Monaco to the French alliance. But these were still going on when Lautrec was killed at the siege of Naples; and with André Doria going over to the Spanish cause and retaking Genoa from the French, in September, 1528, Augustin gave up his attempts to break from Spain.

Formerly he had been obsessed by the urge to avenge his brother; now it was to unburden himself of a responsibility too heavy for his scholarly, priestly shoulders. By a curious chance, Augustin chose just the moment when André Doria was in command of Genoa for proposing to sell Monaco to the Republic, or at least to make an exchange for Ventimiglia. Nothing could be expected to come of it, and nothing did.

However, after the drawbacks and troubles during 1527 and 1528, the following year brought both material and moral satisfaction to the seigneur of Monaco.

On July 14th, 1529, he and Eustaccio Capucio, a representative of the Emperor Charles V, signed an agreement which settled the payments that were five years in arrears, and replaced the subsidies payable only in time of war with the grant of a marquisate in the Kingdom of Naples that carried a revenue of 5,000 crowns. Shortly afterwards, on August 3rd, the Treaty of Cambrai brought the war between France and Spain to an end for a time; and Augustin recovered his benefices of Grasse and the Lérin islands.

Then the Emperor showed how great was his confidence in his ally by landing at Monaco, on August 5th, on his way to Italy for his coronation at Bologna, and being accompanied during his stay by only six halberdiers, six trumpeters, and a single Duke. This small escort was not only flattering to Augustin but also meant that he avoided meeting André Doria, by then a Grand Admiral of Spain.

But his satisfaction did not last very long. Less than two years later he found himself faced with much the same difficulties as before. In addition, Augustin was eager for a cardinal's hat, but discovered with some bitterness that the Spanish faction, headed by Cardinal Doria, was hostile to his advancement—while the French cardinals would have supported and facilitated it. Pressed increasingly by his sister Blanche, who had married the Provençal seigneur of Tourettes, and also by the Grimaldis of Antibes, the Count of Tende, and by Claude of Savoy, Augustin agreed to return to the traditional foreign policy of his family.

He was waiting for the Emperor to return to Spain, in order to put his intention into effect, when death overtook him, on April 14th, 1532. A sudden death, so propitious for the Genoees party that it is difficult not to suspect he was poisoned.

With him disappeared the last of the sons of Lambert and Claudine. Like his two elder brothers, he died a violent death; but like them, too, in spite of a vacillating mind that led him into confused, alternating negotiations, he transmitted the heritage of the Grimaldis of Monaco intact to his successor.

This successor, Honoré I, was ten years of age, and he was to reign for half a century. But for most of this period he was dominated by a forceful personality, Etienne the Gubernant, not a Grimaldi of Monaco but a member of the Genoa branch. Like Lambert before him, and the Chevalier de Grimaldi two centuries later, this man of forty, ascetic, authoritative, and reserved, obtained power and with the support of the population of the three seigniories held it until the end of his lifetime.

Young Honoré's legitimate guardian was his aunt, Blanche Grimaldi; but the Genoese party appealed to Nicolas and Ansaldo Grimaldi, who sent the former's brother, Etienne, to represent them. He reached Monaco in May, 1532. Less than two years later he was in control, having first thrown off Blanche and the partisans of a French alliance and then, although himself a strong hispanophil, got rid of the Spanish representative, Valenzuela, whose supervision was a hindrance to Etienne's independence.

Then he began to rule. At a general assembly held on April 6th, 1534, not only was he proclaimed guardian of Honoré until the boy reached the age of twenty-five, but with the same rights over his ward during that time as if he were Honoré's father. This was the first step towards the astonishing piece of fiction whereby, six years afterwards, on December 6th, 1540—again with the people's approval—Etienne became Honoré's adopted father, and so made sure of always keeping power in his hands.

During those six years everything had indeed gone as the man from Genoa wished. He had given Monaco a life of its own, having managed to throw off practically all the bonds and resisted the pressure of foreign Powers, whether applied directly or indirectly.[1] Although he had no intention of returning to the French alliance, he gradually loosened the Spanish hold until the protectorate was little more than nominal. The Spanish government then reduced its obligations to the strict minimum, but as they had never been properly kept this was small loss when compared to the autonomy that Etienne had gained.

His subjects therefore had reason for being satisfied, and to be happy for him to continue to govern. But it is much less apparent why Honoré I, who was determined as a child, should have accepted with genuine indifference this legal fiction that divested him of his full inheritance.

No doubt the young seigneur had a real affection for his adopted father.[2] Moreover, with the three previous seigneurs having died assassinated, it would have been sinister for the one remaining offspring to succeed to power. Honoré must have been fearful at times, not so much for himself as for his line. . . . One day some years later, after Etienne the Gubernant had married his ward to his niece, Isabelle Grimaldi, the ambassador of Charles V to the French Court was asking an envoy from Monaco, a certain Antonio Raymondo, about the little ally of

---

[1] So prudent was Etienne that in 1536, when the Imperial army commanded by Charles V in person passed through the neighbourhood of Monaco on its way to invade Provence once again, the Gubernant made no move to go and greet the Emperor. He declared that he had sworn never to leave Monaco during the minority of his ward, and he merely sent his doctor to attend Charles V when at St Laurent-du-Var. Two years later he refused to welcome the Emperor to Monaco, and the latter had to set up quarters at Villefranche, a few miles to the west.

[2] A material sign of this affection is the fact that the seal bearing the names of the seigneur and of the Gubernant continued to be used, after the death of the latter and for the remainder of Honoré's lifetime, on the deeds and documents drawn up by the Chancery of Monaco.

the Emperor whose name he hardly knew; and Raymondo gave this description of how Honoré passed his time: 'The seigneur of Monaco occasionally goes out beyond the fortress, but only with a heavy escort. His tastes are such as to keep him within— literature, fencing, games like tennis and other honest pastimes are enough for him. Moreover, with a beautiful young wife, kind and intelligent, he feels no need to seek other pleasures outside.' The ambassador expressed surprise at Honoré not having yet appeared at the Emperor's Court, and Raymondo added that his seigneur would no doubt make it his duty, but was not thinking of going afield until sons had been born to him.

What developments had occurred, by the middle of the sixteenth century, on this Rock where Honoré Grimaldi was so prudently marking time?

On one hand, civil administration had by then been organized in the form it was to remain until the end of the eighteenth century and the upheaval caused by the French Revolution. On the other, the military defences had been strengthened, and the castle was being transformed into a palace (which, a century later, Honoré II improved and converted to give it the aspect it retains at the present day).

After the return of the Grimaldis in 1419, the castellán or keeper of one of the castles, usually the new castle, had gradually combined civil functions with his military duties. He had administrative and judicial powers, and was given the title of *podestà*. Appeals against the findings and sentences of the *podestà*, whether of Monaco, Menton, or Roquebrune, were brought before the seigneur common to the three places.

During the rule of Augustin Grimaldi, the need for centralization felt by most of the great Powers, France in particular, had begun to affect Monaco and the two other seigniories. The office of magistrate was then created, with wide powers. The holder was a kind of duplication of the seigneur; his jurisdiction, too, spread over the three seigniories, and he controlled the administration of the three townships. He was given the title of *baile* or *baile général*—a Provençal term—by Augustin, and this was changed to auditor-general by Etienne the Gubernant. In addition, there was an *avocat fiscal*—a kind of fraud-prevention officer—whose special duty was to enforce the payment of taxes and tolls (the sea-tribute in particular), and generally to protect the seigneur's financial interests and prerogatives.

As the administrative machinery of the Grimaldis developed so had the local government of the commune, the township. Originally a separate institution, since the freedoms granted by Charles I in the fourteenth century it had always continued in close co-operation with the seigneur of the Rock.

The township was represented by four *syndics* who were assisted by a council of twelve. All were elected annually, at Michaelmas, at a general assembly of townspeople. On several occasions the *syndics* and councillors played an important part when matters were grave for their seigneur. Notably in 1457, at the time of the agreement between Lambert and Pomelline; and after the death of Lucien, when the guardianship of Honoré I had to be arranged. And it was the township that, through its general assembly, confirmed the powers of Etienne the Gubernant on three different occasions. This protective rôle towards the Grimaldi dynasty was to be played a last time in 1604, after the death of Hercule I; and then, by an evolution similar to that occurring in France, where the States-General were never again summoned after 1614, the general assembly of Monaco was later eclipsed by a centralized power whose grip remained firm.

Monaco township had not changed much since the fourteenth century. It still consisted of just three parallel streets running along the rocky plateau and ending, by the old castle, in a square about eighty yards wide.[1] But since the siege of 1506 the fortress had continued to be strengthened. The side dominating La Condamine—the harbour front—had been given a second line of defence, and a new stretch of ramparts protected the access up from the harbour. Outposts had been built, and a system of trenches led to the advanced positions. The Emperor Charles V inspected these defence works during his stay in 1529.

On the landward side of the peninsula, where it was most vulnerable, Etienne completed the defences with two large bastions joined by a high curtain wall. And to be sure of a supply of water, in the event of another siege, a great tank to hold

[1] It is still the same today.

56

nearly 400,000 gallons was built in the middle of Foulques de Castello's old castle, beneath what is today the main courtyard of the palace.

Etienne then turned to improving the appearance and comfort of the castle, a matter to which the Grimaldis of Monaco—seafarers and warriors, and often impoverished—had given little thought. Etienne had brought ostentatious habits and artistic tastes with him from Genoa, and he tried to give some kind of architectural harmony to the jumbled mass of buildings that had grown up over the years.

To this end, he built a one-storey gallery of twelve arcades in the courtyard, to screen the wall of the living quarters; a straight staircase gave access to the upper gallery, which was ornamented with a white marble balustrade. (In the next century, this gallery was named after Hercule, the son of Honoré II.) The need to increase the number of rooms for the household led to use being made of a large terrace on the other side of the courtyard. A wing was added there; and over the arcades in front of the vaulted rooms a new façade was constructed—on which Luca Cambiaso painted frescoes during the years 1575 to 1580. The courtyard was then much as it is seen today, except that the Serravalle tower and its rampart were still visible on the north-west.

Etienne the Gubernant died in June, 1561. Honoré then became sole master of the seigniory, thirty-eight years after the death of his father and when he himself was almost forty. The fiction of Etienne's adoption still held; Honoré was the sole heir of the Genoese and succeeded him in effect, the population of the three townships taking an oath of loyalty to him for the fourth time.[1]

Honoré's rule was a continuance of Etienne's in every respect. Monaco's relations with the Spanish government were a monotonous repetition of the same protests and efforts to get its Chancery to keep to its obligations. These demands were always well received and were always without effect. In spite of these repeated vexations Honoré remained faithful to the Spanish protectorate, just as he kept to his sedentary habits. When he

[1] The first time had been in 1523, after the death of Lucien; the second, after that of Augustin, in 1532; and the third at the time of the adoption, in 1540.

died on October 7th, 1581, it is doubtful if he had been outside his seigniories in the last fifty years.

His eldest son, Charles II, succeeded him. Little is now known of this young man, then twenty-six, apart from his physical aspect. A picture in the palace of Monaco shows him as a tall, handsome man with a vigorous build, and very Italian with his almond eyes and thin brown moustache. It would seem, though, that Charles II had a difficult character, and was more like Jean II than his prudent father and grandfather.

Like Jean II, his rule was short; and, like him too, he rashly reopened the quarrel with Savoy over the matter of suzerainty. Charles II died suddenly on May 17th, 1589, without having married.

He was succeeded by his brother, Hercule, who was governing the marquisate of Campagna in the Kingdom of Naples, and who only reached Monaco on June 7th. He was confronted with a troubled and grave situation. Relations with Genoa were strained as the result of quarrels over the sea-tribute, and there were serious difficulties with Savoy; the financial position had worsened because of Spain's incapacity to keep to her obligations, and money had to be borrowed at exorbitant rates of interest to meet the more pressing needs.

It was certainly not due to unwillingness on the part of the Spanish agents, and, to mitigate the failure of their principals, they used their influence to protect their little ally against the claims of Savoy, and helped to smooth the dispute with Genoa. At the same time they arranged a rich and brilliant match for Hercule. His bride, Maria Landi de Valdetare, was a descendant on her mother's side of the Kings of Portugal and Aragón. It was a happy marriage but too short; Maria Landi died in giving birth to her third child, in 1599.

Deprived of his wife's good influence, Hercule Grimaldi began to lead a life of debauchery. So much so, that a certain Stefano Boccone, in the pay of Savoy, found it easy to whip up the anger of outraged fathers and husbands in Monaco. At about ten o'clock on a Sunday evening, November 21st, 1604, Hercule was walking through the town followed by just one servant; the woman he had been to see had given birth a few days earlier to a girl he had acknowledged as his. In an alley by the house of the *podestà* Barthélemy Gastaldi, or Dadino, in the Grand-Rue, five men were lying in wait for the seigneur.[1] They stabbed him to death, and threw the body over the cliff into the sea.[2]

Would this assassination, carried out by men of Monaco as a verdict of the population, cause the age-old link between the Grimaldis and their Rock to snap?

[1] Today, the house is No. 15 rue du Milieu. The alley where the murderers hid now has a shop built on it.

[2] The body was found a few days later, and was buried in the St Sebastian chapel of the church of St Nicolas.

The entry of the death of Hercule Grimaldi in the Monaco parish register is astonishingly terse: '1604. The 21st of November. The most noble and worthy seigneur, Hercule Grimaldi, seigneur of Monaco, marquis of Campagna, called to a better life at the age of about 42. Attacked by five or six in the Grand-Rue, in front of the house of the *podestrà*, master Bartolomeo Dadino, he at once delivered up his soul to God.'

CHAPTER III

HONORÉ II. THE RETURN TO THE LILIES
OF FRANCE (1604–1662)

AS SOON AS THE DEATH of Hercule Grimaldi become known, a spiteful crowd broke into the château and pillaged it. The young Honoré II and his sisters might well have been in danger if they had not been hidden by devoted retainers. The anger of the people soon calmed down, and the town's old affection for the Grimaldis returned. And, too, a fortunate chance brought the captain of a Genoese fleet, Orazio Lercari, into Monaco waters, thus preventing any enterprise on the part of Savoy.

Hercule's intentions for the custody of his children were known, as were his fears concerning the ambitions of his brother Horace; and although no testament was produced (it was only discovered three years later, in 1607), the general assembly of the three seigniories called on Frederico Landi, Prince de Valdetare, the maternal uncle of the seven-year-old Honoré II, to act as regent during his minority.[1]

No doubt the *syndics* and councillors hoped they were getting another Gubernant. They were mistaken. The Prince de Valdetare, a noble of Milan, preferred honours and pleasures to independence and power, and was looking for personal favours from Spain. In no way, then, did he recall the austere Genoese ruminating alone over ambitious plans. Above all, he was not a Grimaldi and could not have that almost mystical feeling towards the Rock and its autonomy which for so many generations had aroused members of the different branches of the House, whether of Antibes, Cagnes, or Genoa, and instinctively drawn them to the aid of the seigneurs of Monaco.

---

[1] Hercule's testament made Valdetare's powers legitimate, and a general assembly —the last ever held at Monaco—appointed three delegates to go and renew the oath of loyalty to Honoré II and his guardian.

This fundamental difference was quick to show itself, and had considerable consequences for the first half of Honoré II's reign.

Valdetare sailed from Genoa on November 30th, 1604, and called in at Finale to take aboard a company of Spanish troops. He wanted to ensure his own safety, and to obtain for Spain a stronghold that Savoy coveted and that France was again showing an interest in. Thus escorted, he reached Monaco on December 2nd or 3rd. But the authorities refused to allow the Spanish troops to land, and Valdetare had to go unaccompanied up to the château.

After this curt welcome he did not stay long on the Rock. He saw that Honoré received the oath of loyalty, had criminal proceedings instituted against Hercule's murderers, and then left his wife to look after his wards while he promptly returned to Milan. And there, no less promptly, he signed an agreement with the Spanish governor that extended the scope of the protectorate and allowed Spanish troops to garrison the fortress, making Honoré II almost a prisoner in their charge.

This solved the problem—in principle—of the upkeep of the garrison; the payments outstanding were settled by bills drawn on the treasury of Milan. The sovereignty of Monaco and the right to sea-tribute were once again recognized. But these were slight advantages when the Rock had been given over to Spain.

Valdetare and Fuentès, the governor of the Duchy of Milan, were fully aware of the importance of the alterations they had made to the terms of the protectorate, and did not inform the Spanish Court until some months later, on March 23rd, 1605.[1] The agreement had by then been put into force, the first contingent of troops having arrived at Monaco from Finale on March 7th. Valdetare returned to Monaco for a few days and then, with the population helpless and the Spanish commander of the garrison installed, he went back to Milan to stay. He took Honoré II with him; the little seigneur was not to see his Rock again for more than ten years.

Although Valdetare, perhaps without realizing it, was a disloyal

---

[1] Even the Spanish Chancery considered the new terms went too far, and wanted to protect the interests of its little ally; and only ratified the agreement in November, 1607, after Fuentès had insisted.

guardian of the Rock's autonomy, he proved to be an affectionate and considerate guardian of young Honoré and his sisters, mindful of their upbringing and ensuring that they received the best education.

Indifferent though he was to the independence of Monaco, the Prince de Valdetare was very conscious of rank, like a good Italian hispanophil; and his two chief concerns—closely connected—about his wards were to arrange brilliant marriages for them and to have Honoré II assume the title of prince.

This title had already been used at the funeral of the Gubernant, in 1561. Thirty years later, Hercule had asked Philip II of Spain, unavailingly, for a principality in the Kingdom of Naples. But not until 1612, when negotiations were begun to marry Jeanne Grimaldi, the elder of Honoré's sisters, to a younger son of the House of Gonzague, was this request presented officially.[1]

From that time, Honoré II began to be referred to in notary acts as 'seigneur, by the grace of God, of Monaco, Menton, and Roquebrune, marquis de Campagna, prince and seigneur.' Honoré himself, from 1614 onwards, assumed the title of prince in his dealings with the Spanish Chancery.[2] Gradually, by 1619, a monarchical formula had been adopted for ordinances and legal documents: 'Honoré II regnant, prince and seigneur, by the grace of God, of Monaco, Menton, and Roquebrune.' The evolution was thus completed; the patronymic was suppressed and the dynastic numeral took its place, the title of prince preceded the enumeration of the seigniories. The same modifications were made to the seals and signets of Monaco.

In the past, the Grimaldis had established the autonomy of the Rock gradually and without any public declaration or formal act. The same House had now substituted the title of prince for that of seigneur, gradually and without any public declaration or formal act; and the ancient stronghold of Foulques de Castello thus became a Principality.

. . . . .

[1] These marriage negotiations fell through, because of inheritance disputes among the Gonzague family. In September, 1615, Jeanne married Théodore Trivulce. She died in childbirth in 1620, and her husband took holy orders, eventually becoming famous as Cardinal Trivulce.

[2] The Spanish Chancery did not recognize this title until 1633, when 'prince' began to compete with 'seigneur' on documents concerning Honoré II.

On October 21st, 1615, soon after the wedding of his sister Jeanne, Honoré II returned to Monaco for the first time since the spring of 1605. A few months later, on February 13th, 1616, he married his brother-in-law's sister, Hippolyte Trivulce. Having made a framework for family life, he then settled down on his Rock.

What manner of man was he, and what was the situation he found after ten years' absence?

Perhaps because of an hereditary likeness, perhaps through a similarity in their lives, the character of Honoré II recalled that of his grandfather, Honoré I. Like him, Honoré II was retiring and shy; probably not very strong-willed but certainly very patient. His grandfather had accepted the presence and control over Monaco of the Gubernant almost with pleasure, in any case with affection. Honoré II had to accept a similar restraint, but one that was not eased by affection or common family background.

The long absence of Valdetare and his ward had given the commanders of the Spanish garrison complete control over the Rock. Although the agreement of 1605 laid down that the garrison commander was under the nominal orders of the seigneur and should be chosen by the governor of Milan from four names put forward by him, this stipulation had not been respected; and the garrison commander, whose orders came from Milan, had become used to acting with complete independence.[1]

Young though Honoré was—still under twenty when he returned to Monaco—he realized that it was useless, alone and unsupported, to begin an unequal struggle. He resigned himself to taking a back seat for a time, leaving all initiative to the Spaniards and seeming satisfied with the baubles they bestowed on him—the Order of the Golden Fleece in 1625, and Commander of the Order of Alcantara, for his heir, in 1628.

During these years of waiting, which were brightened by a happy married life and the birth of a son, Hercule, in 1623, Honoré II was busy taking over the administration of his territories; and, in keeping with the tendency of the times, was

[1] This was so well known that when difficulties arose between Monaco and a neighbouring territory, Nice for instance, the Duke of Savoy did not charge Honoré with the intrigues of the Spanish representatives.

increasingly centralizing the powers of his governor-general—
the same post as the auditor-general of the previous century.

But especially, having been accustomed to splendour and
display during his adolescent years in Milan, the new Prince of
Monaco created a diversion from the annoyances caused by the
Spaniards in starting to extend and improve the look of his
residence. The work went on for thirty years; Honoré spent
considerable sums of money on it, and gave the palace of Monaco
its final aspect.

He extended the south wing, in order to increase the number of
apartments, thereby hiding the old ramparts and towers from
view. A new frontage was formed by a one-storey line of arcades.[1]
And the south-west wing, giving on to the main courtyard, was
extended as far as the ramparts near the Serravalle tower. The
tower became hidden when a building with the new palace
chapel in the middle was constructed in 1656. Near the end of
Honoré's reign the last of these improvements was completed
with the building of 'the Bath apartments,' as it was called; but
this was demolished when restorations were begun early in the
nineteenth century.

In June, 1630, Marie-Anne of Austria, Philip IV's sister who had
married the King of Hungary, was being escorted to Genoa by
a Spanish fleet. The ships put in at Monaco, and Honoré II inaugurated his renovated palace with a magnificent reception for
the cardinals and nobles of Spain and Austria accompanying the
young Queen.

Perhaps the Prince of Monaco forgot that day how much
subjection was concealed beneath this pomp. But before the ships
were out of sight he again felt the bonds chafing him. Each day
they seemed to become harder to bear, and now he thought he
could see a way of breaking free of them.

Cardinal Richelieu had come to power in France six years
previously; and now, having gained the day against the nobles
and the Huguenots, he was turning his attention to foreign
affairs, notably to the struggle against the Hapsburgs of Vienna
and Madrid. Spain's position was most vulnerable in Italy, and

---

[1] Later, Louis I had a large doorway and a gate made in it, to give direct communication between the main and the parade courtyards.

6 Princess Charlotte de Gramont of Monaco, 1639–1678. *Portrait by Sébastien Bourdon.*

5 Prince Louis I of Monaco, 1642–1701.

7 Prince Jacques I of Monaco, 1689–1751. *Portrait by Nicolas de Largillière.*

French intervention there became increasingly active, so that the predominance held by Spain since the battle of Pavia was shaken.

This set Honoré II thinking that perhaps France would help him cast off a yoke that he was not strong enough to loosen by himself—France, with which his House had so many attachments in the past, and which was almost a neighbouring country (the territory of Nice then separated Monaco from France). So in September, 1630, the Prince of Monaco sent two confidential agents—his fiscal attorney, Orazio Rossi, and a Capuchin monk[1] of Menton, Father Gianupero de San Salvatore—to open secret talks with Melchior de Sabran, the new French Resident at Genoa, and to ask him to approach the French King and his Cardinal Minister about ways and means of Monaco returning to the French protectorate.

These overtures were favourably received at the French Court, and at the beginning of January, 1631, Father Gianupero went to Genoa to put forward Honoré's terms. These were: compensation for the certain loss of his Spanish possessions; the French King to pay for 200 foot-soldiers to garrison Monaco in peacetime, for 500 in time of war; the officers to be appointed by the King, but the men to be recruited by the Prince; six galleys charged to the King but under the orders of the Prince to be stationed in Monaco harbour to enforce payment of the sea-tribute; the Prince to receive the French Order of the Saint-Esprit to replace that of the Golden Fleece. These terms had every chance of being accepted (much the same terms appeared in the treaties concluded later) but on March 28th, Sabran received instructions to suspend negotiations, in a despatch from Louis XIII countersigned by Bouthilier, the French superintendent of Finances.

France was about to conclude a new treaty with the Duke of Savoy, and Louis XIII's sister, Christine, was to marry him. It was not the moment to pursue a policy that might cause uneasiness at the Court of Savoy. But the French King instructed Sabran to reassure Honoré's envoy of the good intentions of France, and that he could count on her protection; in short, to await a more favourable time.

.　　　.　　　.　　　.　　　.

[1] The same Order as Richelieu's confidant, the Grey Eminence.

Several years passed before the negotiations were reopened. In the meantime, plague ravaged Monaco, causing the death of a quarter of the population.

It first spread through Lombardy and Provence, and then the pestilence reached the territory of Nice. Some of the inhabitants of La Turbie came to clean infected clothing in a public washing-place at Monaco, and the plague appeared in the Principality at the beginning of July, 1631. Honoré II retired to Genoa with his wife and son, leaving his bastard cousin, Honoré Grimaldi, in charge. This cousin was energetic and resolute, and tried all means to stop the plague from spreading.

The whole population was put into quarantine, and part of the palace buildings was used as a lazaret. No one was allowed out of his house; the church bell was rung to indicate the services, and not until the evening were windows opened and people able to talk across the street. The only persons moving about the town were those with the job of distributing food, and the priest, Dominique Pachiero, taking the sacrament to the dying, and accompanied by the *podestà*, Pierre-Paul Terrazzano, holding the canopy. Twice a day Honoré Grimaldi went round visiting the sick, and changed his clothes in front of a large fire lit in the square before going back into the palace.

Nevertheless the plague kept its hold, and seemed as if it might wipe out all the people clustered on the Rock. But energetic human measures plus help from the skies eventually defeated the epidemic.

Early in October two monks arrived by boat from Nice. They were convinced that the dirt and lack of sanitation in the houses were causing the plague to spread; so they had all the contents, furniture and clothing, brought down to the small cove, the Anse du Canton, and submerged in the water for three days. The things were then washed and put back into the sea for a few more hours. During all this while, the houses were fumigated so densely that the rats fled along the walls and on to the roofs, where they were soon killed.

Measures no less drastic were applied to the people themselves. On a given day, the quarantine was suspended and the whole remaining population went in procession to the Anse du Canton, to stand in the sea for a long time. Then they all returned to their confinement.

These hygienic measures alone might have been successful; but in any case, several days of torrential rain put an end to the seven months' drought, and swept away the last of the germs.

Ever since his return to Monaco in 1615 Honoré II had been resigned to the loss of effective power, but in consequence he placed all the more importance on his position as a sovereign prince being properly respected when he was on foreign soil. There had been much falling short of this during his stay in Genoa. Right from the beginning he had been treated with suspicion, and was officially allowed into the city only on condition that neither he nor any of his household carried swords. There was no lessening of this hostile attitude during the weeks that followed; indeed, on October 10th, when the Prince was crossing the city he was stopped and searched by officers of the law. Honoré II protested to the Spanish ambassador and then left Genoa, going first to Pegli and then to Loano before returning to Monaco.

In the past, the bombardment by André Doria's ships had finally decided Augustin Grimaldi to seek a Spanish alliance; and there can be no doubt that the undignified incident at Genoa —for which Honoré was unable to obtain any satisfaction—when added to his financial difficulties again caused by Spain's failure to pay,[1] was the final blow that drove the Prince to approach France once more.

Honoré II's negotiations with His Most Christian Majesty form a three-act play in which the successive protagonists are of increasing importance. In 1630 the preliminaries had been conducted by Melchior de Sabran and an obscure monk. Two new personalities stepped on to the stage in 1634.

Jean-Henri Grimaldi, the seigneur of Corbons and of Cagnes, was the head of the Antibes branch of the Grimaldi family which had thrown in its lot with France several generations previously. For some time he had had little to do with his cousin in Monaco, but as the result of some incident in 1631 they were drawn closer together. The seigneur of Corbons then heard of the talks that

---

[1] By 1633, Honoré II had been advancing the garrison's pay for fifteen years. The main advantage of the vexatious agreement of 1605 was shown to be very much an illusion.

had taken place with Sabran, and of the fresh inclinations of his cousin. He offered his services as intermediary, and the Prince of Monaco accepted them. He went to see Marshal de Vitry, the governor of Provence, and told him of Honoré's wishes for an alliance with France. In May, 1634, the seigneur of Corbons left for Paris armed with a letter from the Marshal to Cardinal Richelieu.

It was just at this period that Richelieu was intensifying his struggle against Austria and the Hapsburgs, and was seeking alliances in Italy against Spain; his objectives included obtaining the use of ports along the Riviera that were important to Spain's communications with Milan and Naples. Three of these were considered by Richelieu's agents to be of major interest: Monaco, Finale, and Vado. Plans for their capture had even been worked out.[1] The overtures made by the legitimate master of Monaco, could not, therefore, be other than eagerly welcomed.

The negotiations lasted several months, and led to a treaty dated February 24th, 1635, being drawn up by the Grey Eminence and signed by Louis XIII which granted Honoré II the protection of France and all the terms he had put forward in 1631.

It now remained to put the treaty into effect, in other words to turn the Spaniards out of Monaco. Two ways of doing it were proposed. One came from that blunt and tough soldier, Marshal de Vitry: a direct assault on the Rock by 4,000 men supported by eight or nine galleys. But Honoré, a prudent Italian who had led a sheltered life far from any fighting, put forward a less warlike plan and in keeping with the Grimaldi tradition. His idea was

---

[1] The plan concerning Monaco was obviously inspired by the Trojan horse. It is worded: 'Plan for Morgues (Monaco). Can only be taken by surprise or duplicity. To this end, use can be made of fact that there are always 3 or 4 French merchant vessels in the harbour, coming and going, in time of war as well as in peacetime. This number could be increased by 4 or 5 carrying wine; but with soldiers in some of the barrels instead of wine. Each vessel to carry 10 or 12 barrels of wine, and 25 or 30 barrels with armed soldiers inside. Each barrel holding only one man, he could remain inside 3 to 4 days, awaiting the right moment.

'This enterprise could best be carried out on a Sunday morning, during early Mass, when everyone is in church. Ten or a dozen men could easily seize control of the harbour, for the ships to go alongside with reinforcements. Each soldier to be armed with two pistols, two pounds of powder and 50 balls, to defend himself until help arrives. At the same time, 4 or 5 galleys should be waiting at Villefranche, ready to make for Morgues on a signal that could be given from a mountain top between the two places.'

to introduce about sixty retainers or men from Menton into the stronghold,[1] and then with the help of the seigneur of Corbons and of a few well-chosen French officers, Honoré was convinced he could overpower the garrison. This proposition was accepted.

Faced with a decision, the Prince hesitated. Corbons reproached him bitterly that 'for the past four months there has been scarcely anyone in garrison, so that you could easily have carried out what was promised, and you did not.' Eventually a date was fixed, June 3rd. But in the meantime, five Spanish ships loaded with troops, part of a squadron from Naples that had run into a storm and been scattered, put in at Monaco. They remained there for two months.

The favourable moment had been lost. Especially as the Spaniards seized the Lérin islands soon afterwards, thus improving their position along the Riviera and also cutting Monaco's sea-communications with France.

A timid and indecisive man, Honoré II was perhaps thankful that chance had prevented him taking action; and the Spaniards could have possibly exploited his feelings of relief. But those whom the Gods wish to destroy . . . The Spanish agents at Monaco had got wind of Honoré's dealings, and their attitude towards the little ally of their King began to harden. They took away what small amount of authority still remained to him, held back his revenues, seized his stocks, and increased the garrison to 1,200 men. These acts were a direct contrast with the patient attitude of the French, who were still hopeful. Corbons was keeping contact. And the commander of the French fleet in the Mediterranean wrote to Richelieu on October 16th, 1636, from Antibes: 'Monsieur Mazarin has been this way. . . . He asked for some sloops to escort his ship past Morgues, and he was given six fully armed, after having been offered as many ships as he wished. . . .'

For the next few years, however, Honoré II seemed again resigned, and the status quo might have continued were it not for the excesses of the Spanish troops, who were badly paid and

[1] Too many marriages between Spanish soldiers of the garrison and women of Monaco had taken place during the past thirty years for Honoré to feel sure of the support of the local population.

lacking in discipline. Some time in 1639, a notice was stuck up in the main guard-room urging the soldiers to plunder the palace and seize the Prince and his son as hostages. The man responsible for this, a Spanish soldier, was sentenced by the Monaco authorities but the governor of Milan had the case brought before his court and the insult remained unpunished.

Caught between Scylla and Charybdis, Honoré decided that as there was a risk to run it was best to choose the one which could at least lead to freedom; and he reopened negotiations with France for the third time.

For this last act, the part previously played by Marshal de Vitry was taken over by a great nobleman indeed, Louis de Valois, Count d'Alais. This new governor of Provence was a son of the Duke of Angoulême and so a grandson of Charles IX and his mistress, Marie Touchet. He had a well-balanced, flexible mind, and realized that too-warlike proposals would only scare a weak-willed person like Honoré, and so let him and Corbons quietly bring their plan to fruition.

To lull the suspicions of the Spanish, and perhaps to keep a door open in the event of failure, Honoré II gave the impression of drawing closer to the Spanish cause; and this was helped by the marriage of his son, Hercule, to Aurélia Spinola, a grand-niece of his old guardian, Valdetare. Under cover of the preparations for this wedding, Corbons came to Monaco, from Cagnes. As the treaty of 1635 had but to be revived, with only slight modifications, the subsequent negotiations were quite short. A draft treaty was signed by the French King at Péronne on July 8th, 1641, shortly after Hercule's wedding. It was ratified by Honoré II, with various complementary requests, on August 12th. And on September 14th, Louis XIII signed the definite treaty—which was going to regulate relations between France and the Principality for the next 150 years.

The fulfilment of the main terms of the treaty had been fixed by Honoré II for November—perhaps this was a final hesitation before risking his life, and that of his son, in a surprise attack. In any case, this delay made Count d'Alais and Corbons anxious, especially as a series of fortunate circumstances had greatly reduced the stronghold's garrison. At last, on November 4th,

Corbons informed the governor of Provence that all was ready for the 11th. For the past five weeks there had been nothing to prevent the attempt.

But two days later Honoré II panicked; pretending that a leakage might have revealed the plan to the Savoy authorities in Nice, he put everything off indefinitely. Corbons lost patience, and wrote to the timorous Prince in cornelian terms: 'I am forwarding your letters to the King and His Eminence. I know not how the news will be received at Court . . . having learnt that by some miracle the Spanish had withdrawn a hundred men from your garrison; that after this gift from Heaven you waited forty days without taking action as promised, which you could have done twenty-four hours afterwards without danger or difficulty.

'It is a perilous matter to treat such a great monarch so lightly.

'And if Your Excellency would now show the resolution which should spring from a man of your birth, you could easily succeed in the matter; and since it is lost, as greatly appears from what Yr. Ex. says, better to lose gloriously and sword in hand, killing one's enemies, than to perish in shame. . . .'

There can be little doubt that Corbon's fine phrases did less to bring Honoré II round to firmer resolution than did the discovery of a letter from the lieutenant commanding the Monaco garrison to the governor of Milan. Lieutenant Callente wrote that he vouched for Honoré's loyalty, but at the first sign of trouble he would arrest Honoré and his son and send them in chains to Milan.

Suddenly enraged, the Prince seized on an opportunity presented just then by an incident which depleted the garrison, and he did not wait to warn the French. An insurrection, secretly provoked, had broken out at Roquebrune; seventy-five Spanish soldiers were sent there, while about thirty of the rioters were brought to the palace of Monaco. In addition, some men were engaged supposedly for building work in the palace grounds, and others for the preparations of an expedition Hercule Grimaldi was to make against the Barbary pirates. With the thirty from Roquebrune, about a hundred men were thus gathered in the vaults of the palace without suspicion being aroused.

Just at this time a Spanish page picked up some papers that Honoré had lost; they were recent letters from Corbons and the

71

governor of Provence. But the page could not read them, and handed his find to Honoré's major-domo, Jérôme Rey. This happened during the evening of November 17th, while Honoré II was dining with the Spanish officers. . . . After nightfall, when the watchfulness of the Spaniards slackened, the Prince went down to the vaults followed by his son, the major-domo, Rey, and the secretary, Brigati. He read out Callente's menacing letter to the men from Menton and Roquebrune, and called on them to free their sovereign prince. They all made a rush for the weapons that were being distributed, with so much eagerness, and clumsiness too, that several shots went off. But a gale was blowing and the noise did not reach the ears of the Spaniards.

The Prince divided his force into three groups. The first, led by Hercule Grimaldi, captured the Serravalle post; while Jérôme Rey and twenty men easily overpowered the palace guard, shut the rest of the garrison in their barrack-room, and kept command of the position from the loggia above—the loggia that, years before, Barthélemy Doria had failed to capture. With fifty men, Honoré attacked the main Spanish post at the town gate, held by Callente and the best of his soldiers. Three times Honoré was repulsed, but the arrival of 160 men from Menton soon routed the Spaniards.

The next day, November 18th, a Te Deum was sung in the church of St Nicolas. Honoré II wrote to the Cardinal de Savoie: 'I was forced to take this strange decision.' A French point of view was contained in a letter that the *bailli* de Forbin sent to Richelieu on November 20th: 'The news about Morgues has reached me from the governor of Provence. . . . Everything has happened for the best, and Your Eminence has given a hard kick to the Spaniards which makes them go 200 miles farther round to get to Italy.'

The return to the French protectorate marks the culminating point of Honoré II's reign. He was free of financial worries for the last twenty years of his life, with a protector who kept promises scrupulously and liberally. During this latter period the Prince of Monaco was to travel a good deal, to the Court of Louis XIII, and to visit his son; and to become preoccupied with ensuring the future of his line by contracting marriages for his grandchildren.

· · · · ·

In the past, Lambert's sons had appeared at the French Court, and if not all had found a wife there, all had made a good impression. The alliance with Spain, however, had led to hardly any personal relationships. Charles V, the wandering Emperor, had paid a visit to Augustin; but in later years, young Honoré I and the Gubernant had remained on their Rock, while the Spanish King stayed in his austere rooms at the Escorial.

With Monaco liberated, Honoré II was keen to attend the French Court. Honours were to be expected there, but his main desire was to make contacts that would help the Grimaldis obtain high functions or contract brilliant marriage alliances. Louis XIII and Richelieu, for their part, would wish to meet the Prince who had recently placed himself under the ægis of France, and to promote friendly relations in support of the political bond.

So when, in February, 1642, the King stopped at Lyon on his way to open the campaign against the Spanish in Catalonia, he conveyed through Corbons the pleasure it would give him to receive the Prince of Monaco. On March 26th a royal letter confirmed the invitation: 'My cousin, I am ordering the *bailli* de Forbin to have the galley I have given you refitted with all haste, and to send it to you as soon as it is seaworthy, for transporting you to Marseille.'[1]

The Prince of Monaco embarked on April 25th, accompanied by his son, and leaving his daughter-in-law (who was pregnant) to act as regent. The King and the Cardinal were both indisposed just then, and it was not until May 19th that the Prince arrived at the royal field-headquarters in front of Perpignan. Louis XIII had sent a company of a hundred horse to meet him on the borders of Catalonia; two leagues farther on a royal coach was waiting; one league more, and a guard of honour presented arms. The King's welcome to the Prince was most gracious. On May 22nd, Louis XIII invested him with the Order of the Saint Esprit, remarking that the King of Spain had never invested anyone with the Order of the Golden Fleece on French territory as he,

[1] At this period, Monaco was still far from any road, and when mention is made of the seigneurs of Monaco travelling to France it should be remembered that the customary and simplest way was by sea to Antibes or Marseille, as Nice belonged to Savoy.

the King of France, was doing with his Order on Spanish
territory.

After the ceremony, Honoré II had lunch with the Marquis
de Cinq-Mars. Tragedies were not unknown in the Grimaldi
family, but it would no doubt have come as a shock to the Prince
to have learnt that his young, lively, and gracious host had plotted
two months earlier to help Spain against Richelieu; and that only
three weeks after this pleasant meal together Cinq-Mars would
be arrested, and later beheaded.

Honoré II had barely started his journey back when, at Nar-
bonne, he received letters patent made out at the royal camp near
Perpignan which created him duke and peer of the realm, with
title to the Duchy of the Valentinois and its revenues.[1] His son,
Hercule, was given the marquisate of Les Baux.

A month after the Prince's return to Monaco his daughter-in-
law gave birth to a son. Honoré asked Louis XIII to be godfather
to this grandchild; he was encouraged to make the request by
the governor of Provence, Count d'Alais,[2] whose care in acclim-
atizing the Italian-bred and educated sovereign-prince of Monaco
to the ways of the French Court cannot be too greatly stressed.
The King was graciously pleased to accept, and appointed Count
d'Alais to represent him at the christening.

But a whole year was to pass before the infant was named.
During this time the Prince of Monaco made a journey to Paris,
at the end of 1642, as he wished to strengthen his contacts at
the French Court and to put certain financial matters in order.
He also wanted his official reception by the Paris Parlement as
duke and peer of the realm to be held.

He was satisfied on this last point. The ceremony took place
on February 19th, 1643, and the Advocate-General, Omer Talon,
made a high-flown speech extolling the virtues of the Prince.
But on the other hand, once he had taken up residence in a vast

[1] The dukedom could descend to either male or female issue of the Prince, but
the peerage became extinct if a woman inherited. In January, 1643, the *comté* of
Carladez in Auvergne was bestowed on the Prince in addition to the duchy of
Valentinois, bringing the total rent-rolls up to the 75,000 *livres* agreed to in the
Péronne treaty.

[2] The Count wrote to Honoré II on July 26th: 'I do not think Your Excellency
could do better than to ask His Majesty to give his name to the son that God has
been pleased to grant to your House.'

house belonging to the Marquise de Créqui, in the rue Vieille-du-Temple,[1] Honoré II found himself rather out of things, in spite of being well received by Parisian society. The King was dying, the Court had withdrawn to St Germain, and all State business was suspended. Disappointed on the whole, the Prince decided to return south. A few weeks after reaching Monaco he learnt of the death, on May 14th, 1643, of Louis XIII.

The death of the King following that of Richelieu brought Cardinal Mazarin to power. Honoré II had maintained good relations with him since 1636, and had strengthened them during the time spent at Perpignan and at Paris. Both were Italians and got on well together; they were appreciative of each other, and the Cardinal constantly endeavoured to draw the Prince of Monaco into the French orbit.

As the Grimaldi baby had not yet been christened, Mazarin decided that the young boy King, Louis XIV, should replace his father. So on August 16th, 1643, the five-year-old monarch put his name to a fine letter that expressed his satisfaction at the baby being named after him: '. . . which is why, on the advice of the Queen Mother, I am writing to my cousin, Count d'Alais, to tell him to take conveyance to your place and attend the ceremony for me.'

It was in October that Count d'Alais took conveyance, and on the 12th, Louis Grimaldi was christened with much pomp.

By 1646 Mazarin seemed firmly in power, and the Thirty Years War was ending favourably for the French. The Duke d'Enghien had beaten the Spanish and Imperial forces at Rocroy in 1643, and at Nordlingen in 1645. Dunkirk had just fallen. It appeared to Honoré II that the victorious French would extend a warm welcome to their Mediterranean ally. He set off for Paris.

In 1642 the journey had been made in short, slow stages; this one four years later was even slower, but with more pomp and ceremony on the way because the Prince visited his estates in France, Les Baux and the Valentinois. His two secretaries, Charles de Vénasque and Hyacinthe Bressan, have left a detailed account of the journey which gives an interesting insight as to

[1] In the then fashionable Marais district, in the east of Paris. (*Trans. note.*)

how a great lord travelled at that period, and reveals some of the odd things that could happen in France.

The way lay through Aix-en-Provence. There, the Prince was welcomed by Count d'Alais and his wife, and made a speech before the provincial Parlement in which he said 'the fortress of Monaco is a bulwark against an invasion of Provence, which can sleep in safety guarded by its guns.' At Lambesc, the consuls and officers of Les Baux and St Rémy presented the Prince with some excellent wine. When he reached Orange, he was visited by its Dutch governor (appointed by the Prince of Orange) and asked to supply the day's password for the garrison.

On November 2nd the Prince arrived in his Duchy, of which the chief towns were Montélimar and Valence. During his week's stay there were many festivities—torrential rain too—and then he went on up the Rhône valley to Lyon, from where his route took him westwards towards the river Loire, by way of Tarare. 'It was a bad day; the coach was overturned and the litter in which His Excellency was reclining got thrown out, but without hurt to him, against the cliff bordering one side of the road.' On the 16th the travellers reached Roanne and the river Loire, and transferred to a boat 'partitioned into three rooms by hanging tapestries, with windows, and a brazier against the cold.' The river journey took five days, as far as Orléans, and then the Prince took to the road again, through Toury and Etampes to Longjumeau, where he visited the château of Chilly and its many surrounding houses.

Chilly had been built by the Marquis d'Effiat when Superintendent of Finances, and he had insisted on his chief assistants all building houses around it. Effiat had been the father of Cinq-Mars. A religious person like Honoré II must have pondered, as he got back into his coach, on the vanities of men's ambitions.

By November 25th the Prince of Monaco was again in residence at the town house of the Marquise de Créqui. He dare not pay calls at first, because the young son of Elizabeth of France had just died and mourning dress was necessary. But on his second day in Paris Honoré II slipped out by a back door, late in the evening, and called on Cardinal Mazarin, who warmly received him.

His stay in Paris lasted five months, and enabled him to make

a fine haul for distribution among his entourage: four collars of
the Order of St Michael, the appointments of counsellor and
secretary to the King, gentleman of the Bedchamber, chaplain,
and physician to the King. He also had the promise of an abbey
with 5,000 crowns in revenues for his grandson; exemption from
tolls and taxes for all natives of Monaco; and the gift of twelve
bronze cannon for his fortress.

The Prince enjoyed life in the capital very much. 'He found
the company of the ladies charming,' commented Hyacinthe
Bressan. 'They dress magnificently, and although their sex is
naturally eloquent, at the French Court more than elsewhere,
they converse with elegance and great ease.'

However, it was time to think of returning; the Marquis des
Baux had gone back to Monaco a month earlier. The Prince's
departure was fixed for May 1st. On April 29th he attended a
banquet in Mazarin's apartments at the Palais Royal, which was
followed by a performance of Calzabigi's three-act drama,
Orpheus. The young Louis XIV was present with his mother,
Anne of Austria, and so were Queen Henrietta, the wife of Charles I,
and the sixteen-year-old Prince of Wales. As is often the case at
such gatherings the glittering scene in the rooms received more
attention than that on the stage, in spite of the excellent pro-
duction. Eyes were drawn in particular to the Danish ambassador
and his wife, a daughter of Christian IV; the ambassador was
very tall and had red hair, wore a long, black velvet coat and
carried a stick with a silver handle.

After the performance, the rooms were arranged for dancing,
'that H.M. expressed the wish to open, for he dances marvellously
well.' The twenty-four violinists were all ready and waiting, but
'it was almost midnight, and the late hour and the Queen Mother's
firmness were opposed to the youthful wishes of the King.' His
Most Christian Majesty went sadly off to his bed.

The return journey, by a different route for much of the way,
was marked by a fair number of incidents. In spite of cold and
rain the going was easy at first, through Essonne, Fontainebleau,
Nemours, and Briare, until the Prince reached Cosne on the
evening of May 6th. All the lodgings at the inn were already
taken for the wife of the viceroy of Barcelona, Countess d'Harcourt. Honoré II decided to push on another four leagues, but the

servants of the Countess came with an offer to share the accommodation; and everyone settled down for the night comfortably enough.

During all this, the innkeeper's wife was brought to bed of a daughter. The happy father made haste to show the baby to his two distinguished guests, and asked each to stand as godparent. A simple ceremony was held next morning, when the child was given the name of Marguerite; then each got into his or her coach, enriched by a godchild.

At Tarare on the way up the Prince had been overturned; on the way back he was almost drowned. It rained so much that, arriving there on the 13th, he was unable to get away until the 16th. For two days he was confined to the inn, which was 'gradually surrounded by floods and only saved from collapsing by the help of God.' As the waters rose 'the first to make off were the stewards and their helpers in the kitchen, then the coaches and the horses which could have swum around in the stables were got out. The Prince had the good fortune to escape by a service door. . . .'

At St Rémy a triumphal arch and banners greeted him; and then the travellers went on, through the rain still, to Aix and Marseille. In the port a galley was waiting to take the Prince to Monaco. Tired and wet, he was no doubt hoping when he embarked on May 23rd, with a salute of forty guns, that now he was in the Mediterranean which the Grimaldis had always trusted he would be carried without hindrance to his Rock.

But it was then that he had a narrow escape from death. On the evening of the 24th he put in at St Tropez, having met the French barque, *La Royale*, during the day. Next morning, early, his ship was passing under the fort at Agay when it was mistaken for a Spanish vessel and fired on; three men were killed and six wounded. Honoré II was startled from his sleep; his Genoese blood rose up, and he ordered the galley to make for the fort, had its commander sent for, and took him prisoner to Monaco. A few days later, however, he pardoned him.

It was perhaps in the course of this journey, or the one made in 1651—tragically interrupted by the news of the accidental death of his only son, Hercule—that the Prince had his portrait painted by Philippe de Champaigne. The Flemish artist was used to stronger personalities, but seems to have been faithful to his sitter. The picture shows the Prince as an ageing, ponderous man, his round face worn and sagging, but with a firm mouth and dark eyes that are gentle yet express intelligence and doggedness.

Honoré II began to suffer greatly from gout—he died of it in the end—and for the last ten years of his life remained in his Principality. In spite of his bereavements—his wife had died in 1638—the Prince kept a brilliant Court, and festivities were often held at Monaco: Court festivities with full ballet as in Paris, and religious festivals that united the princely family and the people in the same worship. The latter increased to the point where the fifty-two Sundays in the year were supplemented by the celebration of forty-nine different Saints' Days—official holidays—the most important being that of Saint Dévote, the patron saint of the Principality.

The arts had a place of honour. The Prince ordered tapestries portraying the story of David, of Lot, of Alexander the Great, etc., from the famous Gobelins workshops, to embellish his palace, and he collected pictures by old masters—Titian, Raphael, Rubens, Dürer—while also gathering round him local artists like Laurent Gastaldo, Bernardin Mimault, Orazio Ferrari, and Hilaire Pader. The Mint of Monaco was working regularly and producing some fine gold and silver coins; a splendid medal bearing the head of Honoré II was struck in 1648, in bronze and in silver, which was the work of Jean Varin, the chief engraver at the Mint in Paris.

In his desire to uphold the dignity of his rank, the Prince was impelled to maintain a magnificent and openhanded style of living; and it is not difficult to guess that the matter most on his mind was to arrange marriages for his grandchildren. Seven children had been born to Hercule and his wife, Aurélia Spinola: five daughters and two sons. Two of the daughters became nuns at Genoa, and husbands for the other three were found in Savoy or Italy. One son had died in 1652 at the age of four. There remained the heir, Louis, who was sixteen in 1658. His future was of the greatest importance.

Although Honoré II had appeared at the French Court, he

was too old at the time of the Treaty of Péronne to consider
seeking a military or diplomatic career there; and Hercule had
been hindered from doing so by the strife during the Fronde,
and then had met with a premature death. Louis would have to
succeed where they had been prevented. But Honoré II was too
intelligent not to have noticed during his stays in Paris that it
would be imprudent to loose an inexperienced young man on to
the tricky, if not dangerous, ground of the French Court unless
he were backed up by marriage connections which would give
him some solid support. What was needed for Louis was a brilliant alliance with one of the leading French families, one well
placed at Court too.

The widow of old Marshal Guébriant had stayed at Monaco in
1646, on her way back from Poland where she had accompanied
the new Queen, Marie de Gonzague-Nemours. Honoré II had
given a great welcome to the charming widow, and it was she
who had been largely instrumental in deciding him to make his
second journey to Paris. His five months' stay in the capital had
brought them closer together.

Towards the end of 1658, the efforts of the Marshal's widow
and the good offices of Cardinal Mazarin resulted in a great
marriage being arranged for the heir to the Principality of
Monaco. On April 28th, 1659, the marriage contract of Louis
Grimaldi and Catherine-Charlotte de Gramont, daughter of the
Duke of Gramont, was signed in the royal apartment at the
Louvre. The Duke of Gramont was a Marshal of France, the
governor of Pau, and sovereign prince of Bidache, a small
territory in the foothills of the Pyrenees; his wife was a niece of
Richelieu, Marguerite du Plessis de Chivré; as well as being of
excellent family he was a man with influence who could be
of great help to his son-in-law.

Neither Honoré II nor his grandson was present at the signing
of the marriage contract, the Prince being too ill to travel and
Louis too young to go without him. But their interest was very
great. The Prince was in correspondence on the subject with
Hozier, the foremost genealogist of the time, and in a letter
dated May 22nd, 1659, thanked him for his 'pleasant and favourable remarks' concerning Catherine-Charlotte, and added, 'in
the meantime we have been sent a small portrait of her which

has interested us very much here; it is quite well done and most pleasant to look upon, especially by the Duke of Valentinois,[1] my grandson, who keeps it on his bedside table.' Some days later the Prince again wrote to Hozier, expressing pleasure at soon receiving from him 'the quarterings of our young lady. . . . Your news is most interesting, and the felicitous remarks that you add to the general approval of our alliance with the Gramonts cause me no little pleasure, increasing the great satisfaction this honour naturally gives me.'

The wedding of Louis Grimaldi and Catherine-Charlotte de Gramont was delayed by the signing of the peace treaty with Spain and the subsequent mission of the Duke of Gramont to Madrid. But the ceremony took place at Pau on March 30th, 1660. Louis returned to Monaco for a few weeks in November, but it was not until the autumn of 1661 that the young couple went to live there. Did Honoré II begin to think that his new grand-daughter was not taking after the faithful wives that had almost always been the fortunate lot of the seigneurs of Monaco? Perhaps so. But if he felt some doubts about the marital happiness of his grandson, he must have been satisfied by the fertility of the union. A son, Antoine, was born on January 25th, 1661, and a second baby was expected, when on January 10th, 1662, Honoré II died.

His death marked the close of the first stage in the history of the Princes of Monaco. The maritime period had come to an end when Jean I died; then, too, the uncertainty over the Grimaldis' possession of the Rock had ended. Lambert strengthened the title to it by his courage and diplomatic skill, and obtained recognition of the independence of the seigniory. His sons discovered that, even so, they could not remain apart from a Europe that was centralizing its forces, and they began to seek an alliance with a great Power, turning first to France and then to the Spain of Charles V.

For a whole century the Grimaldis remained quiet, tucked into the shadow of Spain and of their Rock, and then with a final

[1] It was not until December 6th, 1659, that Honoré II actually renounced his title of duke and peer in favour of his grandson. For almost 200 years after that date, the eldest son of the Prince of Monaco bore the title of Duke of Valentinois.

bound completed their shrewd evolution. Several generations of obscure Grimaldis were followed by one of the greatest and most intelligent of the line, and one of the happiest too, one who seized the opportunity which both made legitimate and capitalized the work of his forbears.

The first treaty with France had brought subsidies to the seigneur of Monaco, especially the relief of having the garrison maintained by the protecting Power. But Spain, unable to pay cash subsidies because of her habitual financial difficulties, had instead granted large estates in Italy to the seigneur. In addition, consoling him for material lapses by satisfying him on matters of prestige, the Spanish Chancery recognized the title of prince that he had assumed.

When Honoré II completed the cycle by returning to the protection of France, rightly sensing her growing power, the Treaty of Péronne gave every satisfaction to the Prince of Monaco. The French King, too, sanctioned his rank; henceforth, the claim of the Grimaldis of Monaco to be sovereign princes could not possibly be contested. While on the material side the advantages that had resulted from the first treaty with France were restored; compensation was obtained from the French for the compensation given by the Spanish—which was, in fact, having it both ways.

After such success, it seemed that all the hopes of the Princes of Monaco had been realized. They could not increase their territory, hemmed in as it was by great Powers; their security was assured by the protection of France, and the problem of finance was solved since all legitimate maintenance expenses were at the charge of the protecting Power; and the administration of the Principality ran smoothly. How then were these Princes going to occupy themselves, if they did not give way to a life of ease and pleasure?

Spain had never considered making the Grimaldis Spanish, and the seigneurs of independent Monaco had been no more than Neapolitan marquesses. But France had opened her arms generously; by the Treaty of Péronne, letters of naturalization had made this Italian family French. Made them, too, dukes and peers of the realm. This realm was that of Louis the Sun King; and so a new future was opening for the Grimaldis.

THE HOUSE OF GRIMALDI—1297–1662

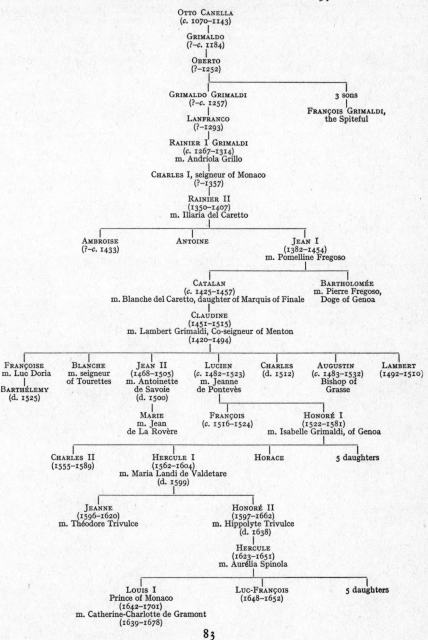

OTTO CANELLA
(c. 1070–1143)

GRIMALDO
(?–c. 1184)

OBERTO
(?–1252)

GRIMALDO GRIMALDI   3 sons
(?–c. 1257)
                                    FRANÇOIS GRIMALDI,
LANFRANCO   the Spiteful
(?–1293)

RAINIER I GRIMALDI
(c. 1267–1314)
m. Andriola Grillo

CHARLES I, seigneur of Monaco
(?–1357)

RAINIER II
(1350–1407)
m. Illaria del Caretto

AMBROISE   ANTOINE   JEAN I
(?–c. 1433)   (1382–1454)
                                    m. Pomelline Fregoso

CATALAN   BARTHOLOMÉE
(c. 1425–1457)   m. Pierre Fregoso,
m. Blanche del Caretto, daughter of Marquis of Finale   Doge of Genoa

CLAUDINE
(1451–1515)
m. Lambert Grimaldi, Co-seigneur of Menton
(1420–1494)

FRANÇOISE   BLANCHE   JEAN II   LUCIEN   CHARLES   AUGUSTIN   LAMBERT
m. Luc Doria m. seigneur (1468–1505) (c. 1482–1523) (d. 1512) (c. 1483–1532) (1492–1510)
             of Tourettes m. Antoinette m. Jeanne   Bishop of
BARTHÉLEMY   de Savoie   de Pontevès   Grasse
(d. 1525)   (d. 1500)

                         MARIE   FRANÇOIS   HONORÉ I
                         m. Jean   (c. 1516–1524) (1522–1581)
                         de La Rovère   m. Isabelle Grimaldi, of Genoa

CHARLES II   HERCULE I   HORACE   5 daughters
(1555–1589)   (1562–1604)
                     m. Maria Landi de Valdetare
                     (d. 1599)

        JEANNE   HONORÉ II
        (1596–1620)   (1597–1662)
        m. Théodore Trivulce   m. Hippolyte Trivulce
                                    (d. 1638)

                     HERCULE
                     (1623–1651)
                     m. Aurélia Spinola

        LOUIS I   LUC-FRANÇOIS   5 daughters
        Prince of Monaco   (1648–1652)
        (1642–1701)
        m. Catherine-Charlotte de Gramont
        (1639–1678)

83

PART TWO

AT THE FRENCH COURT
(1662–1795)

CHAPTER IV

IN THE RAYS OF THE SUN KING
(1662–1701)

'I EXPRESSLY CHARGE THEM never in any event to break with France and leave the protection of His Most Christian Majesty, but always to show zeal and loyalty towards him,' wrote Honoré II in his will and testament.

For the next 130 years or so, until the morning of January 21st, 1793 (when Louis XVI was guillotined), those who succeeded Honoré II abided by his instructions in their various ways. Louis I, through his obedience to them, had his vanity greatly satisfied; for he was authorized by royal decree to bear the title of foreign prince, and his career spent entirely in the service of France was crowned by the appointment of ambassador to the Holy See.

His son, Antoine I, remained in close contact with the French Court, even apparently tightening his connections by marrying into the House of Lorraine; although, with his independent spirit and surly character, he never fitted in with the formalized life at Versailles. Financial difficulties obliged him to leave the Court, and also furnished him with a pretext for not returning. Nevertheless, in spite of the expense and vexation he suffered because of the War of the Spanish Succession, when the marriage of his daughter and heiress to the Principality was being arranged he did not first seek the agreement of the Grimaldi family but the consent of Louis XIV. He no longer recognized that his relatives had the right to intervene in the affairs of Monaco; and by insisting on his son-in-law assuming the name and arms of Grimaldi, he was also ensuring that the French peerage was retained for the family.

His grandson, Honoré III, succeeded him after a very short interval. Relations with the French Court then became slender, and on the personal level the alliance with France was not unlike that with Spain in the time of Honoré I. But although the Court of Louis XV, and even less that of Louis XVI, held little attraction for Honoré III, although his Genoese marriage seemed to be drawing him towards Italy for a while, he was nevertheless very much attached to France. What the marriage alliance with the Gramont family and then with the House of Lorraine had been unable to accomplish was brought about by the Matignon marriage, by a solid Norman connection. Honoré III was bound not just to the monarch but to France. The Revolution could sweep away the throne of the Capets and gobble up the Principality of Monaco, but the Grimaldis of Monaco—unlike some families highly placed at Court, the Rohans, for instance—stuck by France and made a fresh start.

Aurélia Spinola, the widow of Hercule, had not married again but had continued living at Monaco and devoting herself to her children; especially to Louis, who had rarely left her side before going to Pau, in March, 1660, for his marriage to Catherine-Charlotte de Gramont. He was then a youngster of medium height with a gentle face, frank, handsome eyes, and the mouth of a child. Warm-hearted and straightforward, he was cultured and had plenty of common sense.

But in the eyes of a woman of twenty used to the society of the Hôtel de Soissons, the Condé town mansion, that 'school of gallantry, wit, and fashion,' the qualities of young Louis could not make up for his timidity and provincial awkwardness; and he was still only seventeen. With such a handicap, the first few weeks of the marriage could hardly have been happy, even though the bride was charming, had lively dark eyes and a delicate mouth. The picture of her in the palace of Monaco shows her in a bright yellow dress with her throat and neck bare beneath the false modesty of a veil; she looks a creature made for love and pleasure.

In spite of their differences and being strangers to each other, perhaps they would have become fond of one another in time. But the young bride had been forced into the marriage, and was in love with a cousin six years her elder, who had been brought up in her father's house. 'Both having found themselves capable of strong passions, there was nothing comparable to the passion they had for each other,' Madame de La Fayette wrote about the two lovers. And the Grande Mademoiselle commented, 'Her taste was not depraved.' The cousin, 'a small, fair man, well-built for his size, and with lively looks,' bore the name of Puyguilhem at that time, but later became better known as the Duke of Lauzun.

Six weeks after the wedding of Louis and Catherine-Charlotte, the King arrived at St Jean-de-Luz for his marriage to the Infanta Maria-Theresa. In his suite was Puyguilhem, captain of a company of Household troops. While Louis XIV thought of his love, Marie Mancini, and waited without impatience for the Spanish bride he was marrying for reasons of State, the Court amused itself. The new Duchess of Valentinois was at all the fêtes—concerts, Spanish plays, water pageants along the coast—including the garden party given by the King on the Ile de la Conférence. The royal wedding took place on June 9th; and before the eyes of the whole Court, Puyguilhem walked on the right of the King holding the blue baton of his office, all along the flower-decked, tapestry-hung gallery lined by guardsmen and musketeers.

It was a hard school for Louis Grimaldi during those months of fêtes and Court intrigues, on strange and dangerous ground. In spite of the fact that his young wife was soon pregnant there was little real harmony between the two; but in other matters Louis was greatly helped by his father-in-law, Marshal Duke of Gramont—'skilful at keeping on good terms with everyone, especially at making no mistake about those who were to remain in power over others.' Eventually Louis struck up a friendship with his wife's brother, Count de Guiche, 'alone of his kind, a romantic hero unlike any other.'

A year later, Guiche was banished for having attempted a love affair with Henrietta of England, sister of Charles II, who had just married Monsieur, the Duke of Orléans. Catherine-Charlotte, Duchess of Valentinois, who had been chosen by Madame to 'take part in her pleasures,' had had no hand in the matter. But she was fond of her brother, and she had the haughty disposition and quick temper of the Gramonts. 'The hasty character of this lady,' wrote Madame de Motteville in her memoirs, 'caused her to make countless intrigues for the recall of her brother, and even to make disrespectful jeers about the Queen Mother. Madame was very fond of her, and treated this guilty man's sister as one of her favourites. It was only right to make up to her for the faults of her brother, for which she might have innocently suffered. . . . The Queen Mother . . . had her sent away.'

At the beginning of September, 1661, at the time when Fouquet was arrested in Nantes by D'Artagnan, and Louis XIV returned to Fontainebleau, the second Duke of Valentinois and his Duchess started off for Monaco; the former with obvious relief, the latter 'sorely sad.' As for Puyguilhem—'to see her once more, he followed her coach disguised now as a merchant, now as a postillion, or in any travesty which would render him unrecognizable to her attendants.'

It is always refreshing to note the calm, factual manner in which the French gentry and nobility of the seventeenth century accepted the restraints of the times, both temporal and spiritual. The rule for a noble was to be at Court, under the eye of his King. So Puyguilhem did not linger on the road. The Duke and Duchess of Valentinois, who succeeded to Monaco in January, 1662, also knew what was demanded of them by their rank. Louis I legislated, administered, had currency struck; Catherine-Charlotte gave birth to children—three successive sisters for the baby heir, Antoine: Jeanne-Marie-Dévote in 1662, Thérèse-Marie-Aurélia in 1663, and Anne-Hippolyte in 1664.

When the worldly tumult dies and passions fade, Christian traditions reappear; and so pious thoughts came to the exiled young wife. Her idea may have been designed, too, to bring an end to a link between Genoa and the Principality. However, with the full agreement of her husband, she decided to found a convent which would enable the girls of Monaco and the neighbourhood to be educated locally, instead of going away to Genoa or to towns in Provence.

The princely couple chose the recently founded Order of the Visitation, and on August 27th, 1663, an agreement was signed with the nuns of the mother-convent at Aix-en-Provence. Three months later, six nuns and a lay sister arrived in Monaco and were temporarily installed in a house on the palace square. Catherine-Charlotte soon returned to the pleasures of the period, but she always retained an interest in her convent, which was built on the east side of the Rock, behind the ruins of the 'new' castle and on ground where gardens had been.

It was built in ten years, between 1665 and 1675, by an architect from Genoa, Marc Antonio Grigho. In the centre of the vast conventual buildings was a vaulted cloister, and on one side was a chapel.[1] When Catherine-Charlotte died, in June, 1678, she left her heart to the Convent of the Visitation, and a sum of 10,000 *livres* for a Mass to be celebrated perpetually on the anniversary of her death.

But to return to the 1660's. Madame had missed the Princess of Monaco and tried to get her recalled to Court. Monsieur, the perverted Philippe d'Orléans, for his part, 'through feelings that appeared incompatible, was fond of all the Gramont family.' The couple managed things so well that not only was Catherine-Charlotte recalled from her exile, in 1664, but Madame, as an English Princess, was allowed a Lady-in-Waiting to take charge of her Household, and chose Catherine-Charlotte.

Louis let his wife leave for Paris without him. Was this ill-assorted and discordant couple about to separate definitely, and had the husband become resigned to a liaison of his wife's which had roots in the past and might save her from the life of a libertine? It would all seem so; for the Prince remained at Monaco for a year, and only when the outbreak of war against England gave him the urge to take service, and an anonymous letter from an unsuccessful wooer of his wife, the Marquis de Villeroy, told him she had become the King's mistress, did he leave for Paris and appear again at Court.

Puyguilhem was no longer there. He did not at all like women being unfaithful to him, and had shown it. The King, to get him out of the way, instructed him to go down to Pau and see how his regiment of dragoons was getting on. Puyguilhem turned a deaf ear, and 'His Majesty strongly insisting one day he, in despair at leaving his mistress and a little jealous of the King

---

[1] The convent is today the grammar school. But the Place de la Visitation, the present administrative centre of the Principality, is a reminder of it.

besides, replied that he would resign his commission sooner than go away, that his resignation was all ready, and he would never again draw his sword in the King's service.' Louis XIV, with his usual tolerance where Puyguilhem was concerned, told the angry man that he was 'most unwise' and sent him to the Bastille to cool off.

He was kept in prison for six months. Having had time to think things over, he came out determined to take revenge on his faithless mistress, but without running the risk of drawing the King's disfavour upon himself again. He bided his time, until he saw that the King was becoming indifferent to Catherine-Charlotte; then, 'vicious and spiteful by nature, made more so by jealousy,' as St Simon said of him, he acted brutally. It happened on May 18th, 1666. The King himself gave an account of the incident, in a letter to his envoy at The Hague, Count d'Estrades.

'Last Monday, at Versailles, a trinket worth twelve hundred *pistoles* was being played for in the salon, and the ladies had sat down on the floor itself to be all the cooler. I was standing up and watching the play with some interest to see who would win. It so happened that, as I stepped back a couple of paces to have a better view, those who were between me and the wall were obliged to move. Among them was Puyguilhem, and in his haste to make way for me he accidentally stepped hard on one of the Princess of Monaco's hands; she was propping herself on it as she sat on the floor, as I said, but it was covered by her skirt, so no one could see it even, and that makes what happened next most remarkable. The Princess looked at her fingers for a while and showed them to the ladies near her, complaining that they hurt; and then suddenly, having raised her voice, and having seen that it was Puyguilhem who had stepped on her hand, she began to cry, got up from the floor, angrily throwing down a book she was holding, and withdrew into another room where she wept for some time, while several persons tried in vain to comfort her and to make her see it was a pure accident without any intention to vex her and even less to offend her. Puyguilhem, for his part, omitted nothing to show his grief at what had happened, and offered to do anything to make reparation, pure disgrace though that would be, even to throw himself out of the window there and then, if that would satisfy the Princess and convince her that he had been far from any intention to offend her.'

No one at Court was mistaken about Puyguilhem's intentions, though, the Gramonts—who knew him well—less than anyone. But Louis XIV made it known that he 'wished to save two families from coming to harm through a misunderstanding,' and that he would permit no violence; so Marshal de Gramont and his younger son, Count de Louvigny, easily kept their anger within the limits prescribed by prudence and Court servility. But Louis of Monaco, who had hotter blood and a stiffer backbone, hastened to The Hague to find Guiche, who was still in exile. What would the two brothers-in-law, each inflaming the other, have ended by doing? The civil strife of the Fronde was still sufficiently in men's memories for the King to fear they might turn rebels. And so he informed his envoy at The Hague about the incident, carefully and at length, and the mild interpretation he meant to be given to it. This interpretation, this concealed order, was conveyed to Louis Grimaldi; as was the news of the Prince of Condé's intervention and approach to his father-in-law.

Louis, with a stifled sigh, gave way. On May 27th he wrote and thanked the Prince of Condé for his good offices 'in the matter concerning Madame de Monaco. . . . As for the origin of it, that had always seemed to me so exaggerated that I was never able to understand how it could have been an accident, yet I am now completely convinced it was so, seeing that is the belief of Your Highness—who would, I trust, have done me the honour of informing me if I should have taken the matter in any other way.'

His hurried journey to The Hague would therefore have been pointless; but while Louis was staying there, the Dutch fleet prepared to sail to seek battle with the English. Guiche had already volunteered; Louis, without hesitating, like a true Grimaldi, joined him aboard the *Duivenvoorde*, commanded by Captain Terlon. The enemy fleets joined action off Dunkirk on June 11th, and continued for four days. Guiche and Louis fought bravely; their ship was set on fire and they refused to leave her, but the flames reached the gun-room. Clad only in their under-drawers, the two young men were about to jump overboard when

93

they were taken off by the *Petite Hollande*. For another three hours they helped fight this ship, until she too went down. Again they were rescued and, still scantily clad, taken before the Dutch admiral, Ruyter, who congratulated them and had fresh clothing given them.

An equerry of Marshal Gramont had been killed during the battle, Guiche had been wounded in the arm and shoulder, but Louis had escaped without a scratch. This battle initiation aroused his enthusiasm for a military career; especially as he had no liking for Court intrigues, and the love affairs of his wife were becoming so well known that he was content to keep away from Versailles. Moreover, his brave conduct had been noticed and remarked upon. The Duke of Saint-Aignan, who was close to the King, wrote to him a few days after the naval action: 'I was so pleased to hear of the part you played in the sea-fight of the Dutch against the English. And I am charmed by the way it is spoken about at Court.'

It was so well spoken about that on March 15th, 1667, at the beginning of hostilities against Spain, Louis was made an army colonel. He at once raised his own regiment and gave it the name of Monaco Cavalry; with it, he took part in the siege of Lille, where Marshal Gramont distinguished himself at the head of the King's regiment. Lille fell on August 17th; and soon afterwards the Prince of Monaco was present at the siege of Alost, which was taken by Turenne in September. The campaign ended in the autumn, and without appearing at Court the Prince set off for Monaco, where he spent the winter. He returned north for the opening of the campaign in the spring, but peace was signed at Aix-la-Chapelle in May, 1668. He disbanded his regiment, except for the first company which the King kept under arms, and returned to Monaco accompanied this time by his wife, who had found that the atmosphere at the Palais Royal no longer suited her.[1]

They were together for the next two years, residing either at Monaco or Genoa. Their last child, a son, François-Honoré, was born in Genoa on December 31st, 1669.

They returned to Paris in August, 1670, a few weeks after

---

[1] Her affair with the Chevalier de Lorraine was no doubt disliked by the homosexual Duke of Orléans as much as by the Duchess.

the sudden and mysterious death of Henrietta, Duchess of Orléans. The King had a fresh mistress, Madame de Montespan; Puyguilhem—now the Duke of Lauzun—had found a new love in the Grande Mademoiselle; and the Chevalier de Lorraine was languishing in exile in Italy. So it is not difficult to conceive that the Princess of Monaco needed little persuading to return south again. She and Louis were back in Monaco in the spring of 1671. This was her last stay there, and the last attempt of the two to live, if not as a married couple, at least without coming to a public separation.

Madame de Grignan, the wife of the governor of Provence, paid a visit to Monaco in the spring of 1672. Her mother, the famous Marquise de Sévigné, wrote to her afterwards: 'You'll have had much conversation (with the Princess of Monaco), she speaks frankly about herself, even on the most delicate matters,' and went on about the perils of the journey, '. . . to think of it makes me go cold all over. I'd never go there, though I've nothing against those parts, and the thought that you're on your way back makes me tremble. . . . Is Madame de Monaco in despair at being on that side of the Alps? Is she soon expecting to come to Paris?'

The good Marquise—so often sharp and sour—need not have pitied her with such humbug. A few weeks after Madame de Grignan's visit the Prince and Princess of Monaco set off for the north again. Louis went to join the army in the field, for war had broken out against the Dutch; while Catherine-Charlotte went to stay with Madame de Grignan in Provence before going to Paris.

The couple were never to meet each other again. In April, 1673, the Princess was appointed First Lady-in-Waiting to the new Madame of France; she went to live at the Palais Royal and became almost as great a favourite of the Duke of Orléans's second wife, the daughter of the Elector Palatine, as she had been of Henrietta. The Prince divided his time for the next six years between the army and Monaco and travel, avoiding Paris and especially the Court. He took part in all the campaigns in the Low Countries between 1672 and 1678; spent long periods at Monaco; paid visits to Genoa, Rome, and Venice, passing the winter of 1675 in the last place. The following winter he went to London and stayed several months, and was there again in the spring of 1677[1] when he was much in the company of Hortense Mancini, the beautiful Duchesse de Mazarin, who had left her miserable husband for the pleasures of Whitehall. It is hardly likely that Louis Grimaldi succeeded in ousting Charles II in the favours of the lovely duchess but he no doubt tried. In any case, he showed himself generous and blind in her favour. . . . 'Madame de Mazarin is adept at stealing my counters and slipping a card into the pack. . . . I turned to Monsieur de Monaco, who said to me quite seriously and sincerely, "Honestly, Monsieur de Saint-Evremond, I was looking somewhere else. . . ." '

The year 1678 marked a turning point in the life of Louis Grimaldi; in every aspect of it—family, career, and his administration of the Principality.

The Princess of Monaco died at the Palais Royal on June 4th, after a long and painful illness. Marshal de Gramont had been to see his daughter just before leaving for Bayonne. 'He said she would have to think of packing her kit, that Count de Guiche had already gone as an advance party to mark up the billets, and that he himself would soon be joining both of them.' Thus warned, the Princess sent for Father Bourdaloue, of whom it had been said 'he was a good workman for consciences gone to rack and ruin.' She confessed and took Communion, then made her will, 'and with admirable strength of mind made no further reference to death. . . .' Louis Grimaldi was an honest, upright gentleman, but he had been grievously hurt and offended in the past, and he now showed little emotion—which caused plenty of gossip. 'It's very understandable,' wrote Madame de Grignan, 'that he should show so little regret at losing someone who had left him of her own accord.'

In the seventeenth century, worldly life and the spiritual had both a share in each family's existence. Six months after the death of Catherine-Charlotte, her eldest daughter, Jeanne-Marie-Dévote, took the veil and entered the Convent of the Visitation

[1] Louis Grimaldi wrote from London on May 20th, 1677, to the Chevalier de Monceau, who commanded the garrison at Monaco: 'I have come back here to see some friends again, having taken advantage of the journey I recently made to Calais with the King to cross the Channel again.'

8 Princess Louise-Hippolyte of Monaco, 1697–1731. *Portrait by J. B. van Loo.*

9 Princess Marie-Catherine de Brignole of Monaco, 1739–1813.

10 Prince Honoré III of Monaco, 1720–1795. *Portrait by Louis Tocqué.*

that the Princess had founded.[1] This girl of sixteen went to a cloistered life and prayed for God's mercy for her family.

The Prince of Monaco's military career came to an end when peace was signed at Nymeghen. Next time war broke out, ten years later, it would be his son, Antoine, who represented the Grimaldis.

Lastly, the Statutes of Monaco were promulgated on December 23rd. They were the result of long preparation and study of the legislative problems of the Principality. Known also as the Code Louis, there were four main headings—civil and criminal law, police jurisdiction, and rural administration; together they formed an improved set of laws for governing the Principality. Like the Statutes of Menton drawn up in the past by Lucien, the Code Louis was the result of the sovereign prince's own efforts, and was likewise much in advance of the jurisprudence of the time.

The next ten years—the decade between the death of his wife and the wedding of his son, Antoine—were without doubt the happiest and calmest in Louis Grimaldi's life since his childhood on the Rock. Freed from an unhappy marriage that had caused him to be tempted into ways he had no real taste for, he soon established a simple, homely life at Monaco, among his children, and cultivated the company of a few well-chosen friends. He never returned to London, but spent his time either at Monaco or Versailles, where he had a house that he had bought from the Archbishop of Rheims, Charles-Maurice Le Tellier, which he called his 'pavilion' and was in the neighbourhood of the royal stable buildings. He also had a town house in Paris, in the St Germain district.

The education and future of his children were a constant concern of Louis Grimaldi. The eldest, Antoine, came of age in 1682. François-Honoré was then a boy of thirteen, and like many a younger son of noble family in those days he was intended to join the Knights of Malta; this would enable him to follow a military career if he wished, while not excluding the possibility of returning to civilian life if his elder brother died and he became the heir. But François-Honoré was a devout, shy lad,

---

[1] The second daughter, Thérèse-Marie-Aurélia, had asked to be dressed in the habit of the same Order just before she died, at the age of twelve, on February 14th, 1675.

studious and with a love of literature, and soon showed a prefer-
ence for the Church. He eventually became a priest and spent
many years in Paris, in the shadow of the Sorbonne. Louis
Grimaldi's favourite child was his youngest daughter, Anne-
Hippolyte; he was most fond of her, and in later life the two were
on very tender terms.

When in Paris, Louis was always well received at the Palais
Royal, especially by the Palatine.[1] He was on intimate terms with
the Gramonts in spite of the misfortunes of his marriage, and had
good relations with all the influential families at Court, the Le
Tellier, Soissons, Lorraine, and others. The King viewed him
favourably; he attended Court regularly, and was among those
invited to accompany the monarch to Marly and Fontainebleau.

Although Louis Grimaldi avoided Court scandal and intrigues,
and did not solicit office or appointment—he would have considered that incompatible with his rank of sovereign prince—he
was anxious to have the standing and precedence at Court that
he considered his due. For by an anomaly that must have seemed
to him extraordinary, this Prince who had real sovereign powers
found himself less well situated than the members of several
families who held a special position as foreign princes. He was,
of course, too intelligent and shrewd not to admit that 'the
Lorraines,' as they were collectively called, should have such a
privilege. The elder sons of their House, like the Dukes of
Savoy, married daughters of the blood-royal; and a Lorraine,
Louise de Vaudémont, had been the wife of Henri III. But this
discrimination, although accepted with resignation by the dukes

---

[1] Two letters from the Palatine show the esteem and affection she had for the
Prince of Monaco. In one dated September 4th, 1683, her secretary thanked him for
the sympathy he had expressed on the death of the Queen, but the Palatine added a
long postscript: 'If my time had not been so occupied between two different things,
the chase to follow the King around and all the ceremonies to do with the Queen,
I should not have failed to thank you myself for your expression of sympathy; but
the one and the other, although quite different, have in common that they necessitate
some little rest, and so I left the matter to the care of my secretary; but when I came
to put my signature I realized I had too much regard for you to send this letter
without adding a word from my own hand . . .'
Six years later, soon after the death of her stepdaughter, Marie-Louise d'Orléans,
Queen of Spain, she confided to Louis Grimaldi: 'Although her end was so fine and
glorious, and there is reason to believe she is now happier than I am, yet I still
cannot console myself for her loss. I have no doubt, Sir, that you felt sorry too, for
yours is such a good and warm heart . . .'

and peers, touched their vanity and was the cause of many quarrels and incidents—and continued to be so until the end of the old monarchy.

It would no doubt have been simple enough, when the Treaty of Péronne was being negotiated, for the House of Monaco to have obtained the Court privileges accorded to foreign princes, of which one of the most important was a stool for their daughters. But it had not occurred to Honoré II, partly because he was quite satisfied with the very real advantages of the treaty —French protection, revenues and honours, recognition of his title of Prince—and partly because, as neither he nor his predecessors had attended the Spanish Court, he had no idea of the importance that life at the French Court would have for his descendants.

During these ten years Louis Grimaldi was trying, with patience and skill, to find a means of correcting this inferiority of position, through the influential and solid friendships he had acquired by his steadfastness. His efforts met with success when the marriage contract of his son, Antoine, the third Duke of Valentinois, was signed.

Louis de Lorraine, Count of Armagnac, Grand Ecuyer de France, was an important person; he was so convinced of it himself, that people called him Monsieur Mirobolan, Mister Show-off. As for the Countess of Armagnac, who was short and dumpy, St Simon wrote of her in his malicious way that she was 'the finest-looking woman in France . . . with no rouge, ribbons, or lace, nor any sort of jewellery or adornment, always dressed in black or grey, with her gown tucked up like a midwife's, a round mob-cap, her hair unpowdered and uncurled and smoothed down, wearing a collar of black taffeta and a small, low head-dress, whether in her rooms or the King's. . . . She was haughty, loud and pushing, though with little wit or wile . . . was high-handed with Ministers and their wives, spent all her time in her rooms keeping the greatest state of the whole Court, yet waiting on the King as little as possible, and only visited other people on special occasions. Always busy with her household, both mean and ostentatious about things . . . she led her husband by the nose, treated her children like slaves and denied them everything, except for her daughters, whose beauty softened her—she was far from having their looks, and all her life had kept her virtue, as she merited, free from any shadow. Everyone who had to do with her, dreaded it.'

The Countess of Armagnac was a sister of Marshal de Villeroy. Before her marriage she had been a lady-in-waiting to the Queen, but had been banished at the same time as Count de Guiche. This had brought her into contact with Louis Grimaldi; and when, later, they were each seeking a marriage for their children, Louvois, the Minister for War and a member of the Le Tellier family, helped matters by serving as go-between.

The Countess had never really regained favour with the King, who had no liking for her; but her husband stood high in the royal favour. Louis XIV was therefore very agreeable to the marriage of Marie de Lorraine to the Duke of Valentinois; the King not only signed the marriage contract, on June 8th, 1688, but also conferred the rank of foreign prince upon Louis Grimaldi and his heirs male. As an additional favour, the King included the Prince's name among those who received the ribbon of the Saint Esprit in December, 1688, although he was no longer at Court. The Prince had returned to Monaco several months previously, wracked with gout; he was, moreover, putting on weight, becoming increasingly short-sighted, and had almost ruined himself by his extravagances.

'The Duchess of Valentinois was a charming young thing . . . she was spoilt by her parents' fondness for her and by the attentions of the courtiers who frequented the Lorraine house, which was always open day and night; and the beautiful women who were its chief adornment attracted the most glittering young men. Her husband, very sensibly, realized he hadn't the upper hand.' These few lines by St Simon sum up the conjugal life of the Duke and Duchess of Valentinois during the early years of their marriage.

The lack of understanding between them grieved Louis Grimaldi. The letters he wrote to his son between 1690 and 1699, when he was at Monaco and Antoine was with the army, show the affection he had for a son who was intelligent and clever but of a difficult character. They show, too, the father's guiding restraint and understanding, and are the letters of a fair-minded and kindly man whose feelings had not been embittered by the painful experience of his own married life.

The Duke of Valentinois had been commissioned lieutenant in the King's infantry regiment in 1683, and promoted to colonel of the Soissonnais regiment the following year. When war broke out again he went with his regiment to fight in Germany and the Low Countries, and was at the battle of Fleurus in 1690. Throughout that year's campaign his father wrote to him regularly every two or three days, about the war and the news and gossip of the Court, but mainly about the Duchess and how best to come to a happier understanding with her. For instance, in a letter from Versailles dated June 29th, 1690, Louis wrote to his son:

'I still think excuses should be made for your wife because she is so very young (the Duchess was not much more than sixteen then), and that is also why you should bear with her to some extent. I trust that, with time, she will act better towards you and will realize more than she does at present where her true and chief interest lays. Your misfortune is entirely due to the fact that you haven't gained the favour of your mother-in-law, Madame d'Armagnac. She's the stumbling-block . . . as long as you and she don't get on together, you can't expect much tenderness from the daughter. . . .'

Madame d'Armagnac, it must be admitted, made no concessions, especially where her pocket was concerned. When the Duchess of Valentinois was expecting a baby her mother declared it would be too great a financial burden; and so Louis Grimaldi offered the use of his pavilion at Versailles. 'I hope it will be a boy and that he'll remain in my charge, but in any case we shall do well to save your mother-in-law this inconvenience, and it would be a fine thing if that got you free of her.'

Alas, Antoine was neither compliant nor discreet. In camp, at army headquarters, he spoke bitterly and complainingly about his mother-in-law. She got to hear of it, and flew into a rage. 'For God's sake, once and for all get rid of this habit of telling everyone about your domestic affairs,' was the advice given in vain by the Prince of Monaco, who throughout his own uneasy married life had managed to keep on good terms with his wife's family, the Gramonts.

On October 7th, 1690, the Duchess of Valentinois gave birth to a girl, Catherine-Charlotte. Louis Grimaldi was deeply disappointed; still, he expressed the hope that the child would become as lovely as her mother. Though he could not help writing, from Monaco: 'A girl doesn't give our house much to rejoice about. . . .'

The Prince of Monaco would have been even more dismayed if he had known of his son's decision to 'shut himself off from his wife.' Such was the manner in which the couple lived during 1691—a gay round of pleasures for Marie de Lorraine, 'more of an elegant flirt than all the ladies of the kingdom put together,' according to Madame de La Fayette; while Antoine divided his time between the backstage of the Opera and the campaign in Flanders. But in 1692, when the Duke was at the siege of Namur, the Duchess left Paris for Monaco.

The Prince had had enough of the haughtiness and disdain of the Armagnac family; and, moreover, the fact that the future of his line depended on a frail little girl caused him much anxiety. He had no doubt asked the King to remind Marie de Lorraine of her wifely duties; and Louis XIV, who had a liking for Louis Grimaldi, and who was becoming stricter anyway, had given the young Duchess to understand that the air of the Mediterranean would do her good.

A few days after her arrival at Monaco news reached there that the Duke of Valentinois had been badly wounded at Namur. The Prince, in his constant efforts to smooth the way for these two who did not understand each other and felt little love, wrote at once to tell his son that the Duchess had fainted on hearing the news. 'I don't think anyone can have a better disposition or be more good-hearted than she is; the poor girl deserves to be loved.'

The Prince and his daughter-in-law went to stay at Menton in August, then at Genoa until the end of September, when they returned to Monaco to await the Duke. His wound had healed, fighting was over for the year, and his arrival was expected. The Prince was very glad; but although he reckoned a fairly short stay, a month or six weeks, would be enough for essential purposes, he considered that Antoine first needed to show himself at Court. The Prince was also anxious about the future movements of the couple, once reunited. Would the Duke still want to extend his wife's penitence, and leave her behind by the lonely

Mediterranean if he went off to rejoin the army in the spring? It was a matter for husband and wife to argue over themselves, but the Prince pointed out to his son that Marie 'would be in despair if you didn't take her to Paris with you.' This sort of hint was the only kind he allowed himself to give his distrustful and independent son.

'She made all kinds of fine promises,' St Simon recounts, 'and she was taken back to Paris. I don't know who advised her but, while her conduct was the same as before, she insured against having to return to Monaco by starting to spread a vile scandal about her father-in-law. . . .'

No one believed the scandal, but news of it reached the ears of the Prince and his son, and the gap between husband and wife widened. Saddened by all this, and harassed by financial difficulties that were sometimes the cause of peevish letters from his son,[1] Louis spent the whole of the next few years in his Principality, except for a short visit to Versailles in the spring of 1695. He did not even return to Paris for the wedding of his daughter, Anne-Hippolyte, with the Duke d'Uzès, in January, 1696. This was a fine alliance, but an ill-assorted union. She was thirty-two, and looked it; the Duke was only eighteen. But she was wealthy, while he was beset by family debts. It was an unhappy marriage; the Duchess died in childbirth, in July, 1700, leaving two daughters who did not long survive her.[2]

The Prince was away from Paris too, when a few weeks after the wedding the Duke of Valentinois resigned his commission in a fit of temper, resentful at not having been promoted to brigadier. Louis Grimaldi had vainly tried to forestall his son's action. In February, 1696, he wrote to him from Monaco, pressing him to refer the matter to the Duke of Beauvillier and Marshal de Noailles, both level-headed people. The Prince added 'as for the state of confusion in your financial affairs, which you're

[1] Antoine was claiming his 'maternelle,' his inheritance from his mother. Catherine-Charlotte de Gramont had had a dowry of 300,000 *livres*, and in September, 1668, the King had given her some furnished property that had belonged to a certain François de Montbron.

[2] The Prince was in Rome, as Louis XIV's ambassador, when he learnt of the death of the Duchesse d'Uzès. He wrote a sorrowful letter to the King, apologizing for not talking of State business but only of his sadness at losing a beloved daughter. He had 'hastened to San Pastore,' to the Father General of the Dominicans.

thinking of giving as a reason for leaving the army, no one and least of all the King will accept such an excuse; anyway, I wash my hands of the matter, and you may do as you wish.' Of course, the affectionate father went on to say, if the Duke came to Monaco he would welcome him gladly, and 'it will be more proper if you're here with me for a part of the army's next campaign.'

The Duke having committed his grave mistake and resigned his commission, the Prince thought only of how his son could 'wipe out' the bad impression made on the King. Louis Grimaldi knew how great was the influence of Count d'Armagnac, Monsieur le Grand, and did not fail to point out to Antoine that 'what would be permitted from another and forgiven, will be treated as a grave offence in your case.' He wrote to him from Menton, on April 1st, 1696, impressing upon him the need to appear regularly at Court, 'the only good course suitable to the unpleasant situation you're in.'

The Prince's advice was not only sound but timely, as things turned out; for the Grimaldi family was soon in need, once again, of the King's all-powerful mediation. On June 18th, 1696, little Catherine-Charlotte, the only child of the Duke and Duchess of Valentinois, died. The Grimaldis were left without heir or heiress.

A reconciliation between the Duke and his wife was most important, but was difficult to bring about because of the attitude of the Armagnac family. The Archbishop of Paris interceded, and the King intervened in the matter. Towards the end of 1696 the Prince of Monaco, suffering more than ever from gout, travelled sadly and slowly up to Paris. At the beginning of January, however, he was at Marly, and on the 10th announced to his son: 'The King is going to request Monsieur d'Aumont to deal with your troubles. They are being gossiped about here in the oddest way, and Madame d'Armagnac is loud in naming her conditions for agreeing to let her daughter go back to you. It will be a good thing if you made the best of them. . . .'

Wise for once, the Duke of Valentinois made the best of them, and the Armagnac family had to give way. 'On January 27th,' recounts St Simon, 'Madame d'Armagnac accompanied by her son and the Princess d'Harcourt took her daughter to the Paris house of the Duke of Valentinois. Madame de Valentinois had dinner there, slept there, and what was worse, stayed there.'

For several months it seemed doubtful whether this reconciliation imposed by the King would last,[1] but perhaps the Duke was more amenable and his wife more virtuous. In any case, on November 10th, 1697, a girl was born to them, Louise-Hippolyte.[2] And for the next fifteen years the couple lived together, if not happily, at least calmly.

In the spring of 1698 the Prince of Monaco went back to his Rock, mainly to try and settle with the Duke of Savoy the ever-recurring boundary dispute over La Turbie, during a short visit the Duke was to make to Nice. The Prince was still at Monaco when, on August 20th, the King officially announced his appointment as ambassador-extraordinary to the Holy See.

The choice was flattering to the Prince, for the mission entrusted to him was a delicate one. The death of Charles II of Spain seemed imminent, and the three great Powers—France, England, and Holland—had hurriedly made peace at Ryswick in 1697, and were secretly negotiating to divide the Spanish possessions between them. The French Dauphin was to have the Kingdom of the Two Sicilies and to be invested by the Pope. But Pope Innocent XII was over eighty, and at any moment a Conclave to elect a new Pope might have to be proclaimed.

In June, Cardinal de Bouillon, who was representing French interests at Rome, had put forward the suggestion that in view of the expected death of the King of Spain and the possibility of the opening of a Conclave it was desirable for the French monarch to have in Rome an ambassador who was 'both a soldier and a statesman'; and that he, the Cardinal, would be prepared to act under the ambassador's direction. Louis XIV had no love for

[1] In May, 1697, Louis Grimaldi wrote to his son from Marly: 'It's being said around Paris, as it is here, that the discord between you and your wife has begun again, and people at Court are getting some pleasant gossip out of that. However—I advise you to take no notice, and put yourself above it all, if you can; otherwise you'll suffer from the daughter as well as the mother.'

[2] The birth of a baby girl was another diappointment for the Prince. But he had a tender heart, and in a letter some months later, May 30th, 1698, he said, 'I am very glad to hear that my poor scabby little girl is getting better, and I hope it'll help her to be prettier later on. If we were ever to have a grandson, that would compensate us for all our misfortunes in the past.'

Bouillon. 'Terribly vain and with excessive pretensions,' the Cardinal 'looked back with nostalgia to his sovereignty over La Marck'; and it burnt his lips to qualify himself as a 'subject' of the King of France. The lukewarm attitude he had adopted in the Fénelon affair (when that incisive archbishop and tutor to the heir to the throne had dared to criticize the King) had lowered him still further in the estimation of Louis XIV, and even more so in Madame de Maintenon's. Moreover, Bouillon was out of favour with the Pope, who refused to grant him any private audience and did not address a word to him at 'chapels.'[1]

The King took the Cardinal at his word, and appointed the Prince of Monaco.

This choice has been judged a bad one by the historian, Gabriel Hanotaux, who edited and published the 'Instructions to French Ambassadors and Ministers in Rome.' And one certainly wonders what could have decided Louis XIV to appoint a man who had never sought office of any kind, who was no longer at Court, whose health was very poor and whose financial affairs were in a deplorable state. But there would seem to have been three reasons for this 'bad' choice. First, Louis XIV's esteem for Louis Grimaldi, whose zeal and disinterestedness he greatly appreciated. The King regarded him, as did everyone at Court, as very much a well-bred man of the world, upright and fair-minded; his extravagances and love of display were regrettable in a private person but would enhance the prestige of an ambassador in Rome. Secondly, he was a sincere and pious Catholic who showed no leaning towards the Jansenists or the Quietism of Fénelon—and that was a fundamental consideration for the King at this period—and the influential de Noailles had both strongly favoured his appointment, the Archbishop even more than the Marshal.[2] Lastly, the King must have considered that it would be very useful to have in Rome, in that microcosm of

[1] 'Chapels' were held on Fridays and were the Pope's 'receiving days.' The Prince of Monaco, in a letter written on June 29th, said how pleased he was that the Pope 'had become more human' towards the Cardinal de Bouillon, and that 'His Holiness and the Cardinal are now on good terms again, at least on the surface.'

[2] On April 6th, 1699, Louis de Noailles, Archbishop of Paris, wrote to the Prince from Versailles: 'I am much obliged to you for associating yourself with my pleasure at the satisfactory outcome for the Church in the case against Monsieur de Cambrai. It is basically all we could wish, and mistakes have been put right that would never have occurred if you had been in Rome.'

European intrigues, a representative like the Prince of Monaco who was a relative of several Italian cardinals, namely, the two Spinolas, and Pallavicini, Durazzo, and Imperiali, and especially the Secretary of State, Cardinal Spada, whom the King regarded as most likely to become the next Pope; and a representative who, moreover, was Italian by birth and had kept in touch with his relatives and friends all over the peninsula.[1]

This last consideration, however, had its weak points, and these were to have an adverse effect on the whole of Louis Grimaldi's term as ambassador. For one thing, when a remote relative attempts to penetrate into a narrow family circle where suspicion and trickery abound, and tries to sort out the double-dealing, he often arouses alarm and distrust. And then, too, the Prince was much more susceptible to the special atmosphere of Rome than a complete foreigner would have been, and this atmosphere went to his head. He was overcome with matters of procedure and ceremony, and got immersed in petty details, often at the expense of essentials.[2]

Marshal de Villeroy wrote from Compiègne on September 4th, 1698, congratulating Louis Grimaldi on his appointment, and added: 'It seems to me of great importance, in the present state of affairs, that you should come yourself to receive the King's instructions, so I don't doubt we shall be seeing you here soon. . . .' The Prince took the strong hint, and in mid-November set off for Paris. At Valence, on the way, he learnt of the addition to his son's family of 'a third female baby!' 'Imagine how thunderstruck I was by that bit of news. I won't say anything more about it, only that there's plenty of ill-luck in our doings.'

When the Prince reached Paris he attended Court and waited

---

[1] On more than one occasion the Prince had given useful information to the King's Ministers.

[2] For instance, the question of Louis Grimaldi's courtesy call on the Queen of Poland was never settled throughout his eighteen months' embassy to the Holy See. The Queen, widow of Jean Sobieski, and French by birth, would not give an arm-chair to ambassadors when receiving them, as she did to cardinals, only a high-backed chair, at the most—and even went back on this concession, which Louis XIV had found acceptable, much to the Prince of Monaco's annoyance. There were also the household guards of the Spanish ambassador, which made Louis Grimaldi envious; he could see himself surrounded, in the same way, by grenadiers and dragoons—but got little response from the King or Torcy.

on the King, borrowed 80,000 francs from the Duke of Lauzun, and fell out with Torcy[1] over his refusal to address him as 'Monseigneur,' which was how Secretaries of State addressed the Lorraines and the Bouillons, though not the Rohans. This incident foreboded similar ones in Rome. Torcy, therefore, ironic and cautious, began his lengthy, precise Instructions, which were handed to the Prince on January 28th, 1699, with a reminder: 'The honour of serving the foremost King in the world being greater than any title, H.M. believes that those belonging to the Prince of Monaco by birthright will suffice for him to uphold more worthily the authority that H.M. is giving him. . . .'

The Instructions went on to give a sketch of the Pope. 'Those well aware of his character are not disheartened by refusals, and their perseverance is often rewarded by the most difficult favours to obtain.' Torcy next came to the matter of the Spanish Succession and the Partition Treaty which had been signed the previous September. Under this, the French Dauphin was to have the Two Sicilies, as arranged; Milan was to go to the Archduke of Austria, the other pretender to the Spanish throne; and the Prince Elector of Bavaria was to be the next King of Spain.[2] But would the Emperor agree to all this, and what would be the reaction of the Italian States? Torcy dealt briefly and disdainfully with the attitude of the Duke of Savoy,[3] and then proceeded to discuss the expected Conclave by stating the French King's attitude to the *papabili*—the cardinals with the best chances of becoming the next Pope—and by indicating the strategy the ambassador should adopt.

For some, such as the cardinals Acciaioli and Capegna, it should be enough to leave the intrigues to others who were opposed to their elevation. As for Cardinal Marescotti, he was not unaware that 'the King's ambassador and the French cardinals have always been the main obstacles to his election . . . and Rome is not a place where such treatment is easily forgotten.' The

---

[1] The Marquis de Torcy was a nephew of the great Colbert. He had been Secretary of State for Foreign Affairs since 1696.

[2] The Bavarian Prince died in February, 1699, and another agreement was signed in March, 1700.

[3] 'It is impossible to estimate at the moment what the Duke has in mind, except that he wants to draw some kind of advantage from the changes in the European situation that can be caused by the death of His Most Catholic Majesty.'

King trusted, however, that he would not have to take steps to exclude him. In the case of Cardinal Coloredo, 'it is not H.M.'s intention to oppose whoever is chosen as the most worthy; but if difficulties should arise to prevent his election, neither the Prince of Monaco nor the French cardinals are to take any steps to remove them.'

The cardinals to be kept out of the running were followed by those to be aided. His Majesty considered that if the choice fell on Cardinal Barberini it would be a good thing for the Church and advantageous to her interests. 'It seems likely that Cardinal Albani would be his most influential adviser, and this would make the election of Cardinal Barberini even more suitable to the welfare of Christendom.' The ambassador could support Cardinal Cavallerini; and as for Cardinal Castaguti, whose chances would only emerge towards the end of the Conclave, 'H.M., in such an event, has no reason for opposing his elevation, but his limited intelligence and weak morals do not make it very desirable.'

The next three cardinals mentioned were considered too young to be eligible—Cardinals del Verme, Spada, and Albani, the last two especially. But the election of Cardinal Spada would be most suitable to His Majesty, and consequently to the welfare of the Church. Cardinal Albani was the youngest of all three, 'but should he become a strong candidate, the King thinks no better choice could be made. Convey to him . . . that H.M. holds him in high esteem and would be pleased to show it whenever occasion occurs.'

Torcy repeated that the Prince was to avoid formally applying a veto. 'The effects of such a measure cannot be estimated . . . nor what the obstinacy of a faction might lead to. . . . A rupture of that kind would endanger H.M. with having brought about a schism . . . if the cardinals insisted on keeping to their choice . . . H.M. believes it more opportune for the Prince of Monaco to keep this resolve a secret; the fear of a veto being formally applied is sometimes sufficient to cause the cardinals to seek a different candidate.'

There then followed some more advice on conduct which must have given Torcy secret satisfaction. 'He (the Prince of Monaco) was going to a Court where, more than at any other, vanity and self-interest play a great part, in general. . . . It is sometimes not in an ambassador's own power to satisfy the interests of those he may have need of, but when he wishes he can gratify their vanity without much difficulty, especially in Rome where the quality of the French ambassador is particularly respected. . . . H.M. does not doubt that the Prince will use his talents to the best advantage of his embassy. At the same time, H.M. believes he will regard his rank of ambassador as the highest he possesses; and that he will not, therefore, seek prerogatives beyond those conferred on him by virtue of this rank, such an urge being nothing but detrimental to the affairs entrusted to him. . . .'[1]

However, concluded the Instructions, the Prince should precede the Spanish ambassador when attending the Pope's 'chapels,' and the formal calls he made should be returned before those made by the Spanish ambassador; he was not to receive anyone who had failed to observe this rule of precedence. Because of the marriage of the Duke of Burgundy, Louis XIV's grandson, to Marie-Adelaide of Savoy, the ambassador of the Duke of Savoy was to be treated as representing a crowned head; he had to be addressed as 'Your Excellency' and given a handshake. Finally, it was recommended to distrust members of the religious orders. 'They see their superiors become so rich that it is almost impossible for them not to think of ways and means of being raised to similar dignities.'

Although his Instructions requested him to leave for Rome without delay, Louis Grimaldi returned to Monaco in March and stayed there most of the spring, recovering from another and violent attack of gout and waiting for his equipage.[2] He eventually sailed from Monaco on June 9th with the four galleys sent him by the King, landed at Cività Vecchia on the 19th, and reached Rome on the 21st. There he took up temporary residence in a

---

[1] Advice given in vain. On the excuse that neither his forbears nor himself when previously staying in Rome had ever done so, Louis Grimaldi refused to address Italian nobles favourable to France, the *genio francese*, and the nephews of Popes, as 'Your Excellency,' or to receive them with due honours, unless they on their part addressed him as 'Your Highness' and received him with equivalent honours. The result was that the Roman nobility shunned him.

[2] The appointment was worth 72,000 *livres*; but the Prince's equipage cost him 100,000 crowns more. He had twenty coaches needing six or eight horses; also three sets of livery—one alone cost 100,000 *livres*—and a hundred servants to wear them, as well as a great number of lesser minions. In addition, the Prince stripped the palace of Monaco of tapestries, pictures, silver, and the best of the furniture, to adorn the Corsini palace, his residence in Rome.

casin lent him by Prince Pamphili, and later rented the Corsini palace on the Via Lungara where Queen Christina of Sweden had lived.

The Prince's first months in Rome were uneventful. It was summer, and the cardinals and nobles were away at their country villas. All diplomatic business was practically at a standstill. Soon after his arrival the Prince had an audience of the Pope, but then saw little of him; and when, on these few occasions, Pope Innocent XII spoke about 'the Spanish Succession,' the Prince became uncommonly cautious and refrained from preparing his mind for the idea of the Two Sicilies being ceded to France.

At the beginning of November the Pope became ill and his condition soon seemed serious. The Prince had already got himself embroiled in matters of etiquette,[1] and his relations with Cardinal de Bouillon were already cool; the two both claimed to be treated as foreign princes, which set them against each other, and the cardinal had been delighted to thwart the Prince's efforts to be recognized as 'Your Highness,' a recognition he had not succeeded in obtaining for himself.

Louis Grimaldi had too great a diplomatic sense, when some childish vanity did not blinker him, not to become uneasy at his increasing isolation, which meant he would have little influence should there be a Conclave. So he suggested to Torcy, on November 10th, that a few of the French cardinals should come to Rome on some pretext or other. He repeated this a week later, adding that the Pope could not last long.[2]

Torcy seized the opportunity to turn the skirmishes of the winter into a victory over the Prince; he emphasized to the King the inconveniences of the ambassador's requests,[3] and pressed for

[1] In his despatch of November 10th, the Prince again mentioned the claims of Roman nobles to be addressed as 'Your Excellency,' and added that other ambassadors would not admit such claims either. 'Besides, the Dukes Bondi and Mutti, who have no engagement towards Y.M., called on me and took my left hand, did not expect the "Excellency" nor any special reception.' Why then should the Dukes Salviati and Lanti, and the Prince Vaini, expect it?

[2] In fact, Pope Innocent XII recovered from that illness, but died in September, 1700.

[3] The Prince wrote to Louis XIV on December 8th: 'I am only too well aware of the efforts being made to convince Y.M. that by not allowing equality between your ambassador and mere titled persons at this Court I am prejudicing Y.M.'s interests, and that persons are kept away who might be preparing to support them.'

the delicate negotiations in Rome to be put into the more skilful, certainly the more compliant, hands of Cardinal Janson.[1] Torcy was successful; Cardinal Janson left for Rome on the royal mission, accompanied by two other French cardinals, d'Estrées and de Coislin.

The appointment of the Prince of Monaco had no doubt been an unpleasant surprise for Cardinal de Bouillon, and now it was the former's turn to be somewhat put out when he received news of the impending departure for Rome of the three French cardinals. For in his despatch of January 5th, 1700, the Prince could not resist quoting the Pope's comment on learning of it: 'So the cardinals in Italy will have to be summoned to Rome, to be here at our death.' To which the King calmly replied, through Torcy, that if the Pope recovered he would have forgotten his impression, and if he died it would be most important for the French cardinals to be in Rome.

These three arrived at the end of March, 1700; and the French interests in ecclesiastic affairs, and later the policy during the Conclave, passed into the hands of Cardinal Janson.

The second half of Louis Grimaldi's embassy was hardly any happier than the first. Although, in June, 1700, he succeeded in obtaining a cardinal's hat for the Archbishop of Paris, and had his prestige gratified at his ceremonial reception on June 27th and at the public audience of the Pope on July 4th, on the other hand he was still on cool terms with the Roman nobility, and by his precipitation to enforce the sanctions of Louis XIV against Cardinal de Bouillon he annoyed the Pope and the Sacred College.

Louis XIV, as already mentioned, disliked the cardinal. The latter's haughty insistence on his own candidate for the vacancy of coadjutor of Strasbourg, and his intrigues to have the Pope exclude the royal candidate, was more than the King could stand; he commanded Louis Grimaldi to order the cardinal to leave Rome and retire to one of his abbeys in Burgundy, to Cluny or

---

[1] During the Conclave, Cardinal Janson gave the impression he was following instructions from the Prince of Monaco, but this was to keep in with his colleagues; in fact he had a brief from Louis XIV which made him the real interpreter of the royal mind, and he had been given the necessary powers to impose, if need be, his own views.

Tournus. The ambassador was first to inform the Pope and the French cardinals of this order.

Now the Dean of the Sacred College, Cardinal Cibo, was gravely ill just then. In the event of his death the dignity would go to Cardinal de Bouillon, the next senior cardinal, together with the bishopric of Ostia that had been promised him by the Pope; but this was all conditional on his being in Rome. It would therefore have been diplomatic, and in the French interest, for the ambassador to play for time. But Louis Grimaldi was too delighted with this mission not to carry it out with alacrity. Although ill himself, he called for his carriage and hastened to Frascati, where Bouillon was staying. The stricken cardinal pretended to comply with the royal decision, but actually delayed his departure and remained in the neighbourhood of Rome awaiting news of the death of Cardinal Cibo. Meanwhile, Louis Grimaldi requested a special audience of the Pope, and two days later informed His Holiness of the King's action. The Pope and Cardinal Spada made little attempt to defend Bouillon, whose indiscretion they admitted; but other cardinals, among them Albini who was a close friend of Bouillon, were much annoyed at the peremptory treatment of a member of the Sacred College by his temporal master.[1]

By an unfortunate coincidence, the second Partition Treaty having at last been ratified, on that same day Louis Grimaldi intimated to the Pope and then to Cardinal Spada that the Kingdom of the Two Sicilies was to be the share of the French Dauphin . . .

However, on June 27th, a year after his arrival, the Prince of Monaco was at last able to make his ceremonial entry into Rome, accompanied by Cardinals d'Estrées, Janson, and Arquien (the father of the Queen of Poland). The coach he rode in, which was Cardinal Spada's, was followed by those of the French cardinals and by more than a hundred others, each one drawn by six horses. The entry was through the People's Gate, and then the long procession passed right through the city, preceded

---

[1] Cardinal Albini tried to persuade the Pope to issue a memorandum assuring Bouillon of the deanship should Cardinal Cibo die while Bouillon was away from Rome, but without result. Albini and Bouillon approached the Prince of Monaco to help them persuade the Pope, but he declined.

by heralds and trumpeters, with thirty-six flunkeys and a dozen pages escorting the Prince's coach, to reach the Via Lungara and the Corsini palace. There, the ambassador changed into Cardinal d'Estrées's coach, he being the senior of the French cardinals then in Rome, and went with him to have a private audience of the Pope.

A week later, the display was even more splendid. The Prince went to his first public audience with twelve of his coaches, four of them being drawn by six horses apiece; one hundred and fifty other coaches followed, bringing eighty archbishops and prelates, a hundred of the Roman nobility, and many French lords and gentlemen. 'My coaches were thought splendid and handsome, and the fine appearance of my livery was much remarked upon too; the coach I was in was escorted by my pages and officers, and all that stands for France in Rome was present, Sire, in the cortège of your ambassador.' A rumour went round the city that Louis Grimaldi had ordered the horses drawing his coach to be shod with silver horseshoes held in place by one nail.[1]

On July 4th a special messenger arrived unexpectedly in Rome from Madrid with a copy of the testament of Charles II of Spain, which made the Duke of Anjou, Louis XIV's grandson, the next King of Spain.[2] Two days later, the Pope and three cardinals (Spada, Albani, and Spinola San Cesareo) examined and approved the dispositions of the testament. It was at this time that Cardinal de Bouillon, learning that Cardinal Cibo was dying, completed his disobedience of his King by returning to Rome and taking up his quarters at the Jesuit seminary.

The Prince of Monaco refused all contact with the rebellious cardinal, and in agreement with the other French cardinals requested a special audience of the Pope to inform him of the

[1] Louis XIV wrote to the Prince of Monaco on July 19th: 'I have learnt from others more than from the account you gave me that you neglected nothing to make it the most magnificent Rome has seen for a long time, and you must not doubt that I am most satisfied with the impression it made and the manner in which you have upheld the dignity I invested you with.'

[2] Although the Prince soon heard rumours of this—and informed Versailles—he was only told officially on November 26th, by the Spanish ambassador. The latter, no doubt aware of the true situation at the French embassy, had already informed Cardinal Janson.

matter. Innocent XII did not grant it. . . . Disregarding this warning hint, the Prince went to see Cardinal Spada and, pointing out the inconveniences that would arise if Bouillon became Dean of the Sacred College in the existing circumstances, he proposed that the Pope should postpone the consistory.

When the despatch relating these moves reached Versailles, Torcy had little difficulty in convincing Louis XIV of their dangerous aspect, in an atmosphere like that of Rome. On August 1st the King wrote and reminded Louis Grimaldi to be more circumspect: 'It would be serving me better to let him obtain this empty title than to involve me with the Pope by requests that His Holiness feels obliged to refuse. So I count on your prudence . . . either speak to the Pope or else say nothing and by this indifference show disdain for the intrigues of Cardinal de Bouillon.' The King added, however, that if Bouillon stayed in Rome after the matter of the deanship had been settled, the Prince was to go and request him to resign the office of Chaplain-General and forbid him to wear the Order of the Saint Esprit that went with it; the French in Rome were to disregard Bouillon, and he would not be allowed to display the arms of France on his residence.

To be Dean of the Sacred College was indeed an empty title if the holder were not in Rome for the Conclave, which another illness of the Pope portended. Cardinal de Bouillon therefore did stay on in Rome, and on August 17th the Prince of Monaco carried out the orders of the King, although Cardinal Spada had counselled moderation and delay, 'so as not to increase the irritation of the cardinals, who take a keen and sympathetic interest in this matter.'

Pope Innocent XII died on September 27th. The following day Cardinal de Bouillon sent a letter to the Prince of Monaco, in which he assured him that he would act as a faithful servant of the King throughout the Conclave. He gave a first proof of his good intentions on the occasion of the reception given by the cardinals, in the sacristy of St Peter's, before they entered the Conclave. Normally, it was to the Dean that people formally paid their respects. The Prince of Monaco suggested to Bouillon that he should keep away, and the cardinal complied 'out of respect for the King'; so that on October 1st Louis Grimaldi was able to pay his respects—to Cardinal Acciaioli.[1]

Louis XIV and his Foreign Minister were still stressing their support of Cardinal Spada, having no doubt been kept as badly informed by Cardinal Janson as by the Prince of Monaco; but it soon appeared to both the latter that the chances of Cardinal Albani being elected were great. On October 12th, when the Conclave was three days' old, the Prince sent a despatch to say that this cardinal had received a good many votes each time there had been a ballot. A week later he wrote again: 'I am informed by Cardinal d'Estrées that Cardinal Barberini made known to him that if Y.M. were agreeable to the election of Cardinal Albani, he—Barberini—was hopeful of bringing it about very shortly.'

This second despatch greatly interested Louis XIV and Torcy. The King recalled, in a letter to his ambassador on November 8th, that Cardinal Albani had let his ambitions turn him away from France to support the cause of Austria, and that he had obstructed 'the most reasonable requests I made to the Pope.'[2] The King added, however: 'If it is essential to concur in his election, to exclude those I have indicated to you, then I should consider it better for the welfare of the Church than the election of any of those cardinals. But I am convinced this should be the last resource. . . .'

When this despatch reached Rome, much had happened in a short time. At the beginning of November, French machinations had wrecked the chances of election of Cardinal Marescotti; this had aroused some agitation within the Conclave, and before it died down there occurred, on November 5th, the Vaini incident.

St Simon gives this account of it: 'Vaini came of a very ordinary family, and his merits added nothing to it. His affairs were in a bad way, and dissatisfied creditors set the law officers on to him, not daring to seize his furniture because the arms of the King

---

[1] Cardinal de Bouillon kept to his word regarding his conduct during the Conclave. After the election of the new Pope, Clement XI, who confirmed Bouillon's succession to the deanship, the cardinal finally left Rome on February 22nd, 1701, the Pope having unsuccessfully interceded for him with Louis XIV. He retired to his abbeys in France. But he fled the country in 1710, and died in Rome in 1715.
[2] Cardinal Albani was secretary of the correspondence with Heads of State.

were on the door of his palace—for there are only palaces in Italy, no one ever speaks of a house. Vaini fought his way clear of the law officers, who pursued him to his door. Monsieur de Monaco, having been told of what was happening, hurried to the spot and ordered the officer in charge to withdraw from a palace which was no longer Vaini's but his, the French ambassador's, as he was now there. The officer agreed to withdraw; but as some of his men were not obeying him, the gentlemen accompanying Monsieur de Monaco chased them off with their swords, the ambassador desiring that none should be wounded. But when their comrades who had remained in the street saw the others being chased, they fired and wounded a few of Monsieur de Monaco's servants and killed the gentleman he was leaning on, who fell with the ambassador on top of him.'

The excuses and amends made to him on behalf of the Sacred College were judged inadequate by the Prince of Monaco, who decided to quit Rome and withdrew to San Quirico, which was Florentine territory, in spite of the advice of Cardinals Janson and d'Estrées that it was a rash move in the circumstances prevailing. At the next ballot of the Conclave, this escapade of the French ambassador resulted in thirty-one votes going to Cardinal Spinola de San Cesareo, a notorious enemy of Louis XIV.

The Conclave would still have continued for some time, but during the night of November 18th news reached Rome of the death of the King of Spain, on the first of the month. The shock was great, the sudden anxiety profound. On November 23rd the Sacred College unanimously elected Cardinal Albani to the Papal Throne.

Meanwhile, at Versailles, the King had just written to inform the Prince of Monaco of the Spanish King's testament and his own acceptance of it, when despatches arrived from Rome, and so Louis XIV learnt that his ambassador had left that city.

The King's annoyance, expressed in polite form, was sharp: 'I would have much preferred you to await my reply before taking such strong steps as those you inform me of. . . . You ought, in the first place, to avoid involving yourself and exposing the dignity of your office to the insolence of law officers. All that was necessary was to send a large enough number of your attendants. . . . In the second place, you ought to have been satisfied with the cardinals' offer to make an exemplary punishment and with their public disapproval of the treatment you suffered. The letter they proposed to write would have sufficed. . . .'

The following day, November 18th, a letter from the cardinals arrived and shed more light on the matter, and the King dictated an addendum to Torcy: 'In the prevailing circumstances you can do no good to my service by continuing in the way you relate, and you must return to Rome without delay, for your departure and your absence can be most injurious to my service.'

It was a hard knock for a sensitive and sincere man like Louis Grimaldi. In his reply to the royal despatch he recapitulated the reasons for his action and then added sadly: 'All that, however, has done me no good, since Y.M. does not approve of it. I most humbly beg his pardon, and beseech him to believe that if it were possible to die from grief I would be dead by now. . . . Only the Cardinals d'Estrées and Janson objected to what were good intentions on my part, which makes me see that both of them are wiser, more capable, and also happier than I am. . . .'

Though often hardhearted, Louis XIV was touched by this sad letter coming from a man he liked, and his reply would have consoled Louis Grimaldi. 'I have always admitted you had reason for leaving Rome, and I know it was solely due to your zeal on my behalf, and that more strength of mind is needed to take such steps than just to wait calmly and see what happens. . . .' But it was unlikely that the Prince of Monaco had the pleasure of reading those few lines, written on December 20th, which would have been balm to his mind.

He was in very poor health when he returned to Rome, and had then tired himself further by attending an audience of the Pope on December 11th. Two days later, on the Feast of St Luke, he was obliged to be present with the French and Spanish cardinals at a ceremony at the church of St John Lateran, which was followed by a banquet at the French embassy. Then, on December 18th and 19th, at the church of St Louis des Français and amid much pomp and ceremony, he conferred in his King's name the Order of the Saint Esprit upon the two sons of Jan Sobieski, the King of Poland who had driven the Turks out of Vienna.

Louis Grimaldi was a weary man; his doctors bled him repeatedly, and weakened him the more. If he had taken a rest he might have recovered, but he was vexed by not having presented letters from Louis XIV to the new Pope, Clement XI, who, knowing him to be ill, had delayed granting him the necessary audience. Louis Grimaldi now insisted, and had his audience of the Pope on December 29th. He took to his bed on his return, never to rise from it again. He died during the night of January 2nd, most probably of bronchial pneumonia, comforted at the last by Cardinal de Noailles.

Monsieur de La Bussière, who was the chamberlain to French ambassadors to Rome, had known many of them. Several had been shrewder than Louis Grimaldi; and luck, especially, had been with them more. La Bussière said of him, though: 'There never was a more upright and engaging man; he charmed all Rome with his ways and manners. He was the finest conversationalist and the most eloquent in both languages that there's ever been, with a most acute mind, and he was genuinely zealous in the service of the King.'

CHAPTER V

ANTOINE I. THE SEARCH FOR MONEY AND AN HEIR (1701–1731)

THE THIRD DUKE OF VALENTINOIS was forty when he succeeded his father as Prince of Monaco, at the dawn of the eighteenth century.

His subjects knew little of him, for he had spent hardly any time in the Principality since his early childhood, when Louis and Catherine-Charlotte had lived there together during the four years from 1661. When they returned to Monaco for the second time, Antoine was old enough to begin his studies, and in 1668 he had been put in the care of Marshal de Gramont; for the next ten years the Marshal had charge of the education of this grandson whose parents had separated.

When he was ten and a half, in June, 1671, Antoine was sent to Clermont, the Jesuit college in Paris. He was a boarder there for four years, but did not lack comfort; the young duke had private rooms, a tutor to himself, a valet and a domestic servant.

The only career a young lord could follow was a military one; a rigorous preparation was given by the academies for young gentlemen, which were the cadet schools of their time. So in August, 1675, Antoine entered the academy of an Italian named Bernardi.

The following extract from a contemporary periodical, the *Mercure Galant*, gives an idea of the timetable at such establishments: 'The morning is spent in horsemanship and riding-lessons until midday. In the afternoon, fencing and dancing lessons are given, and the young men practise vaulting, have drawing lessons or study military fortifications, according to which master is teaching each week.'

Antoine Grimaldi spent three years at Bernardi's Academy,

and when he left in 1678 the natural course of events would have been for him to enter the Army, attend Court, and get married. But here fate took a hand, moulding the future Prince of Monaco in an individual manner and enabling his strong, independent character to follow its own bent.

His mother had just died; Louis Grimaldi, having recently promulgated the Statutes of Monaco, had come to reside in Paris now that his wife's presence no longer kept him away. Father and son got to know each other for the first time. Antoine, his father was pleased to see, was now a tall youngster with rather marked characteristics but refined, intelligent looks; he had an easy bearing and pleasant, agreeable manners—at least, when his sharp, suspicious nature did not break through.

Louis did not want his son to have the hard, difficult experiences of his own youth, and Antoine did not seem to him to have the makings or character of a good courtier. But this wild youngster had to be broken in. Now, Louis Grimaldi had greatly benefited from his travels in Italy and to England; and while in London he had seen young gentlemen setting off on the Grand Tour without which their education was not considered complete. So, instead of presenting his son at Court, Louis broke with custom and decided that Antoine should go and see something of Italy and Germany and also Holland, lately made accessible by the Treaty of Nymeghen.

Antoine spent a week at Monaco, the first time he had been back there for more than ten years, and then sailed for Genoa on April 26th, 1679, accompanied by a gentleman of whom nothing is known except his name, La Polinière. A year later, Antoine was in Holland, having travelled through Italy as far as Rome, then gone north to Switzerland and Bavaria, and visited Frankfort and Strasbourg.

He kept a diary during his journeys, conscientiously noting down in an unformed hand the daily distances travelled, the names of relatives he met, and their ages. Nothing in these childish entries gives a hint of the assiduous letter-writer he became later, when leading a retired life on his Rock and keeping up a regular correspondence for thirty years with all the leading people in France and Italy. Two characteristics in his young days, though, were pointers to the man he was to become: his great interest in everything to do with military fortifications, and his distinct taste for Italian music.

Antoine, Duke of Valentinois, entered the Army on his return to Paris in 1680. His military career was fairly long but did not respond to his ambitions; he resigned his commission in 1696, as already recounted, and became 'a Paris bourgeois after 15 years' military service,' to quote his own words.

Winters spent in Paris while the army was out of the field, and then his resignation from the service, enabled the third Duke of Valentinois to gratify his taste for music and especially for opera. As a young man he had formed a friendship with the elderly Lulli, and when the great musician died in 1687 he bequeathed one of his conductor's batons to the Duke.

Antoine was not only fond of music, he had a fondness for some of the young ladies of the Opera too. He was not naturally faithful in love, and there had been many impediments in his married life. Shortly before the reconciliation with his wife in 1697 he was having an affair with a certain Elisabeth Dufort. She gave birth to a son, who was christened Antoine, a few weeks before the future heiress to the Principality, Louise-Hippolyte, was born. The boy was legally recognized by Antoine as his natural son, in 1715, and became known as the Chevalier de Grimaldi.[1]

When Louis I died, the Duke of Valentinois was still 'a Paris bourgeois' and had not visited Monaco since going to join his wife in the autumn of 1692. Louis had never encouraged his son to take up residence in the Principality, partly perhaps through wanting to keep all the power to himself, but more likely because he deemed it wiser for the Duke of Valentinois to remain under the eyes of the King. While Louis was in Rome, Antoine had suggested going to Monaco. The Prince had sent him grudging

---

[1] The attestation made by Antoine read: 'that the child baptized in the parish of St Roch at Paris on October 2nd, 1697, as being the natural son of Marguerite Renée and Pierre Baillet, is the natural son of the said Prince Antoine and Elisabeth Dufort.'

Antoine also had a child—Antoinette, who was called Mademoiselle de Saint-Rémy—by a dancer at the Paris Opera, Victoire Vertu, a fatal name. But another child, Louise-Marie-Thérèse Grimaldi, was by a Provençal woman; born on June 2nd, 1705, this girl died at Sospel in 1723, having spent all her short life in the region of Monaco.

permission, just for him 'to have a look round,' and had doubted whether even that was judicious, for Antoine would be the only man of quality not to be attending Court at Fontainebleau just then.

Nothing, therefore, presaged the fact, when news of Louis Grimaldi's death reached Versailles and the new Prince hurried south to Monaco, that he would remain there, far from Paris and the Court, almost without a break until his death in 1731.

It was financial reasons, in the first place, that caused the abrupt departure of the Prince and Princess of Monaco, and then decided them to stay on their Rock. Louis Grimaldi had handed his will and testament to Cardinal de Noailles. When Antoine knew of its contents he resolved not to accept the inheritance unless an inventory were drawn up; for the extravagances of his father in Rome and elsewhere, and the large dowry of his sister, the Duchesse d'Uzès (which was still not entirely paid), had finally endangered the Grimaldi fortune which had been shaky for the past twenty years. Moreover, the marriage portion of Marie de Lorraine had been small[1]—the Armagnac family was not rich—and Antoine was already in debt himself.

A bold decision, therefore, had to be made: to keep away from Versailles and live as much as possible in the Principality.

It was a small sacrifice for Antoine, who was no courtier, though always exceedingly loyal to Louis XIV. But for Marie de Lorraine, who was dismayed at the prospect of being far from her parents, it was an ordeal. Life at Monaco with a surly husband, to whom she was henceforth faithful through duty rather than fondness, seemed a prison to her. She had been indifferent towards her first child, born when she was just sixteen, but was very fond of those who had come after the reconciliation with her husband, when she had turned her back on a life of glitter and flattery. And it was her children who enabled her to support her exile from Paris. On their behalf she was later to find the strength to oppose a husband who had never been faithful nor tender towards her.

The news of Louis I's death had reached Versailles on January

---

[1] In October, 1694, irritated by Antoine's recriminations, Louis had written ironically to him: 'Your marriage has brought such a huge sum into the family that I'd have to squander all I possess to cancel it out.'

11th, 1701. On February 26th, Antoine and his wife were in their palace at Monaco. They found it stripped of the best furniture and decorations, and had to wait three months for their arrival from Rome—with Louis I's coffin.

By the time the couple were able to settle in, political reasons had been added to the financial reasons for remaining at Monaco.

The year 1701 saw the beginning of the War of the Spanish Succession. When the Emperor knew of the dispositions in Charles II's testament he sent Austrian troops to occupy the province of Milan; the French under Catinat, let down by the Duke of Savoy, were forced to withdraw towards their frontiers, and by the summer the mounting Austrian tide was lapping around Monaco.

Louis XIV replaced Catinat by the charming but incapable Marshal Villeroy who, going over to the offensive, was defeated at Chiari in September, 1701, and then captured at Cremona the following February. This ridiculous episode had its fortunate side, however; Villeroy's command was given to the Duke de Vendôme, who restored the situation and stabilized the front.

The Prince and Princess of Monaco then returned to Paris for a while, after more than a year's absence. They took a house in the rue de Verneuil; and the Prince's ceremonial reception by the Parlement as duke and peer of the realm took place. The Princess lost her eighteen-months-old daughter, Marie-Dévote, in October, 1703; little Elisabeth-Charlotte, the 'third female,' the news of whose birth had drawn a cry of despair from Louis I, had died the previous year.

The Princess stayed on in Paris until December, 1703, but Antoine had left for Monaco in the spring. The Duke of Savoy had finally changed sides and become an enemy of the French; Antoine's place was in Monaco, as the rightful commander of its French garrison, even though he had proclaimed the neutrality of his Principality and all the warring Powers had decided to recognize it.

The Duke of Savoy appeared at first to have made an unwise decision. A French army under the command of the Duke de Vendôme captured most of his strong-points in Piedmont, and another French force occupied Nice and the territory around.

It seemed a good moment for the Prince of Monaco to settle the long-standing and annoying boundary dispute over La Turbie to his advantage. Louis XIV was agreeable, and in letters from Versailles dated July, 1705, gave to 'Antoine de Grimaldy, Prince of Monaco, the town and territory of La Turbie, taken from the county of Nice, in recognition of services rendered by him and his predecessors.'

Early in 1706 Antoine journeyed north to thank the King, leaving his wife behind at Monaco. The news of the disastrous defeat of the French at Turin, in September, sent him hastening back to his Principality. He was never to see the King again, nor to return to Versailles. The day he left, Louis XIV dropped his reserve for a moment when bidding him farewell, as though foreseeing that this man who was little of a court-flatterer but most loyal would remain away for good. 'Adieu, Monsieur de Monaco, take care of yourself, and be sure that you have my esteem, friendship, and trust,' the King said loud enough for others to hear, and then went back to his study. The Duke d'Aumont, a good friend of the Grimaldis, looked round with amusement at the stunned and disconcerted faces of the courtiers, and dryly offered 'Four thousand pistoles to anyone who'll go down and repeat to Madame d'Armagnac what the King has just said to Monsieur de Monaco.' History does not say if anyone was daring enough.

Let us pause here for a moment. This autumn of the year 1706 marks a definite stage in the history of the Principality and its then reigning Prince. Renouncing the Court—in other words, France, since there was no real link but with Versailles—Antoine settled down for good in Monaco; and not until modern times did any other Prince of Monaco reside there for so long and continuous a period. The only journeys Antoine is known to have made after this time were to Italy. It is doubtful whether he ever again travelled into France; and yet, when peace returned to Europe, he could have reappeared at Court, where the Regency of his friend, Philippe, Duke of Orléans, might have been expected to attract him.

There were various reasons for his decision. The leg wound he had received at Namur in 1692 had never properly healed. It kept opening up, and in spite of the many doctors who came to attend him, especially from the famous medical school at Mont-pellier, the wound made the Prince a cripple while still middle-aged, and in the last years of his life reduced him to the state of a semi-invalid. He then installed a kind of lift between the ground and first floor of the palace. But the chief reason was surely that he preferred being a sovereign prince on his Rock than an inferior at Versailles. His vanity was satisfied by this independence, and his natural unsociability found comfort in the comparative soli-tude of Monaco. Besides, a person of difficult character is usually more at his ease, more comfortable in his mind, when surrounded only by people dependent on him.

However, Antoine had too lively a mind not to want to keep in contact with the outside world. He had not liked paying court nor calling on the King's ministers, but he liked writing to them; he had been disappointed by the army and then rebuffed, but he was glad to inform its generals. In short, he took up a new rôle when he returned to Monaco for good: through the family rela-tions he had in Italy he obtained much information about events there, and so became a most useful adjunct to communications between Ministers at Versailles, the armies operating beyond the Alps, and the Italian States which had remained loyal allies of France. But he did not merely keep Versailles informed; he entered into direct communication with the French generals and for-warded to them the information he received from his corre-spondents all over Italy.

Peace was signed at Utrecht in 1713, but the Prince of Monaco's correspondence did not cease. He had got into the habit; and his two chanceries, for France and Italy, kept up the pace. He wrote regularly twice a month to the Bishop of Fréjus, later better known as Cardinal-Minister Fleury. Some of the Prince's corre-spondents were not such ready letter-writers, the Marshal Duke of Berwick for instance, and obviously panted to keep pace with him. Thus, although absent from Court, the Prince was not forgotten.

This correspondence filled a large part of his life, but he had by no means forgotten his love of music. He converted a large room of the palace into a concert hall, and there he sometimes conducted the orchestra himself, using the baton bequeathed to him by Lulli. He also got together a company of opera singers; the renewal of its members gave rise to a delightful correspondence spread over fifteen years with Destouches, the manager of the Opera House in Paris.

The Prince's married life became less stormy and gradually entered calmer waters; this may have been partly due to the death in 1707 of his mother-in-law, Madame d'Armagnac, who had always detested him, and partly to the new surroundings and large family. A sixth girl was born in 1708, and three years later there were again hopes of the heir for which the couple had been wishing for twenty years.

But there is often an ironic, bitter-sweet side to life. Not far from the Convent of the Visitation was the summer-house in which Marie de Lorraine spent much time; it was called 'The Desert.' On the other side of the Convent was the villa where the Prince met his acknowledged mistress, who was popular with the people; it was she, no doubt, who was the mother of the Prince's natural daughter born in 1705.

While thus arranging his daily life, the Prince embarked on an expensive, arduous task; a long-term one, but of considerable importance, and it possibly saved the Principality from the covetousness of the Duke of Savoy. After defeating the French at Turin, the armies of Austria and Savoy were free to invade Italy. Antoine Grimaldi realized he could not count on the neutrality of Monaco continuing to be respected, and he turned to the defence of his territory.

The fortifications of the Rock had not been improved nor had any maintenance work been done on them since the time of the Gubernant, in the mid-sixteenth century. A military engineer from Toulon, named Guiraud, recommended by the Duke of Berwick, studied the problem and drew up a report for the Prince in December, 1706. This estimated that work costing 114,000 *livres* was necessary, the most important being to strengthen the defences overlooking the harbour and guarding access to the Rock on that side. Other reports and plans were drawn up the following years, and in 1709 the Spur, the defence-work at the head of the Rock was converted into a fort and named after Antoine. Work on the fortifications continued until 1714 and the final cost exceeded 300,000 *livres*.

Antoine Grimaldi bore this great expense entirely from his own resources. The improved defences quite possibly deterred Savoy from laying siege to the Rock in 1707, when its forces had penetrated as far west as Toulon. But the threat was renewed early in 1709, and on March 1st the Prince sent a cry of distress to Chamillard, the French Minister of War: 'Monaco will soon be cut off . . . no help can reach us by land, and we shall be thrown back on our own defences . . . This Rock is well enough situated for me to say that if I had been able to put 50,000 francs a year into fortifying it, over and beyond the 200,000 I've already spent, which is no exaggeration, this Rock, then . . . need never have been in danger of being taken by force. . . . Since the advance to Toulon of the Savoy troops, I have pledged the precious stones of the Monaco merchants, drawn advances on my small revenues, and melted down 50,000 francs' worth of plate; all I can do now is to send what remains to Aix, with authority to sell, and use the proceeds, as well as bespeaking my future revenues, in stocking this place against a siege. . . . But if this stronghold is still of worth to him (the French king), I beseech you, Sir, do not abandon us when I am doing all that is in my power to keep it for the King.'[1]

That year, 1709, was a terrible one, with its long hard winter, and the reverses for the French armies. But then the tide began to turn. Marlborough was having difficulties with the government at home. The Emperor Joseph died and was succeeded by his brother Charles, the pretender to the Spanish throne, and so England was faced with the choice of supporting the Hapsburgs or the Bourbons; and chose the latter. Peace negotiations began in London in October, 1711. The victory of the French over the Austrians at Denain, in July, 1712, hastened the peace talks which had been in progress at Utrecht since January.

The Prince of Monaco and his friends had no illusions as to the hostility of the Duke of Savoy; the annexing of La Turbie to Monaco in 1705 had reminded the Duke of much older grievances that Savoy held against Monaco, in particular the homage for Menton and Roquebrune that had not been made for nearly two hundred years.

[1] Dangeau noted in his Memoirs on June 11th, 1710: 'Monsieur de Monaco has been away in Monaco a long time, and there helps the King's cause very well. He has even spent large sums on the defences of his stronghold, which is at present one of the best in the realm.'

11 Prince Charles III of Monaco, 1818–1889. *Portrait by François Biard.*

12   Prince Albert I of Monaco, 1848–1922. *Portrait by Léon Bonnat.*

'I have not been out for some time,' Monsieur le Grand, Count d'Armagnac, wrote to his son-in-law on January 4th, 1712. 'I sent to ask the Marquis de Torcy to be good enough to call, which he did. I spoke to him about your troubles as earnestly as if they were my own. He is very well disposed, and will assuredly do his best for you. . . . The passports have arrived, our emissaries leave the day after tomorrow, and we are hoping for a good and quick peace treaty; it seems likely, and if there is and you don't come with your wife and the children to be fondly hugged, I shall never forgive you. . . .'[1]

In April, the claims of Savoy became more specific. Antoine received a letter from his brother, François-Honoré, who was still a priest in Paris, suggesting that he should go to Versailles to plead his cause and look after his interests, or at least send his wife 'who would talk, take necessary steps, and make requests in your place. She's perfectly at home in the atmosphere of the Court. She's quite accepted in that little world, and I'm sure that with her quick wit and winning ways she would be a great help to you in the present state of affairs. . . .' But the King sent word that he was satisfied with the keenness and activity of the Prince, and considered his place was at Monaco. There were indeed grave fears, which were expressed by Marshal de Tessé, writing to the Prince a few weeks later: 'Your neighbour has a big appetite, and no niceties or scruples about it. He'll make do with anything, and if he can't have the daintiest morsels he doesn't disdain the lesser. Throughout the war, I've never suspected him of coveting you, because he had greater things in view. But if he feels this war is drawing to a close he'd much rather seize your Rock, to turn it into a nest of pirates, than miss taking something.'

The negotiations proceeding at Utrecht provided for the return to Savoy of the county of Nice, including La Turbie. The Duke demanded the Principality of Monaco as well, with France to pay an indemnity to the Prince. But Louis XIV made reply that he could not dispose of the property of others, and the Duke—enriched by the cession of Sicily—dropped his claim; but, as a

---

[1] Since the death of Madame d'Armagnac, relations between Monsieur le Grand and his son-in-law had become more normal. The former addressed Antoine as 'Mr Goliath' or 'My dear Goliath,' and asked fondly after his grandchildren, 'Coco,' 'Poupon,' and Chabeuil.

sop to his pride, he insisted on the Prince of Monaco formally
recognizing Savoy's suzerainty over Menton and Roquebrune.

The King of France and the Queen of England were named
as arbitrators; and in June, 1714, their nominees, Amelot and
Prior, gave their decision in favour of the new King of Sicily.
The Prince of Monaco had an interview with him at Nice in the
autumn, and after delaying the matter for another two years was
finally obliged to make homage to the House of Savoy; the formal
act took place at Rivoli, on August 12th, 1716, through a
representative.

While this matter was being settled, one that cut at the Prince's
pride but which seemed to have no real importance,[1] another of
far greater concern for the future of the House of Grimaldi was
causing strife and dissension between the Prince and his family.
It was over the marriage of Louise-Hippolyte, the eldest daughter
and heiress to the Principality.

Louis Grimaldi, back in 1699, had foreseen and been concerned
about the problem. He had referred with annoyance to 'a certain
Claudine,' and later on had concluded 'there can be no doubt
that the rights of succession laid down in my grandfather's
testament cut out your daughters.' But this was not quite correct.
Honoré II, his grandfather, had made no fresh dispositions, only
repeated those in the testaments of Jean I, of Catalan, Lambert,
and Claudine, which allowed female issue to succeed on condition
that they married a Grimaldi or that the husband changed his own
name and arms to take those of the Grimaldis. But Lambert, and
then Claudine, had by-passed their grandchildren in favour of their
younger sons. Jean II had thus been succeeded by Lucien,
instead of by the young Marie (Jean II's daughter); and Lucien
by Augustin. The legitimate heir to the Principality now, therefore, was Antoine's younger brother, François-Honoré—Monsieur l'abbé de Monaco, as he was called—unless he renounced
his rights.

Bound up with the marriage problem was the question of the
Duchy of Valentinois. The duchy itself could be inherited by a
woman, but then the peerage would become extinct. Still,

[1] But, as will be seen later, this revival of Savoy's suzerainty may well have
helped establish the protectorate over the Principality in 1815, and consequently
led to the loss of Menton and Roquebrune.

Monsieur le Grand had the ear of the King, and Antoine Grim-aldi's unwavering loyalty to him gave added reason for hoping that Louis XIV would agree to revive the peerage for Antoine's son-in-law; but, there again, Monsieur l'abbé had first to step aside from the line of succession.

Moreover, this son-in-law had to be wealthy enough to be able to compensate the abbé de Monaco, and to pay Antoine's debts —those that had been left by his father as well as those resulting from the work on the fortifications—and, finally, to constitute dowries for the two younger sisters of Louise-Hippolyte.

In 1711, when Marie de Lorraine had a miscarriage and all hope of a son and heir vanished, Antoine laid these general lines of his plan before his father-in-law. The latter was in agreement, and had little doubt he could get the King to revive the peerage; though at the back of his mind was the idea of marrying his grand-daughter to his own son, Charles de Lorraine. But Antoine, very sensibly, did not think a Lorraine would make a good Grimaldi, and he was evasive on that subject. Monsieur le Grand took offence; after that, Antoine's choice of a son-in-law had to be beyond reproach for his wife's family not to be in any way critical.

There was no lack of candidates, drawn by the prospect of the peerage and the duchy. The choice was narrowed down to two; or rather, Antoine and his father-in-law each favoured a different young man. Count de Roye, the former's choice, was sponsored by Pontchartrain, then Navy Secretary; he was a dashing young officer of twenty-three and belonged to the La Rochefoucauld family. The other, the choice of the Lorraines, was Count de Lux, the sixteen-year-old son of the Duke of Châtillon and a member of the Montmorency family; the Duke was willing to transmit his duchy to his son when the marriage contract was signed.

On December 12th, 1712, Monsieur le Grand wrote a straight-from-the-shoulder letter to his son-in-law: 'Since you twist every-thing I write to suit yourself, I must use the kind of language that leaves no room for mistake. It is not fitting that you, as the father of Mademoiselle de Monaco, should choose a husband for her other than one whose rank is not lower than her own by birth. What are you thinking of, to want to strip yourself of the duchy of Valentinois in order to get yourself a son-in-law whom you will honour by giving him the hand of my grand-daughter? This son-in-law must have a high rank, be possessed of a good fortune in land and property, with no debts attached, but I can only see beggary in the marriage proposed to you;[1] the young man is known as a rascal and to be always in want of money. What kind of marriage are you being pushed into? I had thought that by my referring indirectly to the matter you would see it clearly for what it is, but as you didn't, I must talk straight. I have a great regard for young Roye's father, Count de Roucy, and am well aware of his family connections. The Duke of Châtillon has a title and honours and safe possessions in a family that is one of the highest in the land. I do not see any comparison between the two. I'm telling you just what I think, for your honour is involved; and I know that mine is. Think all this over carefully; I warn you that the blame will be yours alone, and that I shall oppose anything detrimental to the honour of a grand-daughter of a man like myself, to whom you owe some consideration, I think. . . .'

If Antoine had been prudent and sensible he would have given way, accepted Count de Lux for his daughter and so added another duchy to the possessions of the House of Monaco. But he had never been prudent nor sensible, and in addition he detested the Lorraine family, who had always made him feel it was an honour to have married their daughter. So he was obstinate in his choice of a son-in-law, with the result that domestic warfare raged within the palace of Monaco throughout the spring of 1713. The Princess refused to sign the marriage-contract,[2] Louise-Hippolyte refused to have Count de Roye for a husband, and the abbé de Monaco to forego his rights. 'Monsieur and Madame de Monaco are more than ever in disagreement over the marriage of their daughter,' noted Dangeau on May 19th, 1713.

[1] St Simon has this to say of it: 'You never marry your children without putting things down in black and white. Count de Roucy had always been a spendthrift, his Countess up to the neck in debts and lawsuits. They lived from their large estates and large debts, without any order in their affairs, using their wits . . .'

[2] She was strongly supported by her father, who wrote to her from Versailles on April 18th, 1713: 'When you have a good case, stick to it . . . I hope Monsieur de Monaco will stop harrying you, that's all I'm able to wish you and him for the better. If he goes too far, we shall support you.'

He added a postscript: 'Believe nothing you're told about what I'm supposed to have said or done, but only what I write and tell you, and do not sign anything whatever unless I or one of your brothers writes personally to say so.'

'Some time ago he went off to Mantoue (Menton), taking his three daughters. The eldest, the one he's trying to arrange a marriage for, still says she will never sign until her mother does.'

Carried away by his arrogant nature, Antoine Grimaldi lost all sense of proportion. Parting Louise-Hippolyte from her mother had not made either of them change her mind. He sent Louise-Hippolyte to the Convent of the Visitation at Aix-en-Provence, and had her shut up there. His wife reacted to this violent measure by a headstrong act. 'Taking advantage of her husband having gone wenching in Genoa, she fled from Monaco and reached her father's house in Paris,' early in July, 1713.

Let us see what the abbé de Monaco had to say, for he wrote to his sister, the nun, Jeanne-Marie-Dévote, on September 4th, and summed up the matter for her. After referring to the two candidates, and approving of Count de Lux but not the other, he dismissed with an ironic phrase his brother's outbursts against the Lorraine family—'other times, other manners.' Then he mentioned his sister-in-law's flight. 'It's her business and not mine to say what led up to her leaving the Rock. I have no reason to believe that she has ever pretended that my brother turned her out. All I've heard her say is that she thought the time had come to accept her husband's repeated permission to make up her mind which side she was on and to go wherever she considered best. But I leave that as it is. . . .'

In any case, she had received a great welcome from all her family, in spite of what others said.[1] 'The King received her most graciously,' the abbé de Monaco went on, 'and was kind enough to listen to her in a friendly manner for a whole half-hour. This is shown by the orders he gave afterwards to the Marquis de Torcy, telling him to write to my brother about a change of convent for Louise-Hippolyte.' The abbé added that the King had forbidden Pontchartrain to have anything to do with bringing

[1] St Simon repeated these malicious rumours: 'She thought she would reign it as when her mother was alive, and be able as before to wallow in the pleasures of the Court. She was mistaken. Monsieur le Grand greeted her coldly, and began by telling her that a woman who had quarrelled with her husband and thereby come back to her father must not go about in town, must not attend the King except when duty commanded, must visit no one and receive no callers, be satisfied with the high society in plenty around him, but was not to gamble nor paint her face, had to dress plainly, have no elaborate hair style, and avoid parties and pleasures of all kinds. This harangue was not so much a remonstrance as a stern order. . . .'

about the Roye marriage. Mademoiselle de Monaco was entitled to a say in the matter and to have a husband 'pleasing to her and with whom she could be on good terms.'

On receipt of the King's wishes, Antoine Grimaldi had his daughter moved from the convent at Aix to the one at Monaco. A kind of truce then fell between the two sides, each worn out by this first round but tenaciously maintaining its position. A few comfortless letters passed between husband and wife, and Monsieur le Grand and his son-in-law.

'I am in fairly good health, thanks be to God,' wrote Monsieur le Grand on April 6th, 1714. 'I should like you to know just how much I want to see my grand-daughter settled, and therefore the future of your House too. Far from wishing you to change your views, I advise you to study them better than you have done up to now, and as your forbears would wish. Rank and possessions are needed, and Count de Roye has neither. So it is you who should choose another having what he lacks. Make peace with yourself, only that way can you put an end to your troubles. What interest can I have, in Heaven's name, other than yours; what can I obtain from it other than the pleasure of seeing you made happy by your daughter being established in a manner worthy of you both. . . .'

A few months later, in August, 1714—two years after the negotiations were begun—Count de Roucy, the father of the unlucky candidate, realized that the King disapproved of persisting in a marriage project that created division in a family, and decided it was wiser to release the Prince of Monaco from the agreement.

They were back where they started from.

For some while the Lorraine family had had a new candidate in view; but they knew that with Antoine and his ungovernable temper they had to go warily. Whilst Monsieur le Grand was concerned to prepare the way for a reconciliation between husband and wife, and sent mollifying letters to Antoine,[1] a swarm of

---

[1] 'I love Madame de Monaco very much for her sentiments just now . . . she is liked and esteemed, and behaves like an angel. God is my witness to what I say, that she wants only to be in your good graces, her only desire is for the greatness of your House. Let us all do what is in our power to bring peace to our family. . . . Your wife will do what she ought; on your part, do the same.'

fresh candidates came forward; but the favoured one was still
kept hidden in the background. . . . Among the names discussed,
during the summer of 1714, were those of Prince Lanti, a nephew
of the Princess des Ursins, and the Duke of Sesto. Antoine
Grimaldi sought the favour of Louis XIV by rejecting these
foreign suitors; besides, the King would very likely not have
granted the peerage to any of them. There was also question, in
great secrecy and with Fleury, the Bishop of Fréjus, serving as
go-between, of the young Count d'Eu—he was only thirteen—
the second son of the Duke of Maine (who was one of the
legitimized offspring of Louis XIV by Madame de Montespan).
But Antoine doubted whether a Bourbon, even less than a
Lorraine, would make a true Grimaldi.

The ground having been cleared, the Lorraine family thought
the time had come to produce their own candidate; but the Prince
of Monaco then had an idea which was not without merit. He was
considering marrying Louise-Hippolyte to a young relative
belonging to the Antibes branch of the Grimaldis. This would be
following the precedent of the Claudine and Lambert Grimaldi
marriage, and would found the Grimaldis of Monaco once again.
The young man had no fortune, and there was little enough in the
alliance. However, neither the Lorraines nor Antoine's friends
dare obstruct him directly this time. 'Your choice is worthy of
you,' Marshal de Tessé wrote to him from Fontainebleau on
October 14th, 1714, 'and to want to retain your name and possessions in a senior branch of your family, through having no
heir of your own, is only natural and right. I congratulate you,
and hope most heartily that for your satisfaction and ease of
mind this project will attain the success you desire, since you have
had the King's approval in the past. There is every hope that His
Majesty will keep to the arrangements agreed on then, which
means you hold a strong hand.'

Tessé, used to the life and atmosphere at Court, had ended
with a reservation—the King's consent was necessary. This was
what the Lorraines were counting on, and they took steps to
ensure that it would be refused. Six weeks later, Tessé wrote
and seriously warned the Prince of Monaco. 'Certainly nothing
can be more specious than to want your name to be continued
within a senior branch of your family; but do you think it would

have been out of place to have first consulted the King's wishes before following your own? It seems that people of your rank and birth carry out this preliminary, in contrast to those who are not attached to him in so many ways.'

Antoine Grimaldi, busily occupied in congratulating himself on his plan, took no notice of the warning. His daughter, bored with her convent and eager to get in touch with her mother, seemed resigned to the marriage with her relative. However, this was just a pretence, to play for time until the King's decision was known. Louis XIV was explicit; the young man fulfilled none of the conditions necessary for the royal approval. With this encouragement, Louise-Hippolyte changed her mind—and was sent back to the convent.

When the curtain fell on the second act of this comedy-drama it seemed to have come to an end for lack of cast—for lack of suitors. But neither the Lorraines nor their candidate and his family were discouraged; they took advantage of the interval to prepare the third act. There was no question of putting forward the name of Jacques de Matignon themselves; knowing the Prince of Monaco, that would have meant failure straight away. So they arranged for the preliminaries to be made through the Duchesse de Lude, who had previously been the wife of Count de Guiche, and Marshal de Villeroy.

In spite of Antoine Grimaldi's aggressive instincts, he was no doubt tired of this struggle which had lasted more than two years. Besides, he felt the disadvantage of being so far from the centre of things, especially while his wife was at Versailles. He realized that the time had come to give way. Moreover, the young man proposed to him by the Duchess and the Marshal was likely to be acceptable to all parties.

Jacques de Matignon, Count of Thorigny, was twenty-five and the only son of Count de Matignon. He had commanded one of the royal regiments in 1710, and in 1713 had become Lieutenant-Governor of Normandy. Even more satisfactory than his career were the standing of his family and the state of his fortune. The Matignons were one of the best French families of the old nobility, though not ducal. They had come originally from Brittany; one of their ancestors, Jean de Matignon, a relation of Du Guesclin, had settled in Lower Normandy on marrying the heiress to the Thorigny estates.[1] Early in the sixteenth century a Joachim de Matignon had obtained the hereditary position of Lieutenant-Governor of Normandy; his son, Jacques, was a loyal supporter of Henri IV and carried a Sword of State at his coronation, and later became a Marshal of France and held Normandy for the King against the Leaguers.

The Marshal's son, Charles, married a Longueville daughter; when the male line of the Longuevilles became extinct, the Matignons had hoped to succeed to their duchy of Estouteville which could then in principle be handed down through the female line. The present Count de Matignon had attempted to claim it, but as he would have become the senior duke of the realm the other dukes opposed him, with the pretext that his relationship was too far removed. This failure was sufficiently fresh in his mind for him to agree with alacrity to the sacrifice of his name and coat of arms, if it meant obtaining a duchy for his son and family, through an alliance with the Grimaldis.

As for the fortune, it was great and untouched by any mortgage, represented by vast estates in the most fertile and richest province of France; and backed up, from the point of view of obtaining ready money, by an old friendship with Chamillard, the Minister for Finance and for War. So Count de Matignon was able to accept the financial demands put forward by the Prince of Monaco.

It did not take Antoine long to decide in favour of this new candidate, but he asked for the negotiations to be kept secret from the Lorraine family. Marshal de Villeroy proposed trying to bring about a reconciliation between the Lorraines and Antoine Grimaldi, and the latter was prepared to accept it if his wife admitted she had been in the wrong, and if she and her family agreed in advance to the 'unknown' son-in-law he had chosen.

The Lorraines freely gave way, naturally. 'I have always had the notion, Sir, that your good sense and feelings would put things right again,' wrote Monsieur le Grand to Antoine Grimaldi on Christmas Eve, 1714. 'It gives me great pleasure, and I greeted your representative as though he were bringing an olive-branch from you. Although he did not explain about the choice you have made, I don't doubt it is a good one, judging by the manner in

[1] In the west of Normandy, just south of St Lô. The locality is now called Torigni-sur-Vire.

which you write to Marshal de Villeroy. I shall not sing the praises of my daughter here—the way people speak of her is pledge enough, and must be very pleasing to you. I am your father-in-law, let us all draw sincerely together. Madame de Monaco is only waiting for you to command her, in order to comply . . . as she puts no limit on following your wishes, I ask you to welcome her and treat her kindly, as she deserves. I will speak for her, she has been conducting herself in an exemplary manner, God has had a hand in it. . . .'

The same day Marie de Lorraine also wrote to her husband. 'I cannot describe to you the joy I felt, Sir, on learning from Marshal de Villeroy that you were kind enough to allow me to renew my expressions of respect and affection towards you. If I have had the misfortune to displease you, it was only in acting too impulsively for what I thought the best for us, and for the honour and greatness of your House. Forgive me, Sir, if I have done something wrong, for the sake of my respect and obedience towards you and of my love for my children . . . I ask your pardon, Sir, and to be allowed to come and tell you myself, more strongly than I can ever do by letter, how willingly I shall meet your wishes for the rest of my life. My father is kindly telling you how he himself feels about it all. . . . I beg you to kiss my children for love of me. I hope you will again be able to feel affection for me through the fondness you have for them. With regard to your choice over my daughter's marriage, I am only too convinced of your affection for her and of your high regard for your House not to give my complete consent in advance. I am grateful to you for your kindness in wishing me to concur with you, and I ask with all my heart, Sir, for your affection, and beg you to believe I shall never be unworthy of it.'[1]

Contented with what he thought was 'his victory,' Antoine Grimaldi condescended to be gracious. His reply, on January 8th, 1715, was dignified—and inconsiderate.

'As it is the marriage of the Count of Thorigny to my daughter which is the means of reuniting us, the earlier that is depends

---

[1] Some years later Jacques de Matignon filed away the family letters. He had bitter-sweet memories of his father-in-law, and made ironic notes on many of the letters. On this one is written in his hand: 'Suitable style from a wife to her husband, but little used.'

solely on you, madam. . . . I shall see whether it is followed up by the obedience you promise me, that I dare to say you owe me, and I am prepared to believe you are ashamed for having cut yourself off from it in such a scandalous manner. I have no desire at all to go over the past, you know there would be far too much for me to say. I draw a curtain over a sad picture, so as to start a peaceful life with you and the children again. You can judge if I'm a false or perverse man. Come back, madam, come back in all good faith and with as sincere a heart as mine. That being so, all will be well; you will be cordially welcomed. If, when your rebellious behaviour was at its worst, I paid you back in the kind due to a mistress of a household, what can be awaiting you as mistress here when your conduct is satisfactory. I kissed our children for you with all my heart. They are eager for your return; give them satisfaction, and I shan't be the least to mind, provided that my conditions are observed. And I add this to them—if necessary, in stronger terms—I forbid you to see my unworthy brother and to have any dealings directly or indirectly with him. Farewell, madam, and may God make this year as happy a one for me as you have failed to make those preceding it, but enough of that now.'

Three weeks later, his wife replied to this matrimonial epistle: 'Your desire for the marriage between the Count of Thorigny and my daughter is so much more pleasing to me, Sir, as you make it the means of reuniting us, and being deprived of that has been very painful to me. . . . I wish I were already on my way to tell you how grateful I am to be again in your good favours, indeed I am extremely impatient to be with you and our children, and I beg you to kiss them for love of me.

'Though I should have been most sorry, I would not have failed to obey your commands concerning your brother if Marshal de Villeroy had not considered it best to suspend them for the good of the matter in hand. Kindly believe, Sir, that I wish only to please you and to have you return my affection, that I have made an inviolate rule to obey your commands and to prove that my feelings for you are full of genuine and respectful affection.'

The families were now agreed, so it was time to take action. There was the marriage-contract to be negotiated, and the royal consent to be obtained for the Valentinois dukedom and peerage to be transmitted to the Prince of Monaco's son-in-law.

The discussions over the financial arrangements were long and complicated. The abbé de Monaco made a hard deal for renouncing his rights; the Prince obtained huge concessions in his own favour, including the payment of 700,000 *livres* of debts and 600,000 as dowries for his two younger daughters.

As for what was required from the King, St Simon has explained it all in biting phrases: 'His (the Prince of Monaco) affairs were in a bad way, he put all his hopes in the influence of Monsieur le Grand, and was not mistaken. The chief obstacles to the transfer of the ducal coronet were overcome, and the rest seemed of small consequence. . . . The duchy of Valentinois carried a peerage, but for heirs male only . . . a prior difficulty for transmitting the dignity to a woman. It still existed in the person of the Prince of Monaco, so was not extinct, therefore could not be revived. . . . All that, however, was conceded to the Prince of Monaco, but as no bounds are put to enormities once legitimate barriers are surmounted, here are other concessions that he obtained. Should the Prince of Monaco have a son, the dukedom and peerage would revert to him, and even with the seigniority dating from 1642; the Count of Thorigny would remain duke during his lifetime, but his son would only succeed to the Matignon estates and title. The Prince of Monaco thus sold his dukedom and his daughter at a high price, but with a reservation on the former should he have a son born to him.'

On March 21st Tessé wrote to the Prince of Monaco to announce with pleasure that 'This marriage which has been so much wished for, and on which your peace of mind and that of your family depend, has just been announced. Count of Thorigny, on entering into your family, is to become Duke of Valentinois and peer of the realm.' And Monsieur le Grand wrote on the following day to say with cautious triumph: 'You know that what I have done, my dear Goliath, has only been for the greatness of your name and family; if I've acted contrary to your sentiments, it was to bring you victory. You see you have no truer and firmer friend than me. I've acted as I had to, and I've done it with pleasure. Now let us think only of reuniting. . . . Your wife has been behaving like an angel, the King and all France are unanimous on that, she lives only for the moment of going to join you, which she will do as soon as she possibly can. . . . Show much affection for her, I entreat you, she's my daughter and I love her, treat her kindly, for she deserves it, she always has tears in her eyes when she speaks of you and the children. So be happy, my dear Goliath, since we have cause to be. The Count of Thorigny, moreover, is the most upright and honourable youngster there is in France, he has all kinds of good qualities, as everyone acknowledges; his manners are most dignified, and his attitude to me is most agreeable. I like him very much. Well, God has rewarded us for our good intentions, mine have always been very pure. . . . May there be tremendous high jinks at the wedding, to make Goliath strain himself to do the honours of his house.'

It did indeed seem that the wedding could be held fairly soon. The Princess of Monaco and her prospective son-in-law made preparations to leave for the south, and the engaged couple exchanged their first letters. But there was still Antoine Grimaldi and his difficult character to be reckoned with.

When everything ought to have been going happily forward, he showed himself solely concerned with the financial arrangements for his younger, favourite daughter, Marguerite-Camille; he kept making further demands in her favour, which the Matignon family found impossible to accept. The pitcher was taken too often to the well, and after negotiations had been several times held up they were finally broken off altogether in July.

On the 11th, Monsieur le Grand had tried to overcome, once again, his son-in-law's obstinacy. 'We have at last reached the end of our difficulties, my dear Goliath,' he wrote, 'and although both of us are weak in the legs we have not ceased plodding on. . . . We are all agreed, and there is only this trifling matter which is Madame de Monaco's affair. . . . Do consider that this match and the arrangements made are the sole suitable for my granddaughter. Monsieur de Matignon has agreed in general to everything you desire. Kindly allow me just to say, as your father-in-law, that I wish things to happen as arranged, and as the most loyal and zealous friend you will ever have I ask and implore you to conclude this business. . . . Personally, if it went wrong now I should regard it as an everlasting disgrace. Matignon is acting most honourably over it all; my Goliath will tell him so. You have gained what you wanted, if it were not so I should be a thousand times more peevish than you. Let us get together, now your daughter is settled in the way befitting your lineage, and to the satisfaction of all of us, including that of the King our master; let the others grind their teeth with envy, that's soothing to those who get their own way. One could wish for no better young man than Thorigny, who is amiable and much appreciated in every sense, I pledge you my word. So send a reply promptly, for your wife—who is my dear and worthy daughter—to go and join you. . . .'

The Prince, alas, did not reply; and although the King agreed, on July 24th, to have a warrant drawn up containing 'all those monstrous concessions,'[1] two days later Monsieur le Grand received a visit from Count de Matignon who, discouraged and perhaps uneasy for his son's future with a father-in-law like Antoine Grimaldi, had decided to release the Lorraines from their engagement.

Never had such a situation been known at Versailles. The 'monstrous' favours of the aged, autocratic King looked like being dismissed as unwanted. Monsieur le Grand asked Matignon to delay his decision until August 15th, and then acted swiftly. Well aware of his son-in-law's distrust of him, no doubt he considered it best for a third party to open the attack. So it was Marshal de Tessé who wrote to Antoine, on July 29th, in the following terms: 'Without wishing to enter into an argument that I do not know the details of, I am informing you bluntly and as your servant what I hear about the marriage arranged . . . I do not know whether the cart's been put before the horse, as you wrote . . . but when a matter is so far advanced, and the King has given his approval with many signs of friendship for you and the others concerned in it, how can you then expect, my fine Prince, such a matter to be called off? I've too much affection for you not to say frankly that you give the impression of treating the establishment of your daughter in too light a manner, and I don't know whether the King would accept the reasons which might seem excellent to you but not appear so to him.' Tessé followed this reproach and preliminary reminder by saying that one should not ask for the impossible when others were doing all they could, and ended with a clear warning. 'I do not think there is now

---

[1] The phrase is, of course, St Simon's.

anyone in France but Monsieur de Matignon who would do for you and the Princess all that he is said to have done; and neither is it thought that the King would be prepared to accord to another the gracious facilities granted to him.'

This first onslaught was followed next day, the 30th, by a letter from Monsieur le Grand expressing his extreme grief over the latest difficulties in the way of the marriage. He added that the King had been informed, and did not consider the reasons valid. Finally the King himself, no doubt through Torcy, made it understood that he would not tolerate the arrangements being broken. Grudgingly, the Prince had to give way.

On September 5th, 1715, four days after the death of Louis XIV, the Regent and the young Louis XV signed the marriage-contract between Mademoiselle de Monaco and the Count of Thorigny. These were their first official signatures of the new reign.

So then Marie de Lorraine set off for Monaco. She was never to return to Versailles, nor to see her father again. There was still little encouragement forthcoming from her husband before she started out. On September 10th she wrote to him sadly: 'Your continued silence, that I take as a sign of your anger with me, is spoiling my pleasure at the prospect of going to rejoin you and of seeing my daughter settled in accordance with your desires and my own.'

This letter crossed one from the Prince, dated September 13th, which ought to have reassured her a little when she received it. 'I defy you to be more pleased than I am at the marriage arrangements. They have been concluded with all suitable propriety, both as to the conditions and the authority I am entitled to wield as father. So let us now think only of finishing the whole business and spending our days calmly in friendship. I trust you are already on your way here, and that our future son-in-law will follow a day or two later. . . . Do not try to deceive yourself, through an affection as inordinate as it is blind; you will spoil everything, though with the best of sentiments. I quite believe yours are, but I fear for your partiality. Everyone has his own way of showing love; mine is never forbearing in certain matters. . . .'[1]

[1] The Count of Thorigny wrote in the margin of this letter: 'A sensible, decent letter. How could there be so much dissimilarity in one and the same man.'

Calm never lasted for long between these two, in spite of the steadfast good-nature, the humility at times, of Marie de Lorraine. What could that avail against the violent tempers of Antoine Grimaldi? On September 26th he wrote a letter that he sent to await his wife at Aix-en-Provence, and which was hardly likely to comfort her.

'I know of your great affection for Coco (Louise-Hippolyte) and of your friendliness towards her sisters, but have I not some reason for doubting the affection you say you have for me? A further proof is the kind letter that you caused Monsieur de Torcy to send me just recently. . . . I had reason to congratulate myself that you had had time to repent from using this sort of means for attacking me, that you had realized I am not amenable to rough handling. In brief, it is charming for your father to make out that by using his influence he forced me into arranging a marriage that I have always wished for more than anyone. That is not the kind of thing, believe me, likely to soften my heart towards him. . . . Sorry experience has taught me that I was blind to put my trust in you. You know you had it completely, and my affection too, during the last six or seven years we spent together before your fine journey up to Paris. Don't preen yourself about the good marriage that ours is; chance and my good fortune have brought it about. . . . I had as good a reason for preferring Count de Roye to Count de Lux as I should have been wrong not to accept Monsieur de Thorigny before all others if he had thought of marrying my daughter then. And that, it seems to me, is talking sense. Admit, therefore, in the same way, that Count de Lux would have had my daughter if I had wished to give him her, and that the sole defect you found in Count de Roye was that he had been chosen by me. . . . I end this digression in which I unconsciously let myself be drawn, happy however if it should cause you to admit, as you desire, that you have been completely in the wrong towards me. That would at least convince me that you are repentant. I only hope so, to give you all my affection again.'

The Count of Thorigny's comment written on this letter is: 'What a charming expression of gallantry from a husband, in this last sentence.' One must agree.

However, the Prince's family seemed united when the wedding

took place between Jacques de Matignon and Louise-Hippolyte de Monaco, on October 20th, 1715. The young couple liked each other from the beginning, and there were hopes that the palace of Monaco would shelter a smooth, lasting union, with many children, after the two previous unhappy marriages.[1]

Antoine Grimaldi and his wife appeared to have made a truce and established a *modus vivendi*. The fourth Duke of Valentinois (as Jacques de Matignon now became) was easy-going and had a friendly nature, and soon conquered his irascible father-in-law. He went to great trouble to do this. For instance, knowing the Prince's love of music, he engaged maids for Louise-Hippolyte of whom 'the first played the harpsichord, the second sang, and the third could dance if necessary. . . .'

Monsieur le Grand expressed the relief of all Antoine Grimaldi's family and friends when he wrote on November 10th, three weeks after the wedding: 'It is a great satisfaction to know you and my daughter are well reunited; this gives me more pleasure than I can say. I am strongly convinced that it will last, for Goliath is an upright, honourable man, his wife thinks only of pleasing him, it's her only aim, she is charmed by you, and I thank you with all my heart. I am sure you will find our son-in-law just as I described him, he's a fine fellow, he's sensible, and our dear Coco is a pleasant child; he wrote and told me he's delighted. . . .'[2]

No disappointments occurred over the royal favours either. Although Louis XIV was dead, the warrant dated July 24th had been drawn up during the monarch's lifetime and had made his concessions public. Neither the Regent, Philippe, Duke of Orléans —well disposed towards Antoine Grimaldi, moreover[3]—nor the Council of Regency found any difficulty in giving effect to them. In December, 1715, letters patent creating the new duchy and peerage of Valentinois were drawn up. The official recording of them by the Paris Parlement, and Jacques de Matignon's ceremonial reception as Duke and peer, should have followed almost

---

[1] Tessé said he was preparing a whole book of questions for the husband, 'as big as the Thousand and One days. I took care not to make my comparison with the Thousand and One nights, for naturally I leave them to the young couple.'

[2] Monsieur le Grand died in June, 1718, at Royaumont.

[3] When the Duke of Orléans became Regent he had expressed the wish that the friendship he had formed with 'Goliath,' as he too called the Prince of Monaco— a friendship formed chiefly backstage at the Opera House—should continue for the general good.

at once; but were adjourned owing to quarrels over precedence between the Parlement, the dukes and peers, and the royal princes. Nearly a year passed before they were smoothed over, relatively speaking. On September 2nd, 1716, the new duchy of Valentinois was officially recorded, and on December 15th the fourth Duke's reception by Parlement was held, none of the princes being present. 'They had all promised him not to go,' Dangeau remarks, 'in order to avoid any dispute between themselves.'

Although Antoine Grimaldi was a difficult husband and a tyrant of a father,[1] this bad side of his character did not appear in his relations with the people of Monaco. He had poured money into improving the fortifications of the Rock, and he was no less generous towards his subjects in time of peace. Under him, the Principality was governed in a liberal manner—he could in fact be called a prototype of the enlightened despots—and his reign was, from the people's point of view, a happy and peaceful one.

Relations with the outside world were quiet until the end of Prince Antoine's life. Once the bitterness over the homage made for Menton and Roquebrune had been forgotten, the best of relations were maintained with the House of Savoy, which ruled the new Kingdom of Sardinia. An agreement over deserters from its armed forces was concluded.

Plague broke out in Marseille in 1720 and spread through Provence, but the Principality was saved by its remote position and difficult access by land. Four years later, the Prince had a carriage-road made between Monaco and Menton.

Although the Principality in general was going through a happy and peaceful period, life at the palace did not remain so for long. Marie de Lorraine had been modest in her triumph, but her husband was too intelligent not to perceive that the Lorraines had got round him—for his own good, no doubt—yet a nature like his could not easily accept it. Besides, were not the members of his family his normal enemies? Having made it up with his brother in 1716, the Prince then began to take a dislike to the

[1] Even his favourite daughter, Marguerite-Camille, experienced this tyranny. He called her back from Paris, without rhyme or reason, and in spite of the protests of his family and friends, during the negotiations for her marriage to the Prince d'Isenghien—whom she married in 1720.

Duke of Valentinois. Was it a valid reason for reproach, that the Duke should stay by his pregnant young wife instead of paying a visit to the Duke of Savoy? The Prince ought to have realized that if it had not been for his son-in-law's homely nature he would have shown much less willingness to remain at Monaco. The Prince ought to have remembered, too, that he himself had not taken his father's advice when he had announced his intention of leaving the army, and that Louis had not held it against him. But especially, it would seem, the Prince was annoyed by the harmony that existed between his wife and the young Valentinois household; the three of them breathed better in his absence. If he went to stay at Menton, they remained behind at Monaco on the slightest excuse. But was it not his tyrannic attitude that made them draw together?

A son was born to the Valentinois couple in December, 1717, at Monaco. Great was the joy, which turned to great sadness when the baby died three months later. The atmosphere at the palace became heavier than ever, and the Duke and Duchess could stand it no longer; in May, 1718, they went to live in France, away from Antoine's outbreaks of temper, and stayed there almost continuously until his death.

Louis Grimaldi must sometimes have thought that the rank of foreign prince had been dearly paid for; and if the Valentinois couple had not been so happy, the Matignons would have thought the same about the duchy of Valentinois. The Duke's difficulties with his formidable father-in-law appear strikingly similar to those that Antoine Grimaldi had with his formidable mother-in-law, Madame d'Armagnac. Could he, after thirty years, have been taking a belated revenge, and on an innocent person?

For some years, outward appearances were saved by this separation and distance between them, and by the patient tolerance of the Duke of Valentinois.

Even in the spring of 1725, just prior to their greatest difficulties, the Duke wrote to his father-in-law: 'With regard to the arrangements you write to say we shall have to make together, I don't see how there can be any, for you will always be the master so far as I am concerned, and in that way our affairs are not difficult to settle.' A month later, uneasy over the other's demands, he civilly wrote: 'You mention the state of your affairs as though you wish me to do all I can to ease your situation. I will willingly help . . . on condition, if you please, that you take no steps to prejudice the future interests of your grandson, the seigneur des Baux (born in 1720, destined to become Honoré III). He is such a bonny boy that nobody could think of playing a dirty trick on him.'

Marie de Lorraine had died in October, 1724, and before long a series of lawsuits began over the inheritance. They were still in progress when, in May, 1726, the Prince's youngest daughter, Marie-Pelline, Mademoiselle de Chabeuil, died; and they were given fresh impetus by the dispositions of her will.

The Prince was claiming the usufruct of his wife's possessions, but this was disregarding certain stipulations in the marriage contract. As for Marie-Pelline, he had caused her to make a will in his favour, though she was still a minor.

These lawsuits continued for several years, until the end of Antoine Grimaldi's life and even beyond—for his case was taken over by his second daughter, who had become the Princess d'Isenghien—and in spite of efforts by Cardinal Fleury to reconcile the parties. Incidentally, the cardinal's friendship with the Prince often caused him to be unjust towards the Duke of Valentinois.

In August, 1730, though, when the Prince was recovering from a very serious illness, he seemed prepared to make the peace, in response to the increasing insistence of Cardinal Fleury, who had become Prime Minister in 1726, at the age of 72.[1] 'God has helped your recovery,' the cardinal wrote to him on August 11th, 'and it seems to me that the first use you should make of it is to forgive not your enemies but your children, who wish for nothing more than to put right the misfortune they have had to displease you. . . .'

On August 18th the Prince assured Fleury that the Valentinois couple were back in his good books and that they could come to Monaco. That same day he wrote to Louise-Hippolyte— since the opening of the lawsuits in 1725 he had addressed her as

[1] On July 11th, 1726, Fleury thanked the Prince for his congratulations, and mentioned his own sacrifices for the King, and the heavy burdens laid upon his shoulders. The fourth Duke of Valentinois wrote in the margin—'This is a letter from the greatest hypocrite there ever was.'

vous instead of the familiar *tu*—'I can only say that however much I may have had to complain of your conduct, it has never entered my head that you were indifferent to my recovery. So you can judge whether I was comforted by your letter of the 5th, in which you express no less strongly than Monsieur de Valentinois sentiments so much in line with his.'

Was the reconciliation sincere? Hardly, for that would suppose Antoine Grimaldi's feelings had quickly altered, which was not in his nature. Indeed, less than three weeks earlier he had written a very different kind of letter to his brother, François-Honoré, Archbishop of Besançon since 1723, who was proposing to stay with the Valentinois family while in Paris.

'It was against all my wishes and with great reluctance,' ran the letter, 'that they (the lawsuits) were started with the amiable Monsieur de Valentinois and his wife, who, not content with failing in every kind of propriety towards me, and in their promises to end our differences amicably by arbitration . . . have been humbugging me more than ever, since Madame de Monaco and my poor Chabeuil died, using the most unbelievable underhand tricks. What it all amounts to is this—they are following the fine system they adopted right after the deaths of those two, which is to see me die with rage in my heart because, thanks to them, my situation is no brighter. But they'll find they will pay for it all one day. My other daughter and son-in-law, the Isenghiens, act very differently, and you will never find that they have written and dared to suggest that I forced my poor Chabeuil to benefit me as she did, which is unbelievable.

'So I leave you to judge for yourself, my dear brother, whether in all decency you can accept their offer of hospitality, considering how my relations with them are, and are bound to be. . . .'

The Archbishop had broken with his brother for some years following the negotiations over Louise-Hippolyte's marriage, and had then broken with the Valentinois couple at his brother's request, but in defiance of him had later made it up with them; Antoine's letter now made no impression on him. Besides, he was far away. . . . In short, on August 11th he serenely announced to his brother, from Paris: 'I arrived here last Tuesday and found Monsieur and Madame de Valentinois, whom I thought were in Normandy. They told me they had decided to come here in order to receive news of you more promptly. I could not be better looked after than I am here, I have every reason for praising their arrangements. Both husband and wife are most desirous to have the honour of regaining your favours, and they seem to me entirely disposed to agree to whatever it may please you to direct. It is in this state of mind that Madame de Valentinois is leaving for Monaco with one of the children. . . .'

The Duke of Valentinois was by no means anxious to discuss family affairs with his father-in-law, so he excused himself on grounds of ill-health, and only his wife went to Monaco, taking their second son, who had been born in January, 1722, and had the title of Count de Carladèz. She stayed there for several weeks, and the reunion appears to have been a happy one. The Prince, who had wished so much for a son, quickly grew fond of the fair-haired, fresh-faced and pleasant boy that Louise-Hippolyte had brought to see him. Antoine showed his affectionate side, and his strong, eccentric character overawed the young and perhaps not very bright woman, whose husband had been wrong, on the whole, not to accompany her. Louise-Hippolyte had lived happily for many years far from Monaco, but now she suddenly and passionately felt she belonged there.

The Prince, with his intelligence, could not fail to note this victory over a son-in-law who was to him an enemy and a stranger.[1] It was a last triumph for him; he was very sad when his daughter left to return to France in January, 1731. He wrote her an affectionate letter on February 9th, but was unable to finish it. He caught a chill on the 13th, and died during the night of February 20th, 1731. His doctor sent the unfinished letter to Louise-Hippolyte with an account of the Prince's last hours.

With the death of Antoine I, the male line of the Grimaldis of Monaco came to an end. His reign had been a happy one for the Principality; the sovereign prince had resided there almost continuously, and had governed with intelligent liberality.

---

[1] Financial matters had in the meantime created more bitterness. 'I'm dreadfully sorry,' François-Honoré wrote to his brother on December 22nd, 1730, 'to hear that no agreement has been possible between you and Monsieur de Valentinois, as was hoped for. . . . Yet it seems to me that it should be easier to come to an agreement just now, as Monsieur d'Isenghien has thanked you for your 15,000 francs, which was the item in your demands that most grieved Monsieur de Valentinois. . . .'

CHAPTER VI

THE PLEASURES OF LIFE (1731–1795)

THE LONG LIFE OF HONORÉ III was marked by three women—his mother, and her brief reign; his wife, who was the chief interest of his middle years; and his charming daughter-in-law, Françoise-Thérèse, whose cruel death hastened his own.

Not a great deal is known of the character of Louise-Hippolyte, Duchess of Valentinois, who became Princess of Monaco at the end of February, 1731. What chiefly emerges from the letters of Antoine to his wife and to his daughter is the great affection Marie de Lorraine had for the child born from her reconciliation with Antoine, and the powerful influence she had over the somewhat timid girl, who was scared by her father's powerful and harsh character. There is however a portrait of Louise-Hippolyte, done by the Provençal painter, Vanloo, when at Monaco in 1712. She has rather irregular features, bright eyes and a fresh complexion, and her mother's gentle looks; but Marie de Lorraine was gay and lively in her youth, while her daughter at that age appears a little sad and with a touch of anxiety.

If one considers what the years of family quarrels must have been like, and her confinement to the convent previous to her marriage, it is understandable that her health should have been affected—later improved by the peaceful family life in Normandy, in spite of her several pregnancies—and that she should be susceptible to outside influences.

The main influence upon her came naturally from her husband, a handsome, jovial, vigorous Norman. Life had been good to this ruddy-faced man with sandy hair (and so his nickname was 'Sandy'), who had been brought up in a happy, very wealthy family, his parents' only child. His sole ambition was to lead a pleasant, peaceful life, cultivating his artistic tastes, far from the army now that peace had come, far from the Court, too, which he disliked; sharing his time between his town mansion in Paris and his estates in Lower Normandy. And—something rare among his class at that period—this brisk and merry man with a lively mind wanted to be constant and faithful in his love for his wife.

For fifteen years the two were perfectly happy together. Seven children were born to them after they had lost the baby son; and six survived. There were two girls, Charlotte and Louise-Françoise-Thérèse, born respectively in 1719 and 1728; and four boys, the future Honoré III, Charles-Auguste, François-Charles, and Charles-Maurice, born in 1720, 1722, 1726, and 1727. This happy family can be seen in a portrait by Gobert at the palace of Monaco. Father and mother are looking proudly from left and right upon the group of fine, alert children; the heir, the young seigneur des Baux, stands in front, dressed in a yellow costume and holding a dog; the elder daughter, Charlotte, grave and serene, has a slightly absent look, perhaps listening to the call that was soon to draw her into the cloisters.

Nothing in February, 1731, hinted that a rift was soon to appear between this long-united couple—unless it were the effect that Antoine Grimaldi had had on his daughter during her recent stay at Monaco.

As Antoine's brother had renounced his claims to the succession in favour of Louise-Hippolyte and her husband, the latter should have ruled the Principality with her and become Prince of Monaco under the name of Jacques I. This would have conformed, moreover, with the precedent of Claudine and Lambert. Yet as soon as Louise-Hippolyte learnt of her father's death she did not wait for her husband, who was detained in Paris by the reading of Antoine's will and the early complications over the inheritance,[1] but set off for Monaco with one of her children, François-Charles. In the opinion of a previous biographer, L-H Labande, she had already decided to have herself alone proclaimed as sovereign princess, and had hidden this intention from her husband. Another writer, Gustave Saige, basing himself upon a study of the Princess's correspondence, believes she still then had every

---

[1] The will, dated October 14th, 1726, made Antoine's younger daughter, the Princess d'Isenghien, his sole heir.

intention of sharing the rule. But the Duke apparently made a grave mistake in allowing his wife to go alone, and be influenced by her father's officials; in particular by Bernardoni, the auditor-general, who had been the confidant of Antoine Grimaldi for the past thirty years and knew of his personal grudges.

It would seem, though, that such influence had already been applied during her previous stay at Monaco; otherwise its action was surprisingly rapid, as Louise-Hippolyte and her husband were apart for only six or seven weeks.

Whatever her intention on leaving Paris—and Labande seems nearer the mark—Louise-Hippolyte had the oath of loyalty made to her for Monaco, Menton, and Roquebrune, very soon after she arrived on April 14th, and without any mention being made of her husband. Moreover, the local lawyers were given instructions that henceforth acts and documents were to be headed by her name alone.

The Princess had an edict prepared, however, that associated her husband's name with hers in the governing of the Principality; but being no doubt drawn up by officials who had served under Antoine, when the Duke arrived at the end of May he found it almost insolent in its wording.

That was the opening skirmish. He then soon discovered, without any difficulty, that he was considered a hindrance; that the chief officials of the little State were encouraging his wife to exclude him, either through love of power for themselves, or because they remained faithful to Antoine's memory and continued his antagonism towards his son-in-law. The Duke was a realistic Norman, and it seemed to him that if a choice had to be made between a struggle for power on the Rock of Monaco and a carefree life in the elegant surroundings of the Matignon town mansion in the rue de Varenne, then there was nothing to hesitate over. And besides, as a disappointed but loving husband, he probably thought that by leaving at once, before an irreparable scene occurred, his wife would recover her independence of mind all the sooner—and her affection for him. So he returned to Paris.[1]

[1] Madame de Simiane, a grand-daughter of Madame de Sévigné, wrote in October, 1731: 'It is said that there has been a quarrel between Monsieur and Madame de Monaco, because he wished to be named with his wife in the proclamation of accession, and she did not wish it; and that they have separated, he returning to Paris, she staying at Monaco.'

Her husband's departure no doubt caused the Princess to think things over. She did not venture to widen the breach between them, and the new reign was announced to foreign Powers under both their names. But it was in her name alone that Monsieur de Gourdon, a relative officially representing her, made homage for Menton and Roquebrune to the King of Sardinia; and it was she alone who received the investiture, on December 3rd.

How would matters have turned out between them? Would the healing hand of time have had its effect? Unfortunately, Louise-Hippolyte had little time left; and the rift between her and the Duke still existed when, on December 29th, 1731, she died of smallpox.

Soon after learning of his wife's death, the Duke held a family council and was legally appointed the guardian of his children's rights. Then he left for Monaco, where the legal authorities had given the opinion—referring back to Etienne the Gubernant—that he ought to rule at least while Antoine's brother, François-Honoré, was still alive;[1] at the latter's death, he ought to remain ruler during the minority of the heir, which meant until Honoré reached the age of twenty-five. The same jurists even expressed the wish, the 'ardent wish,' that the Duke should govern as long as possible, that the son should abdicate in favour of his father and thus follow 'the example of those who relinquished to their father the command of their fiefs inherited through the mother.'

And so the Duke of Valentinois was recognized as sovereign prince of Monaco by all the people; though he did not ask for the oath of loyalty to be made to him. The people accepted this Norman converted into a Grimaldi and showed no impatience for his son to succeed, but he himself soon came up against the same difficulties and worries as the year before—the antagonism of the old officials of Antoine Grimaldi, the hostility of Cardinal Fleury and therefore of the French authorities, and the refusal by the King of Sardinia to recognize his rights over Menton and Roquebrune.

The fourth Duke of Valentinois could certainly not be called ambitious or persistent. A few weeks of struggling against such

[1] He resigned his archbishopric in 1731, and lived until 1748.

difficulties were sufficient to discourage and defeat him. On May 20th, 1732, he appointed the Chevalier de Grimaldi, the natural son of Antoine I, as governor-general of the Principality with very wide powers, and he returned to Paris—to his pleasant life there in his fine house, among the art collections he was assembling. From there, he continued to negotiate with the Sardinian government without eagerness or success. In the end, he had to accept his position as the Duke of Valentinois, legal administrator of the possessions and rights of his son, the Prince of Monaco.

On April 15th, 1733, the Chevalier de Grimaldi, officially representing the young Honoré III, made homage to Charles Emmanuel, Duke of Savoy and King of Sardinia, and was invested with Menton and Roquebrune. A few months later, on November 7th, Jacques I formally abdicated, though retaining the regency and the administration of the Principality during the minority of Honoré III.

The Duke of Valentinois returned to Monaco for the last time in May, 1734, taking Honoré III to be presented to his subjects and to receive their oath of loyalty. The absence of this affable, very wealthy man, prepared to be generous, was perhaps regretted by then, and the officials who had opposed him were perhaps thinking they had been mistaken in their policy. For his arrival with the young Prince was greeted with much pomp and ceremony, and by acclamations of loyalty that confirmed the official nature of Jacques I's reign and that he had been generally accepted as the legitimate sovereign prince during those two years.

It was a tardy demonstration of political acumen on the part of the local authorities. Too much so. In spite of it, the Duke of Valentinois left Monaco for good this time. He had no reason for liking the place, since it reminded him of the bitter quarrels with his father-in-law, and of the sadder, most unexpected, disagreement with his wife. This definite absence, though, affected his sons. The younger ones do not appear to have set foot in Monaco again, but remained fully occupied with their military careers and life in Paris; while even Honoré III did not return to his Principality until fifteen years later.

The Chevalier de Grimaldi had his powers renewed in May, 1734, and continued to govern for half a century, until his death in 1784. It was a peaceful period for the Principality, but a some-what stagnant one; the isolated territory had to fall back on its own poor resources. It felt the lack of its Prince's presence, as a centre of attraction and also for the prosperity which the rich landowner, having vast estates in the Valentinois and in Nor-mandy, could have brought in his train. The posthumous triumph of Antoine Grimaldi over his son-in-law resulted, in effect, in a material loss for his Principality.

The Duke of Valentinois began to organize a comfortable life and to arrange for the education and future of his children; and to settle the lawsuits with the Isenghiens. On December 4th, 1735, young Honoré wrote to his grand-uncle, gravely signing himself as Prince of Monaco, to say: 'My affairs with my aunt d'Isenghien have been settled by agreement. It was all arranged without difficulty yesterday, when my father agreed to all she was asking for, to get peace. We are giving her half a million *livres*. . . .'

With this matter settled, the Duke arranged the shape of his existence. He established himself at his town mansion in the rue de Varenne, and had some tapestries, pictures, and *objets d'art* sent up from the palace of Monaco. In June, 1736, he acquired two twin pavilions linked by a stone balustrade, at Passy, just outside Paris; they stood in a large park and were approached down avenues of trimmed lime-trees.[1]

The Duke divided his time between Paris, Passy, and his country seat at Thorigny. His children were growing up, but he was to lose three of them in the next few years—four of them, if the elder daughter, Charlotte, is included, for she took her vows and entered the Convent of the Visitation in the rue St Jacques, at Paris, in January, 1738. Her sister died in 1743 at the convent-school where she was a boarder. The four sons all took up military careers. Charles-Auguste, Count de Carladèz and later Count de Matignon, who, when a boy, had been taken to Monaco by his mother to see Antoine I, became colonel of his regiment and was advanced to brigadier when the War of the Austrian

---

[1] The Duke eventually gave this country folly to one of his daughters-in-law, the Countess of Valentinois. She held *fêtes galantes* there, some of which were attended by Madame du Barry. Later, Benjamin Franklin stayed there on several occasions.

Succession ended, in 1748. But he died the following year, while down near the Spanish frontier.

The younger brother, François-Charles, was intended for the Church, but he lacked the vocation. The Grimaldis were sincere Catholics, and the family had never forced sons to enter the Church; and the Duke was too affectionate a father to start doing so. He purchased a commission in the Royal Infantry regiment for the youngster. But François-Charles died at the age of seventeen, while serving in the garrison town of Mouzon, in the Ardennes.

The youngest son, Charles-Maurice, had the title of Chevalier de Monaco. He was to join the Knights of Malta, but the death of François-Charles in 1743 altered his future. He entered the army instead, became captain in a cavalry regiment in 1744, and transferred to the King's gendarmes early the following year. A few months later he was at the battle of Fontenoy, where he distinguished himself and was wounded in the thigh. At eighteen, the Chevalier de Monaco was a likeable, frank and even-tempered young man, much sought after in Court society. Voltaire, in his poem on the French victory at Fontenoy, gave a line to the young Chevalier—a privilege envied by not a few women—'Monaco lost his blood, and Love sighed over it.'

In December, 1749, a few months after the death of Charles-Auguste, the Duke of Valentinois arranged a brilliant match for this one son remaining to him apart from Honoré III, and who was then called the Count of Valentinois. By a peculiar stroke of fate, the bride was the only daughter of the Duke of Ruffec and the grand-daughter of St Simon; and so the heritage of the famous, sarcastic memoir-writer passed to the descendants of the Grimaldis he had so greatly detested.

The Duke of Valentinois obtained royal approval, on the occasion of this marriage, for his younger son to become Lieutenant-Governor of Lower Normandy in his place, together with the governership of Cherbourg, Granville, Saint Lô, and the Chausey isles, all of which were hereditary posts of the Matignons. The Duke had every reason for believing he had assured a fine future for his favourite son.

But the marriage turned out to be unhappy, and childless. The Countess was pretty, but sour-tempered and fickle. She got into the Pompadour set, and later that of Du Barry. The couple separated in 1766, and from then on the Count de Valentinois—who seemed to have his father's homely, gentle nature—lived mostly in Paris. He became involved in the quarrels between Honoré III and the Princess, as will be seen later, and took the part of his sister-in-law.[1]

The chief concern of the Duke of Valentinois was of course the future of the young Prince of Monaco. After being educated by Jesuits, Honoré III became a musketeer in the King's Guard at the age of fifteen. His father soon tried to get a regiment for him—the Duke himself had been bought the command of one when he was thirteen—but met with opposition from Cardinal Fleury, who had no liking for the Duke.

In a letter to Honoré's grand-uncle on September 1st, 1737, the Duke expressed his bitterness on the subject: 'He (Honoré III) has now been a musketeer for nearly two years, and this seems a long time to me. I've spoken and written to Cardinal Fleury about having a cavalry regiment for him, but I've only received vague replies. If it were a request on my own account I should not have been at all surprised . . . after the fine services that rascal Bernardoni did me with His Eminence . . . but it concerns my son, who ought not to be made to suffer because of alleged faults of his father. I wrote to tell the cardinal that if he should not be favoured among those wishing for a regiment he would be obliged to remain in his natural position, which is that of a sovereign prince who will one day have an income of a hundred thousand écus; to judge by His Eminence's reply, he is not used to receiving such pressing applications. He ought also to have considered . . . that the one man of France most able to dispense with favours from the Court is Monsieur de Monaco. I've decided to say no more to him on the matter, so I have the honour of writing to ask you to try and find out what his intentions are . . .'

The ex-archbishop liked his peace and quiet above everything, and promptly replied that he was no better placed at Court than the Duke; who had to wait patiently.

[1] The Count of Valentinois's town house was behind that of his sister-in-law in the rue St Dominique, built by Brogniart.
The Count emigrated with her after the French Revolution, and he died in 1793.

Honoré III was given the rank of lieutenant in the King's regiment; and finally obtained an infantry regiment, which was then named after Monaco, in October, 1739. It cost his father 55,000 *livres*.

Having ensured Honoré's military career, the Duke then turned to the matter of getting him married. In March, 1740, he began negotiating for the hand of the daughter of the Duchess of Maine. He wanted Honoré to be granted the style of foreign prince, on the occasion of such a marriage, following the precedent when Antoine married Marie de Lorraine. But Cardinal Fleury, still hostile to the Duke and therefore to his family, and perhaps remembering Antoine Grimaldi's protests on the subject not so many years previously, opposed the granting of the title, and the negotiations were broken off.

The Duke was not discouraged, and fell back on the Duke of Bouillon's daughter. Agreement was reached on the terms of the marriage contract, the King's approval obtained, and then at the last moment Honoré III refused—on a poor pretext—to sign on the dotted line. The Duke began to think his son was decidedly 'a most capricious individual and most independent in his behaviour.' Perhaps he found, too, that on reaching man's estate Honoré was remarkably like his grandfather, if not in appearance at least in character.

To punish him for this disobedience, the Duke obtained a *lettre de cachet* from the King and had Honoré confined to the fortress of Arras for some months. He came out embittered and on somewhat bad terms with his father, who gave up attempting to arrange a marriage for him; he had no liking for the Court, and showed it, which increased his resemblance to Antoine I.

Although the unsociable side of the Grimaldi character appeared to be coming out in him, his family's courage and loyalty to France were not lacking either. It seemed probable that a brilliant military career was ahead of him, which would cause him to forget his grudges. He was given command of a brigade on May 1st, 1745, a few days before the battle of Fontenoy, at which he too, like his brother, distinguished himself. He was wounded during the campaign in the Low Countries the following year; and in 1747 he had his horse killed under him while leading his brigade at the battle of Lawfeld. In May, 1748, he was appointed brigadier-general by royal warrant, when still only twenty-eight; but less than a month later, for some misconduct or other, he was thrown into the Bastille. He was kept there for several months, during which time peace was signed at Aix-la-Chapelle. Although his appointment was officially confirmed in December, 1748, and so he could hope for a return to favour, Honoré III had lost all ambition, and the second internment had increased his dislike of the Court. He resigned his commission, and went off to Monaco for some fresh air.

During the War of the Austrian Succession, diplomatic relations between Monaco and the Sardinian government had been broken off, and the Principality occupied by belligerent troops; and a British cruiser had appeared off the coast. But after these alarms, all had become happy and calm again under the liberal trusteeship of the Chevalier de Grimaldi. Honoré III was given an enthusiastic welcome by a population proud to have their Prince among them again and grateful for the generosity constantly shown by his family. Moreover, the young man cut a very dashing figure. His lively dark eyes and high forehead gave him something of his mother's looks, but his bearing and build came distinctly from the Matignon side. He had an elegant manner, yet with his tall, strapping build went an air of authority and decision.

He began to take an active part in the administration of the Principality, but did not stay very long at Monaco. The more or less enforced absence of the third Duke of Valentinois and his family in the past continued to have unfortunate effects. Honoré III, who resembled his grandfather in many respects—by his intelligence, his independent spirit, and lonely nature—could very likely have taken root in Monaco as Antoine I had done; but he had been away for too long a time. It had been easy for Antoine to settle down in his Principality; his early childhood had been spent there, he had no establishment to detain him in France, and the political situation had been such as to enable him to make full use of Monaco's situation between France and the Italian States. In addition, his temperament and tastes had been Italian, and he had been satisfied with a sedentary life.

But Honoré III, although having no more liking for the Court,

13 Prince Louis II of Monaco, 1870–1949. *Portrait by P. A. de Laszlo.*

14 Princess Charlotte of Monaco, 1929. *Portrait by P. A. de Laszlo.*

and with a similar feudal outlook that looked to Versailles only for honours and not for rewards, had grown up between the Matignon mansion in Paris and the wide-open spaces of Normandy, the thousands of acres of pasture and forest of his father's estate. In that rolling, lush and leafy countryside, he had developed a taste for an open-air life, for hunting and shooting, and training the yearlings on the stud-farm. Moreover, the Grimaldi-Matignons had far fewer links with Italy, and the French political axis had shifted from the Mediterranean towards Germany; the importance of Monaco, whose harbour and, later, fortress had been of value to rival Powers, was now much diminished, and by the middle of this eighteenth century the Principality was entering a period of great calm and peace. Honoré III could only have been held there by strong personal connections formed by years of habit, of the kind that often prove the strongest of all. But there was none; and besides, others of a different kind had been formed. And so Honoré III, and then his successors during the next hundred years, made only short stays on their Rock; though they always maintained a deep interest in the happiness of their subjects and acted with much generosity towards them. The responsibility for this long absenteeism, though indirect and unknowing at the time, must be laid upon the entourage of Antoine I.

It was at Versailles, in 1750, that Honoré III first met the Marquise de Brignole-Sale.

She came of a great Genoese family, the Balbis. Though a fine-looking woman, and intelligent, she had a haughty manner and a hasty temper. Her marriage had not been a success. The Marquis de Brignole-Sale was immensely wealthy—he was descended from a line of Doges—but though good-hearted he was slow-witted and had a rugged character. His wife's whims and fancies irritated him, and he gave way to her with surly resignation. This ill-assorted couple had one child, a girl named Marie-Catherine, then eleven years old.

The Marquise had left Genoa and the marble-fronted Palazzo Rosso to spend several months in Paris. Her breeding and fortune brought her a flattering welcome at Court, and her educated mind made her equally acceptable in the salons of the most intelligent and cultured women of the period, such as those of the Marquise du Deffand and of Madame Geoffrin. She became very friendly with the latter's daughter, Madame de La Ferté-Imbault.

The Marquise lived in an age and among a society, especially, in which passions came to the fore. When a woman falls in love with someone much younger than herself, and for the last time, she does so deeply and passionately; and, when she has a bounteous heart and unlimited devotion, her affection is friendly and motherly too . . . So it was with the Marquise de Brignole, almost at first sight, when she met Honoré Grimaldi. There was something sharp and sensual about this Norman-Italian which must have attracted an experienced, intelligent woman like the Marquise. Yet behind the assurance of the sovereign prince she perceived the child whose mother had died too soon and who had known family quarrelling too early in life. His troubled boyhood and then his imprisonments had given him an uneasy mind and a jealous heart, more inclined to be suspicious than affectionate (only a long life and its disappointments were to soothe all that away). He was, in short, the kind of man that women often find attractive and are often hurt by.

Honoré Grimaldi and the Marquise arranged matters so that appearances were saved; and an uncommon understanding developed between these two strong-minded people. If she gave the greater love—while he let himself be loved—it was because she was forty and he but thirty.

In 1754 Honoré III went to Monaco and also spent several months in Genoa, staying at the Palazzo Rosso. The Marquis de Brignole had no liking for his guest, whose elegances irritated him, and considered his courteous indifference to be just sly hypocrisy. But Honoré did not let himself be put out by his host's animosity. For he had discovered that behind the mother was a daughter of budding fifteen. Marie-Catherine was tall and slender, already well developed, and graceful in her movements. A blonde with dark blue eyes and a fresh, pink complexion, she was as lovely as an angel, according to Madame de La Ferté-Imbault.

For the past fifteen years Honoré had rejected all idea of marriage, but when he left Genoa to return to France it was quite likely that he no longer scorned such an idea.

On the death of his father in 1751, Honoré had become the fifth Duke of Valentinois; and his official reception as duke and peer of the realm by the Paris Parlement took place on March 17th, 1755. The Prince of Monaco was showing his awareness of dynastic needs and of the urgency to ensure the continuance of his line. For his brother, the Count of Valentinois, still had no children after more than five years of marriage.

On her side, the Marquise de Brignole must have realized how matters were developing, for she spent the summer and autumn of that year in France, and brought her daughter with her. The whole attitude of the Marquise, and the letters that passed between her and the Prince of Monaco during 1756, indicate that she was aware of and allowed the written promise of marriage that Honoré III had received from Marie-Catherine on November 29th, 1755. It read: 'I, the undersigned, declare and promise to the Prince of Monaco never to marry anyone but him, whatever may happen, and never to listen to any proposal that might tend to release me.'

The consent of the Marquis had still to be obtained, and that was difficult. If his daughter had dared to face him herself and declare her love, as she did eighteen months later, she might well have got his consent at once, for he was fond of her. But she was very young, and left it all to her mother. And the sweeping demands and outbursts of the Marquise probably made him firmer in his refusal.

So the weeks and months went by, and the situation was still the same in the spring of 1756. Honoré III became discouraged, and started discussions with the Duke de La Vallière for the hand of his daughter. The Duke was in much favour at Court, and seemed quite sure that he could persuade Louis XV to grant to his future son-in-law and descendants the rank and honours previously held by the Grimaldis, but which had lapsed with Antoine I, the last of the male line. Honoré wrote to the Marquise at Genoa, on May 3rd, to tell her of these negotiations. He could no longer expect to overcome the Marquis's opposition, after so many months of perseverance, and Mademoiselle de La Vallière represented his only prospect of obtaining advantages from the French Court. A month later he received a reply from the Marquise; it contained no reproach, merely the hope that Honoré was making a choice that would be a happy one for him.

It was not without regret that he turned his mind away from the Genoese alliance. The close vicinity of both parties seemed to him an assurance of security; Marie-Catherine's good looks and pleasant nature seemed assurances of happiness; and her family fortune an assurance of power. And so he let another month go by before taking the matter with the Duke de La Vallière any further. Early in July, without having seen the daughter nor signed anything with the Duke, he came to an agreement with him, and the Duke placed the application before the King.

At first, everything appeared to go well. On July 8th, an official of the King's Household, Count de St Florentin, announced the royal approval to the Duke de La Vallière—the Prince of Monaco and his heirs would be granted the rank and style of foreign prince. But as soon as news of this favour became known it aroused a cry of protest from the dukes and peers. Honoré remained confident, however, and like a gallant gentleman returned the written promise of marriage to the Marquise de Brignole.[1]

It was a courteous and chivalrous gesture, but imprudent. The peers renewed their protests more strongly, and Louis XV refrained from making public the favours he had been prepared to grant. On July 27th, Honoré III wrote to the King—at the request of the Duke, who hoped to force the royal hand—and reminded him that an authenticated copy of a letter to his ministers informing them of the favour granted was sufficient for the marriage contract to go through, and that otherwise he, Honoré, would 'make no proposal for any closer agreement with you beyond that existing between us.'

This had no effect. On July 30th, at Compiègne, the King wrote to the Duke de La Vallière: 'Cousin, I came to my decision after examining all the communications from Monsieur de Monaco, and I do not wish to change it at all. I shall be grieved if this causes the marriage to fall through, but you will lose none of your rights nor any of my kindness towards you. I pray that God's good mercy be upon you, cousin.'

[1] The envelope containing it bore the words: 'This belongs to Madame Anne Balbi de Brignole, of Genoa, and must only be given into her hands, or against an order signed by her. At Paris, this 19th of July.'

The following day, the marriage negotiations were broken off.

It was a great disappointment for Honoré III. A wrathful letter from Madame de Brignole arrived to make matters worse. Although she had been informed, and had been acquiescent, now that she thought the La Vallière marriage was practically arranged she wrote to tax the Prince with ingratitude. He replied to her point by point, on August 7th, in a letter that ran to thirty-two pages. 'You accuse me of so many dreadful things that I'm obliged to defend myself. I may even find good reason for attacking you. . . .' He reminded her of their letters of May and June, and was surprised at her anger, since he could believe himself to be free, and there was nothing to cause him to expect 'the reproaches you think you have a right to make now.' After persevering for seventeen months, 'there were no signs of Monsieur de Brignole being won over.'

The Marquise had one of those tempestuous and lofty minds that do not believe in half measures. A triumphant Honoré greatly annoyed her; a Honoré defeated by a clique aroused her active sympathy. He had left Versailles for Monaco. The Marquise wanted him to have a striking revenge that would enable him to return to Court in triumph. Marie-Catherine had very likely heard nothing of the La Vallière episode nor knew of the return of her promise, which she was as ready as ever to keep. Her mother made further attempts, with fresh energy, to get the father to consent to the marriage.

The Marquis sulked, and kept to his own rooms. Honoré III, aware of his prospective father-in-law's hostility, became very exacting over the terms of the marriage contract. For by the end of October, 1756, matters had nevertheless reached that stage; though the Marquis carried out valiant rearguard actions, and his wife only just managed to prevent a decree being published which would have forbidden the Brignole heiress to transfer her wealth outside the Genoese Republic.

By March, 1757, the Marquise believed the end was in sight, and she wrote to Honoré's agent in Genoa, Chabrol: 'My daughter is greatly obliged to you, and will never forget how much the marriage is due to your efforts.' But a few days later all was unsettled again. 'It is yes and then no, following each other so fast that there's nothing to be said,' the Marquise wrote to tell Honoré, and added, 'You can't see the way clear at all.'

However, by the 21st all was arranged. The Marquis and his daughter had a talk together, just the two of them, that lasted for a couple of hours. He was worried over the difference in age—Honoré was nineteen years older than Marie-Catherine— and he feared the Prince had a difficult character. But he appealed to his daughter to confide in him, to tell him her 'intimate thoughts'; if she sincerely wished to marry the Prince, he would overcome his dislike. Marie-Catherine could only talk in one way, of her love, and the Marquis gave his consent. A week later Marie-Catherine wrote to her future husband: 'I deserve no praise for obeying papa, for the consent he has just given you in no way preceded mine.'

There were still a few difficulties, on Honoré's part this time, to the despair of the Marquise; but at last, by June, they were all smoothed over, the contract signed, and the jewels sent to the fiancée and acknowledged to be 'most admirable and of perfect splendour.'

Seventeen-year-old Marie-Catherine again wrote to her fiancé: 'It is as flattering to me as it is pleasant, monsieur, that you should feel as I do about this conclusion on which my whole happiness depends; it will be perfect if I can indeed hope that yours does too. Please believe that I will always do all I can to contribute to that. Although mama must have sent you my thanks for your beautiful presents, I cannot allow myself not to repeat them. . . .'

The wedding took place by proxy in Genoa, on June 15th, 1757. The young bride 'went aboard a splendidly decorated galley, accompanied by her mother and relatives and a large retinue. Ships of the Republic escorted it ceremoniously as far as the territorial waters of Monaco. . . .' Then the whole arrangements practically broke down. The Marquise de Brignole-Sale, highly conscious of her birth and rank, maintained that the Prince should come out and greet his wife on the galley. But Honoré, a sovereign prince, refused to 'go any farther than the landing-stage.' The Marquise was indignant, negotiations were begun, and continued for days.

A delightful account of this episode is contained in a letter written by one of Honoré III's household to a friend, several days later:

'You'll remember that when you left Monaco, the Genoese boat had dropped back to outside our waters, taking the precious charge, the object of our regrets, with it. These proud republicans still persisted in wanting the Prince to go and collect his Princess from their boat; and the Prince remained unshakeable in his determination to do nothing of the kind. After six days of useless negotiations, of letters and messengers being sent back and forth, the famous Colonel Millo was deputized to come to an arrangement over the final expedient proposed by the Genoese. This was to make a bridge out from the Condamine landing-stage to join one let down from their boat. The next day, Colonel Millo's embassy having settled the matter, a general post was sounded, we all took up our positions for the great event, the fleet arrived in the harbour, the palace guns fired a salute, the Prince and his Court came down to the shore, the galley drew near our bridge and started to lower another, as had been agreed, when the Prince grew tired of waiting for the end of what seemed a long job, and became impatient to embrace his darling bride. He jumped into a boat, followed by his most intrepid courtiers, and in spite of the fuss reached the galley's ladder; he had scarcely put foot on it when the Princess came down followed by her mother, three uncles and a cousin. The flags and banners were hoisted, the galley-slaves saluted, the guns thundered, and the people shouted with joy.

'They're now at the Prince's summer-house at Carnolès, where we find the peace of the countryside a relief after the tumult of the capital. There are six or seven officers, Monsieur le Chevalier de Grimaldi, a lady-in-waiting, some gentlemen, and myself, among the elect. The bride's family has gone back to Genoa, except for the Marquise de Brignole, who is a woman of much spirit and merit. The bride is charming, kind and lovely, and she is making her husband happy. . . .'

She continued to make him happy for several years; and could have gone on doing so, if the effects of old family quarrels, and the clash of character, had not caused these two people to drift apart.

For three years Honoré III wisely stayed by the Mediterranean, sharing the time between Genoa and his Principality. They were tranquil years, as happy as could be, for him and his wife. On May 17th, 1758, Marie-Catherine gave birth to a son, who was named Honoré-Anne-Charles-Maurice.

But once again the effects of the departure of the fourth Duke of Valentinois with his family in 1734 began to be felt. Honoré III took an interest in his Principality, and kept aware of its needs; in 1760, for instance, he founded the printing-works of Monaco. His generosity towards his subjects did not lessen. Yet the administration remained essentially in the hands of the Chevalier de Grimaldi, as it had of yore in those of the Gubernant. Honoré I, 'married to a beautiful young wife, kind and intelligent,' had felt no urge to seek pleasures outside his territory. Honoré III, though, had spent neither his childhood nor his adolescence at Monaco, and he had tasted a different sort of life. In middle age, could he have settled down in his Principality? It would seem that he did make an effort, hopefully, but the call of habits long-formed and of old friends was too strong for him.

In the summer of 1760 he journeyed north to Paris and the Matignon town mansion, then to Normandy and the Thorigny estate, finally attending Court—looking forward to the proud moment of presenting the new Princess of Monaco, who was to join him later.

The letters written by Marie-Catherine to her husband during this first period apart leave no doubt as to the harmony existing between them, nor the young wife's sure and tender love for him.

'My dear love, I swear I feel as deeply as you how cruel it is to be separated from the one you love most in the whole world, and although I am very happy to be with my parents, who are most kind to me, my sorrow at your absence is ever with me. I'm only truly happy when dreaming, for then I've always the feeling of being with you . . . and I'm always happy to see that you respond affectionately to the signs I give of my tenderness for you; but waking up is cruel, for however much I look, I don't find you. . . .'

It was in December that Marie-Catherine reached Paris, having left her son with her parents. She was soon presented at Court and had a great success. But, happy to be again with a husband she loved, she accepted with indifference the gallant attentions paid to her; even those by the young Prince of Condé, the owner of Chantilly, who had recently lost his wife after three years of a love-marriage.

The months passed. . . . Marie-Catherine, who had had hopes of another child during 1760, was again expectant in the summer of 1762. She and the Prince were overjoyed. It was then two years since she had seen her son or her parents, and she left for the Mediterranean; while Honoré attended Court and visited 'the farm' (the vast Thorigny estate) and the stud there, in which he —who enjoyed the open air and had independent tastes—was taking an increasing interest.

'I arrived here at three o'clock, my dear love,' the Princess wrote from Savona, on August 4th, 1762. 'Monsieur Sigaldi will give you the news of our son, who did not know me. He's got amazing strength and vigour, he's big and a lovely child, with the eyes, forehead, and nose of his papa, and the mouth and chin of his mama. I found my mama has got fat, but papa is still as thin as ever. Goodbye, dear love, with my fondest kisses. . . .'

Some days later, Marie-Catherine heard that her husband was slightly ill, and expressed her concern: 'Look after yourself, I beseech you. It worries me to be so far from you, for I know you don't take care of yourself. Do not eat any fruit, or at least very little, there's nothing so bad for the health. . . . Our little boy sends kisses to his dear papa of Monaco, which is what he calls you. You'd love him dearly if you knew him.'

Honoré III was strong and healthy, his wife was delicate. She had a miscarriage, and he hurried down to Monaco. In October he brought her back to Paris in a doleful state. It was perhaps a mistake on his part to leave her and go off to Fontainebleau and Thorigny, just when his young wife had been through a sad time. But men often forget women's need to feel protected and looked after. Husbands may be quite sure of their own feelings, but neglect to show them. 'You are fogetting about me, dear love, the pleasures of Fontainebleau take up all your time, this is the third letter I've written to you and I've only had one from you. That's not very nice, make up for your mistake promptly by sending me your news. . . .' After Fontainebleau, it was Thorigny that kept the Prince from his wife. He spent his days with his horses, carelessly dressed, 'without stockings or breeches, wearing a light dressing-gown,' exercising his yearlings in the grounds of the château. Did he not think of 'a wife who loves him and would be happy to see him again?'

On September 10th, 1763, Marie-Catherine gave birth in Paris to another son, who was baptized Joseph-Marie-Jérôme-Honoré at St Sulpice a few days later. Then the first differences began to appear between husband and wife, mainly due to their separate tastes. She had always been used to life in cities, and was not happy in the Normandy countryside; and she refused to return to Monaco, where she had been ill. There was still nothing serious between them, and though her letters reflected a certain sadness they remained affectionate in tone, expressing the hope that her husband would soon return from Thorigny. On April 30th, 1765, she wrote: 'Fortunately, I can still give you nothing but very good news of our child; he comes and has dinner with his mama every day. . . . Everyone is busy preparing for the Court going to Marly, the day after tomorrow; Paris will be rather deserted. I don't regret at all not going, and am quite content to stay with my son. I hope you are coming to keep company with him too, your absence is a long one, how does your brother manage about it, I was hoping he would have decided you to return earlier.'

Lady Sarah Lennox was in Paris in June, 1765, and met the Princess of Monaco, whom she described as having 'a round face, with a sweet and charming expression. Her complexion is lovely, and she's got the best figure of any woman I know. She is the only one here not to paint her face, all the others dab rouge on in a horrible manner.'

At a Court where everyone was dependent on the King and sought his favours with servility, a wealthy and independent person like Honoré III brought disparity and aroused jealousy. As a husband with a loving and beautiful wife, he had seemed invulnerable and the envious had fretted impatiently; the men were vexed that their attentions to the Princess should make no impression on her, and the women were irritated by a rival who seemed uninterested in conquests and even ignored the faithful love of a prince of the blood royal. . . .

Moreover, the Countess of Valentinois had not looked upon

the coming of a sister-in-law who was wealthier, better-looking, and younger than herself, without some feelings of spite; and the brotherly affection that the Count of Valentinois showed towards Marie-Catherine completed her discomfiture. Was it she who urged on the malicious-minded? So Marie-Catherine believed, and complained about it. Be that as it may, the basest means were employed—Honoré III was showered with anonymous letters that were coarse in expression and insulting in matter.

He ought to have ignored them, being sure of his wife; but that would be overlooking his suspicious nature and uneasy mind. Moreover, he was beginning to show himself something of a misanthrope, a trait probably inherited from his grandfather, Antoine I. The consequence was that the innocent wife was treated as though guilty.

She submitted meekly; and stayed in Paris, at the Matignon mansion, throughout a long visit that the Prince paid to Monaco during the summer of 1767. She patiently accepted this retirement demanded of her by a jealous husband, occupying herself with her children and writing regularly to Honoré. 'I've no complaint to make of your letter of the 30th,' she wrote on July 10th, 'as I could have done of others that were decidedly short and sharp. I thank you for this one, which is more fitting, and for the permission you kindly give me. . . . I'm bored, and I'll be bored, but it's a misfortune that occurs in life sometimes . . . I'll have the consolation of being with my children, they are both very well, the elder has not been so unreasonable this week . . . I kissed them for you with much pleasure, they are really delightful children and they and their mother send you kisses too.' Two days later she was writing: 'It's with pleasure that I'm punctual with my letters, for I hope this will make you be. . . .'

Soon afterwards, on August 24th, she was mentioning an important decision to her husband—to have the four-year-old Joseph vaccinated. In this matter, too, she showed complete confidence. 'Doctor Tronchin came yesterday and examined our little boy, and found he is in the best possible condition for being inoculated.' Three days later she wrote to the Prince: 'As you say nothing about your return, I don't know when you will be back here, but I hope that when you do come you will find the little boy very well and completely recovered from his slight sickness. I myself am fairly well, and am most grateful for the kindness you show in enquiring after my health.'

The Prince was preparing to return to Paris when he received news that George III's brother, the Duke of York, intended to visit Monaco. He was an affable man, but not over-bright nor very strong; but he had an eye for a pretty woman. He was in Paris, and about to go to Compiègne, when he heard that a lady he was in love with was staying in Genoa. Without losing a minute, he set off for Italy.

At the end of August, 1767, the Duke reached Toulon. The governor of Provence, the Duke de Villars, gave a splendid ball in his honour. The royal Duke danced a great deal, and caught a chill. When he arrived at Monaco on August 31st he already had a temperature and was obliged to keep to his bed. The room he had at the palace was one with a gilt alcove that Antoine I had had decorated; it has since been known as the 'York bedroom.'

The Duke was ill for a fortnight, and died on September 17th in spite of the efforts of doctors called from Nice. According to a popular legend, the ship that had brought him to Monaco was followed by a yacht that dropped anchor off the headland on the other side of the bay, the Pointe de la Veille. A beautiful young woman left the yacht and went and hid in one of the grottoes on the headland, while the yacht sailed away. Each day throughout the Duke's illness, the graceful figure of a woman in white sat on the headland and looked across at the palace.

The body of the Duke was taken aboard the *Montreal*, while the palace guns fired a last salute; and when the ship with its flag at half-mast disappeared into the sunset, the ghostly lady in white gave a great cry and cast herself into the sea. For many years after that, the Pointe de la Veille was said to be haunted, and peasants crossed themselves whenever they went near it.

George III wrote to thank the Prince of Monaco for his kindness; and, on being informed by the British ambassador in Paris of the Prince's great interest in horse-breeding, sent him two of the Duke of York's racehorses and some hunters. The King also invited him to London.

On March 26th, 1768, Honoré III left Paris for London, accompanied by Colonel de Millo. He was received with the ceremonial given to a Head of State, had an audience of the King, and met the royal family. The Prince of Monaco stayed in England for two months, being made welcome in London society and journeying into the country. He attended the races at New-market, visited various studs, and was shown over the arsenals at Portsmouth and Woolwich. He also happened to be present at the riots over John Wilkes, the reformer and pamphleteer, which could not have failed to arouse the interest and curiosity of the sovereign prince.

On his return to France, Honoré found that the slander campaign against his wife was still in force. Friends, or relatives, tried to intervene but made matters worse. The Prince became exasper-ated, and had one or two affairs, perhaps with the intention of arousing his wife's jealousy. Marie-Catherine, on her part, having been patient and long-suffering, sought elsewhere the support lacking in her husband. The two gradually drifted farther apart, though without any incident occurring between them. In July, 1769, the Princess left the Matignon mansion for a retreat in a Paris convent. Once there, she requested permission of the Archbishop of Paris to retire to the Convent of the Visitation at Le Mans, where the Bishop was a Grimaldi of Antibes and a childhood friend of Honoré. This prudent retreat made nothing irreparable, and gave both husband and wife the time and opportunity to reflect.

In the autumn, Marie-Catherine had to go to Genoa, to attend to legal matters connected with her inheritance, the Marquis having died earlier in the year. The Marquise did her best to make the peace between the couple. 'My daughter is by no means fickle, and she loves you steadfastly,' she wrote to Honoré. 'Open your heart to me; if you think there is something about her conduct that can be improved, let me know. But have you nothing to reproach yourself for? What you write to tell me pierces me to the heart. . . . Will you have the courage to add to the horror that's upon me, you, my kind son? Don't embitter the little time I still have to live!'

For a while, she seemed to have succeeded. In January, 1770, Honoré having enquired affectionately about his wife's health, the Marquise replied to him: 'I congratulate you on the ending of this matter. The eagerness of your wife to rejoin you has, I think, largely caused the sacrifice she has made in her interests here. If you are satisfied, I shall be too. . . .'

There was in Honoré III's character, as there had been in his grandfather's, a suspicious bluntness that combined with a hastiness of temper to serve both these men badly on occasion, in spite of their intelligent and generous mind. In 1757, Honoré had been punctilious over the clauses of his marriage contract; some years later, his intervention in the tracing of the frontier between Monaco and La Turbie had not been fortunate. And now, when his wife rejoined him, he took offence because he had been given no say in the power of attorney she had signed for the administration of her inheritance. The Senate of Genoa rejected his claim—the laws of the Republic gave Marie-Catherine sole control over her fortune, except for the dowry—and this annoyed him more. He lost all sense of proportion, and instead of making the most of Marie-Catherine's return, which should have been considered the important matter in his life just then, he concentrated on minor details and blamed her for certain financial dispositions in the settling of her father's affairs—which were perfectly legal and had perhaps been deliberately inserted by the Marquis, who had never got over his dislike of Honoré. Finally, he spoke of taking his young wife to Monaco.

Marie-Catherine became completely dismayed. Sure of the Prince of Condé's feelings towards her, she decided to break with Honoré.

On July 19th, 1770, she made legal application in Paris for a separation, on the grounds of 'the cruel conduct' of her husband. Official notification reached the Prince on July 26th, towards the end of the afternoon. At eleven that morning Marie-Catherine had left the Matignon town house for good, and moved into a convent close at hand, in the rue de Bellechasse. She moved to another the following day, and remained in that convent until January 16th, until after a judgment had been given in her favour.

Honoré III took a lofty view of the matter and alleged that the French legal authorities had no jurisdiction over him; his quality of sovereign prince, recognized in every treaty, did not allow him to submit to their judgment; and so he was obliged to protest that any order made against him was null and void.

He presented a memorandum to this effect to Louis XV, who returned it to Choiseul, the Minister for Foreign Affairs, with instructions to give no reply and to classify it as secret.[1]

The proceedings followed their painful course. The Prince was not represented, maintaining his logical attitude, but evidence was given on his wife's behalf.

Judgment was due to be pronounced by the Parlement on December 10th. But three days beforehand the King suppressed the Parlements, on the instigation of his new Minister, Chancellor Maupeou.

The Prince of Condé intervened and used his influence to get the authorities to meet just to pronounce the legal separation of the Prince and Princess of Monaco. This took place on January 9th, 1771, and on the 14th the Prince wrote to inform his mother-in-law: 'Your daughter will no doubt be telling you, my kind mama, that her wishes have been granted. This event affects her reputation too greatly for me to be indifferent to it; but it makes no change in the state of things, for she abandoned her house and her children six months ago. Nevertheless, my legal advisers wanted me to pass an act at Monaco recalling her to her duties. I do not flatter myself that would turn her from the bad path she has taken, and I think the only thing left for me to do is to cry over her.'[2]

The next twenty years of Honoré III's life were as peaceful and serene as the previous thirty, from 1740 to 1770, had been restless and agitated. By a kind of paradox, the failure of his marriage seemed to calm him down, to make his harsh but honourable nature more amenable. For a few years he bore an

[1] 'I am returning the memorandum of Monsieur de Monaco to you,' the King wrote to his Minister on August 13th. 'If it were shown to the Procurator-General I think he would be able to contradict several of the points in it. But secrecy is the essential thing, which it would be best to keep. Send the memorandum to the secret archives of the Foreign Office.'

[2] Henceforth the Princess of Monaco divided her time between Paris and Chantilly, the Condé property. She bought the château de Betz, in the region south of Compiègne, not far from Chantilly; it had magnificent gardens arranged in the classical manner by Hubert Robert. Her sons often went to visit her there. At the Revolution, this still beautiful woman went into exile with the Prince of Condé, and poured the whole of her great fortune into helping the royalist forces. Some years after the death of Honoré III she married the Prince of Condé, in 1808. She died on March 28th, 1813, near London. This once wealthy woman was then so poor that the Prince Regent paid for her funeral.

excusable grudge against Marie-Catherine, but it gradually disappeared. He had less and less to do with Court circles, and lived the life of a just and liberal-minded sovereign prince at Monaco, of a great lord in Paris, and of an understanding, charitable landowner at Thorigny. After the turbulence of his youth and middleage, his later years flowed like a broad, smooth stream.

Marie-Catherine had been a gentle and kind mother, and for a long time the sons appeared to prefer her to their more reserved father. Honoré III did not take offence, and gave much thought to their upbringing. To avoid similar consequences of the mistakes made in his own case when young, he took his two boys down to Monaco in 1773, for a long stay. The heir, Honoré, reached the age of sixteen the following year, and his father obtained a sub-lieutenancy for him in the Regiment of Carabiniers.[1] Three years later, Honoré III thought he had arranged a brilliant match for his heir by marrying him, at the age of nineteen, to Louise-Félicité-Victoire d'Aumont, who was eighteen months younger. She was the heiress, through her mother, to the titles and possessions of the Dukes of Mazarin; the considerable Mazarin possessions had been transferred by the Cardinal to his niece, Hortense Mancini, when she married the son of Marshal de La Meilleraye.

The Mazarin duchy and peerage had been invested in Hortense Mancini and her husband, together with the name, and could be handed down through the female line. Thus it had passed to the grand-daughter of the last Duke of Mazarin, who had married the Duke d'Aumont. It was their daughter that young Honoré married, and who brought into the House of Monaco the possessions of both the Mazarin and d'Aumont families. On the occasion of this marriage, Honoré III severed the last links he had with the French Court by transferring the dukedom and peerage of Valentinois to his heir, who then became the sixth Duke.

By all appearances it was a splendid, rich marriage; but because of bad management in previous generations, the Mazarind'Aumont possessions were encumbered by mortgages and tied

---

[1] He was appointed captain in May, 1777, a few weeks before his wedding. In 1782 he was second-in-command of a regiment, rose to colonel in 1788, and when he left the army on grounds of ill-health in 1791 was given the rank of *maréchal de camp*, or brigadier-general.

up in a number of lawsuits, which the heiress succeeded in increasing after she came of age in 1781. The character of the new Duchess of Valentinois, moreover, was not compatible with that of her mild husband, who was beginning to suffer from ill-health.

In May, 1789, when the Duke was undergoing treatment at Lausanne, the Duchess announced to her father-in-law that she intended to apply for her own fortune and possessions to be legally separated from her husband's, because of the increasing disorder in her affairs. The letters that Honoré III wrote to his heir on this subject during the following twelve months, and which are in the palace archives at Monaco, have much psychological interest. They reveal how greatly the trials and troubles of life had changed Honoré III, and brought his good points to the surface. They are the letters of a just, fair-minded man, affectionate, and with an upright, balanced attitude. He was obviously very fond of this son whose state of health gave anxiety, but he did not shut his eyes to the facts—personal debts amounting to 1,390,000 *livres*, which 'at first glance do not indicate a wise or enlightened management.'

A 'fair and prudent' judgment was given by the courts on March 25th, 1790. The Prince, who had been at Monaco for the past six months, wrote to the young Duke on April 4th to say he was leaving for Paris 'the day after tomorrow at the latest, to come and congratulate you and to work out with you a better management of your affairs for the future. Goodbye now, son, I'm most impatient to see you again.'

The younger son, Joseph, gave every satisfaction to his father. He had risen from ensign in 1778, when he was fourteen, to be second-in-command of a Breton regiment ten years later. In April, 1782, he had married Françoise-Thérèse de Choiseul, a daughter of Marshal de Stainville. She was a pretty, sweet girl, and a virtuous wife, and the two were very happy together; the old Prince had a very tender spot for this daughter-in-law. In 1785, Joseph and his wife had spent several months at Monaco, staying in the summer-house at Carnolès; and the local people, too, had taken to the young, blonde Françoise-Thérèse, who seemed to spread happiness around her.

The Principality of Monaco soon felt the effects of the French

Revolution. The population of the three towns demanded reforms, and in February and March, 1790, the Prince agreed to councils being formed at Monaco, Menton, and Roquebrune. But they gave little satisfaction, and petitions for changes in them were sent to Honoré III, who had left for Paris—destined never to see his Rock again. His edicts granting the fresh, limited reforms were published in the Principality on January 15th, 1792. They satisfied the traditionalists but not the progressive elements, and seeds of discord were sown that before long were to result in the Principality losing its autonomy for nearly twenty-two years.

Honoré III had gone to Paris in April, 1790, not only to congratulate and see his son, the Duke, but also to watch over his own threatened interests. On August 4th, 1789, the Constituent Assembly had abolished all feudal rights and taxes. But the Prince of Monaco protested that his revenues from the duchy of Valentinois were, in accordance with the terms of the Treaty of Péronne, compensation for the loss of the estates in the Kingdom of Naples.

In September, 1791, the Assembly recognized the Prince's claim and issued a decree allowing him an indemnity and charging the King's government to negotiate the amount. This was fixed at 273,786 francs, and was about to be sanctioned when the King was arrested and the fall of the monarchy followed.

The Prince's administration was still in control at Monaco, but unrest was growing. When French troops entered Nice in the autumn of 1792, following the outbreak of hostilities against the Sardinian Kingdom, the unrest seethed dangerously; but it was the Convention's decree ordering its generals to establish a republican régime in all territories they entered with their armies that caused the storm to break. General Brunet, the commander of the French troops advancing against the Sardinian government, applied the decree in the Principality of Monaco— which was friendly territory, whereas the decree was intended to apply to enemy countries.

In any case, on January 13th, 1793, the people's councils of Monaco, Menton, and Roquebrune, formed a Conventional Assembly that declared the Prince's reign at an end, and asked for union with France. General Brunet had this request conveyed to Paris, and on February 14th Carnot presented a report to the

French Convention recommending the union, but he ended with a somewhat unexpected compliment to the Prince of Monaco. . . . 'However, since it appears that the ex-Prince did not declare himself an enemy of France during the Revolution, and since he has always claimed her protection as a friend and ally, your committee is of the opinion that in abolishing his honorific and feudal revenues you ought to accord him protection and safeguard for what he may possess as an ordinary citizen.'

By a decree issued the following day, the Principality of Monaco was annexed to the newly formed *département* of Alpes-Maritimes; and on March 4th, 1793, two Commissars of the French Republic arrived in Monaco to make the decree public. The lozengy standard of the Grimaldis was not to fly from the palace again until June, 1814.

If Honoré III had been less courageous, and his son Joseph more prudent, perhaps their futures would have been different. But, sure of his rights and having been publicly certified a good citizen by Carnot, he remained at the Matignon town mansion and busied himself with his various claims. At Thorigny he would certainly have been safe, for the local people were prepared to welcome him.[1] After all, another fair-minded and charitable land-owner, the Duke of Penthièvre, a grandson of Louis XV, went on living peacefully and unmolested in Normandy, at Vernon, until his death in 1793.

However, having given his horses and carriages to the military and donated to patriotic funds, Honoré III had stayed unmolested for much of the Terror, in spite of denunciations by the local Committee of Public Safety. Then the 'Law of Suspects' was

[1] The following report was made by the people's union of Thorigny, on the 10th and 11th Frimaire of Year II (November 30th and December 1st, 1793), to a delegate of the Committee of Public Safety for the sector in which the Matignon Paris mansion stood: 'The citizen Grimaldy . . . very different from other seigneurs of the old order . . . has always shown himself kind, just, and understanding . . . always affable, sympathetic, and generous; mindful of the farms, he never went hunting and shooting over them except when no harm could be caused.' He had fines imposed under the game laws refunded, he allowed poor people to gather wood from his park, had 900 loaves sent every week to families in want, and gave a number of other doles, pensions, and help in kind. . . . The local council and the people's union concluded the report by asking for his release (the Prince of Monaco was arrested in September, 1793) and that he should come and live at Thorigny, when they would be responsible for him.

voted, and relatives of those who had emigrated became liable to arrest.

Now Honoré's younger son, Joseph, who was greatly influenced by his mother and sympathetic to the emigrants, had made several journeys outside France since 1790, trusting that his family's rank of foreign prince would save him from interference. These comings and goings had not failed to draw attention upon him, and upon his family too. After the arrest of Louis XVI he again left the country, this time taking his wife, Françoise-Thérèse, with him and leaving their two young daughters in the care of a devoted governess, Madame Chenevoy. His wife returned to Paris in November, 1792, worried about her children and unable to bear a longer separation from them, and took up residence again in her house in the rue Monsieur. Her husband continued to stay out of France, and his name was added to the list of royalist émigrés. This was hardly surprising, for his activities with the royalists were no doubt known about in Paris. Had he not been to Condé's headquarters in the Rhineland and handed over 300,000 francs for the royalist forces that his father had given to him? And then allowed himself to be named an aide-de-camp to the Count of Artois? These imprudences exposed members of his family to reprisals. The 'Law of Suspects' was passed on September 17th, 1793, and on the night of the 19th the Prince of Monaco was arrested and imprisoned in the barracks in the rue de Sèvres. He was to be detained there for over a year.[1]

His son's actions cost the Prince this long and unpleasant loss of liberty; but they cost charming Françoise-Thérèse her life. For a few months she had no reason to regret returning to France. But then, as the wife of an émigré and having herself been out of the country, she was arrested in the spring of 1793. Honoré III intervened on her behalf then, and no doubt paid over some money; she was released against surety, her claim of belonging to the family of a foreign prince having been admitted.

When she was arrested at her house for the second time, in

[1] The inoffensive Duke of Valentinois, who had never left France after his return from Lausanne in March, 1790, was arrested and kept in prison for fifteen months; while his wife, although she had obtained a divorce in June, 1793, was put in prison with her younger son, eight-year-old Florestan. She was saved by the Grimaldi family doctor, Désormeaux, who contrived a release order and then hid her and Florestan at his house until the end of the Terror.

September, 1793, she had no illusions. On some pretext or other she was allowed to go into an adjoining room, and from there managed to flee. She hid at first in the home of a Madame Davaux, and then succeeded in reaching the convent in the rue de Belle-chasse. The congregation had been dissolved, but a few nuns were still living there, and Françoise-Thérèse stayed with them for several months. Someone must have denounced her, for she was arrested a third time early in 1794 and taken to the Plessis prison, which served as waiting-room for the Conciergerie, and so for the guillotine.

But the months went by, and there was hope—the only hope possible—that Françoise-Thérèse had been forgotten in the swarming prison. It was not to be, however, for her husband's imprudent actions again drew attention to her. On the seventh of Thermidor (July 25th, 1794) she received an order to appear before the Revolutionary Tribunal at ten o'clock the following morning. 'She showed not the slightest sign of emotion,' recounted a prisoner who was fortunate enough to escape execution. 'She shared out her money among those without any, whom she usually helped, kissed her maid, and took leave of us just as though parting from fellow travellers whose company has been pleasant and agreeable during a long journey.'

It was the period when large batches of prisoners were being sent daily to the guillotine; they were composed of a strange variety of people, representing all the elements of a France being torn bloodily apart. There were thirty names on the list in which Françoise-Thérèse's appeared: some priests and a bishop, a State counsellor, a restaurant-keeper, a grocer, an ex-noble without occupation, the Duke of Clermont-Tonnerre, and the Marquis de Crussol; and women such as Marie-Anne Leroy, aged twenty-one, of the Feydeau Theatre, the Princess of Chimay, Madame de Narbonne-Pellet and her maid. Numbers 28 and 29 were Françoise-Thérèse Stainville, wife of Grimaldi-Monaco, aged twenty-six, and Adrien-Denis-Benoit Viotte, agent of the ex-Prince of Monaco.

All were declared to be enemies of the people, and condemned to death. Françoise-Thérèse did not falter on hearing the verdict. But when they were led into the records office—only a few steps from where the dreadful tumbrils were waiting—her courage failed her for a moment as she thought of her young daughters. It was then that someone—perhaps the faithful Viotte—suggested she could put off the fatal hour by declaring herself to be pregnant. Her husband had been away for nearly two years, that was well known, and she was proclaiming her unfaithfulness. But she accepted that, and was taken back to the Conciergerie.

There, she hastened to do what she wanted. She had allowed herself to steal one day's respite, but no more; the lie would be unbearable if it lasted longer. She broke a pane of glass and cut her fair hair herself, then wrapped the locks in two letters, one addressed to her daughters and the other to their governess, Madame Chenevoy. Afterwards, she wrote a note in a firm hand to the Public Prosecutor, Fouquier-Tinville: 'I should be obliged if citizen Fouquier de Tinville would come and see me here for a moment. I earnestly ask him not to refuse this request.'

But the Public Prosecutor was busy with the next day's list of victims, and did not go. The night passed quickly, and dawn appeared. Françoise-Thérèse hastily wrote another note: 'I give you notice, citizen, that I am not with child. I wanted to tell you, and now, having no hope of you coming, I inform you in writing. I did not soil my lips with this lie for fear of death nor to avoid it, but to give myself one more day so that I could cut my hair myself instead of having it cut by the executioner. This is all I could leave to my children; it had at least to be clean.'

On the outside of the note she put, 'Very urgent.'

Then she waited, dressed and ready, her cheeks rouged—she hardly ever put any on—for fear of appearing pale as she mounted the steps of the guillotine.

She did not have to wait long. When Fouquier de Tinville received her note, the batch of victims for the day—the ninth of Thermidor—was already prepared; forty-one was the total. But another would make little difference, they would just have to squeeze together more in the tumbrils; and the smooth, cold-blooded man—who had little time left to live himself—added Françoise-Thérèse's name to the list, the last one on it.

By five that evening, the forty-two heads had fallen. At the same hour, the Convention overthrew Robespierre, and the Reign of Terror came to an end.

Two months later, Honoré III was freed from prison and returned to the Matignon town house. But he had lost all hope and desire to struggle; with the death of Françoise-Thérèse had disappeared his joy in living. He died on May 12th, 1795, less than ten months after her.

The long reign of Honoré II—nearly sixty years—had fore-shadowed and then prepared the way for the period of close relationship between the Princes of Monaco and the French monarchy. Honoré III's even longer reign of over sixty years saw the end of that period. The Principality had known a happy and peaceful time, thanks to its wealthy, generous, and liberal-minded Princes. They themselves had suffered from marital troubles, but had made brilliant alliances and gained honours at the French Court.

The male line of the Grimaldis had ended with Antoine I, but the family had drawn renewed vigour from its grafting on to robust Norman stock. The Grimaldi-Matignons survived the storms of the Revolution, and were to find a new use for their reduced Principality, bringing happiness and prosperity to the Rock of Monaco; and, moreover, its Princes were to acquire international renown in the realms of science and the arts.

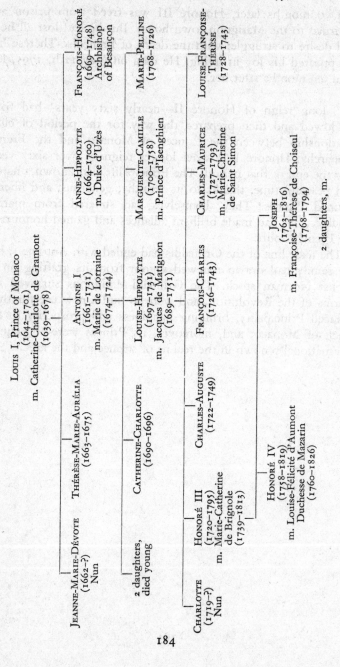

PART THREE

THE PRINCES OF MONACO
(1795-1961)

CHAPTER VII

FROM ONE FRENCH REVOLUTION TO THE NEXT (1795–1848)

THE END OF AN ERA in the history of a country, a race, or a family, is sometimes marked by an obscure period, while deeply rooted strengths are being husbanded for a fresh drive forward. The seigneurs of Monaco had experienced such a period when, after the death of Charles I in 1357, Rainier II had abandoned their Rock. For more than half a century afterwards, the Grimaldis had struggled to survive and then to take over Monaco again; and their fruitful marriages during the fifteenth century, admitting strong-minded Pomelline and then wise Lambert, had enabled the family to flourish afresh.

They experienced another such period of half a century, from the death of Honoré III in 1795 to the assumption of power by Charles III in 1848. Again the Grimaldis struggled to survive, and then to take over Monaco. In a world shaken by the French Revolution and being changed by the Industrial Revolution, and with the day of large organizations looming ahead, the Grimaldis would very likely have met with failure—if a fortunate and happy marriage, to an intelligent and energetic woman, had not eventually provided the clever and enterprising man of which the ancient family stood in need.

In December, 1794, two months after his release, Honoré III had applied for the sequestration on the Thorigny estate to be lifted. The application had been refused, pending proof that his son Joseph had returned to France; but Joseph had remained absent. A month after Honoré's death, however, his heir, the sixth Duke of Valentinois—the title he continued to be known by—succeeded in obtaining temporary control of his father's property, on condition that his two nieces were given shares in the inheritance.

The invalid Duke led a quiet, retired life, dividing his time between the Matignon town house and the country estates of Thorigny and Valmont, near Fécamp. He left all his business affairs in the hands of his brother Joseph, who returned to France at the end of 1795, and of his elder son, Honoré-Gabriel.

Honoré III had ensured that this grandson, born in 1778, should have a peaceful childhood and adolescence, in spite of his parents being separated, by putting him in the care of a country priest and teacher in Normandy, where the troubles of the Revolution had scarcely penetrated. The letters Honoré-Gabriel wrote to his father in 1795–6 show him as an affectionate, trusting son, treating his invalid father as a comrade, and as a youngster satisfied with his country existence.

But his uncle was soon obliged to leave France again,[1] when laws against returned émigrés were brought back into force in September, 1797, and Honoré-Gabriel had to take over all the affairs of the family, and make the many applications and claims that the troubled times necessitated. He was helped in this by his mother, who since her divorce was known as the Duchess de Mazarin; a help that was often odd and fanciful, but always backed by intelligence.

The Duchesse de Mazarin had recovered most of her possessions, and although badly managed and encumbered with law-suits—which ended by ruining her—she could have aided her two boys; but she was a difficult woman to please. Florestan was alternately spoilt and treated severely; and Honoré-Gabriel had to use subtle methods with her. In December, 1797, he was going to rejoin his father in Normandy when his mother, who had a bad cold, asked him to remain with her. 'If I refuse,' he wrote to the Duke, 'I fear it will be difficult to get on good terms with her

---

[1] Joseph Grimaldi tried to get Talleyrand to intervene on his behalf, but that unscrupulous Minister had not been very energetic about it. 'Joseph Grimaldi, son of the ex-Prince of Monaco, submits to the Citizen Minister for External Relations that . . . his position as a foreigner having been recognized by the Constituent Assembly . . . his name should not be included in the list of the 19th of Fructidor, Year V. However, as he has always wished to obey the laws of this country, he hopes the Citizen Minister will kindly send his just claim forward and inform him what action he should take. . . .' Talleyrand confined himself to asking Fouché, his 'dear colleague' at the Ministry of the Interior, to give his opinion as quickly as possible. Fouché was explicit—'Everyone on the list must leave France by the date given.'

again afterwards.' A few days later he was able to announce the success of his diplomacy. 'I eat at her house every day and stay with her for a time, and she doesn't now seem to want another quarrel. Florestan is always talking to me about you, and asks me to send you his regards.'

Mother and son were still on good terms in May, 1798, when he came to Paris on business—more overtures to make—and then went to see her at Chilly, the Effiat château she had inherited which Honoré II had visited in the course of his journey up from Monaco in 1643. 'Mama welcomed me with open arms and was delighted to see me again. She could not be more friendly towards me, she had been making many applications for your name to be struck off the list (of proscribed persons) and the matter is well forward now. . . .' A fortnight later, the young man proudly announced that his father's situation had been satisfactorily cleared up, and that his residential permit had been sent 'all in order with the last decade.'

Honoré-Gabriel could therefore believe that his father would be able to live peacefully, with what remained of the enormous Matignon fortune, while he himself, heir to a Prince without a Principality, chose a career. He chose to serve France in her army as so many of his forbears had done.

He joined the 23rd Light Cavalry on December 21st, 1798, and entered upon this new life with courage and good humour. But he found it tough, and soon fell ill. At one moment, his family thought he was dead; he heard of this, and was amused by it: 'I'm disgracefully hungry now, and eat all day long.'

A few months later he was a sergeant, and then was promoted to second-lieutenant the following year. After campaigning with his regiment in Flanders, he was sent to the Grisons region of Switzerland to fight against the Austrians. Taken on to Marshal Grouchy's staff, he went with him to the Army of the Rhine and was badly wounded in the right arm at the battle of Hohenlinden in December, 1800. Soon afterwards he dictated a letter, from his billet in Munich, to reassure his father. His wound, he said, would leave no after-effects, 'but just now I've so little control over my arm that I can only sign my name, and rather badly too.'

In fact, this wound and the military life for which he had been little prepared greatly changed the young man's character.

Previously he had been frank and affectionate, but the suffering and unexpected shocks he experienced—and perhaps even more so the poor health he subsequently had—turned him into a severe, distant man, who remained apart from his family and shut himself up in an ivory tower. Though he was always thoughtful for his fellow-men—as he showed at Thorigny and later at Monaco—he gradually discarded personal contacts for theory, and developed into a lucid, unhappy misanthrope.[1]

Joseph Grimaldi's name was taken off the list of émigrés in October, 1801. He returned to France, and became actively engaged in recovering legal possession of the family property that had not been sold, and in settling the family affairs in general. His meddling and his powerful influence over his weak brother appear to have been additional factors in separating Honoré-Gabriel from his father, whom he had always helped as much as possible.

The task Joseph Grimaldi had taken on was no easy one. On one hand, there were the outstanding debts incurred by the sixth Duke prior to the Revolution, and those contracted by Honoré III after it, during the six years until his death in 1795; and there were also borrowings at interest rates that had been made over the years to meet expenses. On the other hand, the family estates in Normandy had been badly managed while under sequestration, the Thorigny château and the Matignon town house had not been kept in good repair. Much money needed to be spent on them; and Joseph Grimaldi—with the blind agreement of his brother—decided to sell up.

The hôtel de Matignon was bought by an English speculator named Crawford for less than 200,000 francs gold, in 1804; the

[1] His military career extended over fifteen years. He was promoted lieutenant after the battle of Hohenlinden. His health kept him out of active service for a few years, then he joined the army in Prussia in 1806, and reached the rank of captain. Appointed aide-de-camp to Murat, he was wounded during the Friedland campaign, and awarded the Legion of Honour in July, 1807. He went with Murat to Spain in 1808, and on his return to Paris became an equerry to the Empress Josephine, and was made a Baron of the French Empire in August, 1810. He was recalled to active service in 1811, but his old arm-wound obliged him to be put on the retired list the following year. He then rejoined his post as equerry to the ex-Empress, and remained there until her death in May, 1814. At the Restoration, he was nominated battalion-commander but put on half-pay.

Valmont house and estate went for 1,300,000 francs in 1805, and Thorigny for a million a year later.[1] In 1807 the family recovered some five thousand acres of forest which had been part of their estates of Valmont and Thorigny, and these were put up for auction in 1810. The whole business was disastrous, and the fault was mainly Joseph Grimaldi's; it was badly managed, and placed in the hands of dishonest agents, and in the end did not even raise enough money to pay off all the debts.

Joseph did not come too badly out of this—he travelled about France after the death of his second wife in 1806, an English-woman he had married in London in 1798—and his daughters had made good marriages, as well as inheriting from their mother; but his brother was gravely affected by it. The Duke's health necessitated expensive treatment, but he was reduced to living on an allowance from his elder son and his brother, which the former apparently paid more regularly than the latter.[2] The Duke was then living in Paris, at a house in the rue d'Enfer, and probably spent the summers in Normandy, at a small place just outside Bayeux that belonged to Honoré-Gabriel. The two sons had been badly hit too, and Honoré-Gabriel bore his uncle an ill-will that later found expression when, in 1814, at the restoration of the Principality to the Grimaldi-Matignon family, Joseph Grimaldi again wanted to elbow aside the heir apparent.

During the twenty years the Principality had been blended into the Alpes-Maritimes *département*, life there had been peaceful but far from prosperous. As a French commissar remarked in his report, the people were not in great want, but the resources of the territory were poor and few were in comfortable circum-stances. In this blessed climate, suicide was practically unknown, and the priests were tolerant. The report concluded that public morale was fairly good and that when peace came it would be better.

[1] Talleyrand bought the Hôtel de Matignon later, and then sold it to Napoleon in 1812 for 1,280,000 francs. It is today the official residence of the Prime Minister.

Thorigny was again sold in 1815, to the local municipality. Until 1944 the magni-ficent château was a show-place, but was badly damaged during the battle of Normandy. It is now being gradually restored. (*Trans. note.*)

[2] Honoré-Gabriel wrote to his father in January, 1808: 'You say your brother is unable to help you, and I must admit that remark surprises me. You can't be unaware that the sums paid over to you come from my account and not from my uncle's. . . .'

But peace was a long time in coming, and the last years of the First Empire were hard for everyone; especially so in the Principality, whose exports were reduced by the Allied blockade. And then, in the exceptionally hard winter of 1813–14, the lemons and olives suffered badly from frost. When the news of Napoleon's abdication was received, great was the joy; and the Restoration of the Bourbons brought hopes of the return of the Grimaldis, who had always shown themselves to be generous.

The instincts of the people had not misled them. Joseph Grimaldi's activities in 1814 were, for once, of great advantage to his relatives. The Grimaldi family had at once petitioned Louis XVIII, in April, 1814, to 'allow them of his gracious kindness to enter into their rights and possessions again, and to deign to take the Principality of Monaco under his powerful protection.' It is unlikely that alone would have had effect, in view of the avid designs of the Sardinian government, which had recovered its territory of Nice and was about to absorb that of Genoa. But Joseph Grimaldi made energetic representations to Talleyrand, who by a stroke of his pen had just given up fifty-three occupied towns, from Danzig to Antwerp. With another stroke of his pen, and the same nonchalance, he resurrected the Principality of Monaco by an addition to paragraph eight, article one, of the Treaty of Paris—France renounced all sovereign rights over territories outside the frontiers fixed for her, the Principality of Monaco returning, however, to the status obtaining prior to January 1st, 1792. It was a return to the Treaty of Péronne.

The Duke of Valentinois, who then took the title of Prince of Monaco and the name of Honoré IV, was too much of an invalid to assume any of the responsibilities and burdens of his new State. He renounced the duchy of Valentinois and the peerage in favour of his son, Honoré-Gabriel, but delegated full powers in the Principality to his brother Joseph. His brother at once nominated a governor-general—Louis de Millo, son of the man who had served Honoré III so well—and ordered him to organize a provisional government until his own arrival, which he declared would be soon.

Joseph Grimaldi no doubt remembered with delight his stays at Monaco before the Revolution. Without realizing that customs and outlook had changed in the past twenty-odd years, and with-

15   View of Monaco—the rocky acropolis jutting into the Mediterranean carries all the main buildings of the Principality.

16   The Casino at Monte Carlo.

out thinking that the Grimaldis were no longer wealthy princes keeping their State alive but poor princes needing to be kept alive by their State, Joseph repealed the existing laws and re-established the edicts and ordinances prevailing up to January 1st, 1792. Was he hoping that he could thus wipe out twenty-two years of the Principality's history, which was the whole of the younger generation's? This upheaval in the life of the people was also ill-advised because the official language became Italian again; and the moment was not propitious for this additional reminder of affinity with neighbouring Piedmont.

The return to the past was one mistake, and Joseph Grimaldi made another and more serious one by not urging the sending of French troops to garrison Monaco, in accordance with the Treaty of Péronne. Those stationed there during the war had evacuated the territory on May 17th, 1814, and a small company of sixty Austrians had replaced them. The Austrians left early in July, after handing over to the local guards. Fearing a shortage of food, the governor-general, in full agreement with Joseph Grimaldi, adopted delaying tactics to hold up the arrival of the French military garrison; a few officers merely came to inspect the barracks and military stores. No blame could be attached to the Royalist government, which was quite prepared to fulfil its responsibilities, in the interests of its protégé, as France had always done in the past. On September 26th, the King appointed Joseph Grimaldi his military commander of the citadel of Monaco, which conformed with the Treaty of Péronne. But months went by and he was still in Paris, busy with his various personal affairs, while his presence in Monaco became increasingly necessary. The economic situation there had grown acute, due mainly to more frosts; and in January, 1815, people refused to pay their taxes.

It was then that the situation took a new turn. On February 23rd news reached Monaco that the heir apparent, Honoré-Gabriel, was on his way there, and that he would govern in future.

Honoré-Gabriel had been occupied with his appointment to the ex-Empress Josephine at Malmaison, and with personal matters;[1]

---

[1] A natural son had been born to him on June 8th, 1814. Oscar Grimaldi was legally recognized by his father, and was later given the title of Marquis des Baux by Charles III of Monaco. He died in 1894.

he was probably satisfied with his dukedom and peerage, and so had not protested against power being delegated to his uncle. But Joseph's reactionary policy, and the fact of his remaining in Paris, angered the heir and caused him to take steps to have matters in his own hands. Through the Duke d'Aumont, a cousin of his mother, he obtained the ear of Louis XVIII. The Duke d'Aumont, who had gone into exile with the royal princes, had recovered his functions at Court at the Restoration and had daily access to the King.

Joseph Grimaldi was obliged to give way. He wrote to say as much to his brother, to whom he had been a faithful and attentive friend, it must be admitted: 'Your son having again approached me through several people, and as I want to put an end to the discord in the family, I have consulted with your friends d'Aumont and d'Esclignac (a nephew of Talleyrand) and together we have drawn up the document I am submitting to you; by it, your son will be bound in such a way, and in accord with the family council, that I do not think he will be able to deviate from these agreements. By this means there will be peace in our family again, and you will have sufficient income to live comfortably. Say whether you're agreeable to it; I did nothing without d'Aumont's consent, and you know of his friendship for you.'

By a procuration signed at the d'Aumont town house on January 18th, 1815, Honoré IV passed the exercise of his sovereign rights to his son, not retaining any at all; he delegated to him full administrative, legislative, and financial powers.[1]

Honoré-Gabriel informed the French government of this, and requested his appointment as military commander of Monaco in place of his uncle. Then he promptly set off for the south.

By March 1st he was nearing Monaco, preceded by a messenger in red livery named Milowski, who had been with him at Malmaison. In the middle of the afternoon Honoré-Gabriel passed through Cannes, and his carriage was rolling towards Antibes when it was stopped by an advance-guard—of Napoleon, who had just escaped from Elba and landed at Gulf Juan. . . .

---

[1] The effective reign of Honoré V therefore began on that date, January 18th, 1815, although his father lived another four years, being accidentally drowned in the Seine, on February 16th, 1819. Joseph Grimaldi died previously, on June 28th, 1816.

'The guard had caught a messenger of the Prince of Monaco,' recounted Marchand, Napoleon's valet, 'and brought him to the Emperor, whom he assured that once through Provence he would find everyone ready to follow him. These words of a man of the people confirmed what the Emperor thought himself. Approaching Cannes, the Emperor met with the Prince of Monaco, who was embarrassed at first, but ceased to be when he found himself greeted like someone the Emperor knew. . . . A big fire was lit, and he and the Emperor went and stood near it. All the while they were speaking together, the Prince kept his hat in his hand. The Emperor wished him a happy journey as they parted. This Prince did not hide from the Emperor how risky such an expedition was. The fairly wide circle we had formed around the two prevented us from hearing what they said, yet the Emperor's good spirits gave cause for thinking he was satisfied with the details he got about Paris and the state of mind in France. The Prince had given him the opinions of the drawing-rooms; the messenger, the outlook of ordinary people, who would rise as one at the Emperor's approach.'

The next day, even before he reached Monaco, Honoré-Gabriel wrote a long report and sent it off to the Minister for War, Marshal Soult. The Prince emphasized, with his clear-sightedness and precise mind, that as Provence was for the monarchy a few troops at Cannes would have sufficed to prevent Napoleon landing. . . .

In spite of the wounds he had received fighting bravely with the armies, Honoré-Gabriel had not been treated by Napoleon with any particular favour during the Empire, and its fall does not appear to have affected him personally. Nevertheless, the glory surrounding the name of the prisoner on St Helena having grown with the years, when Alexandre Dumas published a fantastic account in June, 1841, of that meeting between Honoré-Gabriel and Napoleon, the old Prince of Monaco seized his pen and rectified the matter with a few biting phrases:

'Sir, I have a painful duty to perform . . . but the conversation you give as having taken place between the Emperor and myself is a travesty of the truth. . . . He did not keep saying to me "Good morning, Monaco," he never asked me to follow him, and I did not reply that I awaited his orders. . . . You must admit that your

imagination has been too fertile. I have certainly had nothing
to complain about when reading your novels, but history requires
the truth. . . .'

Before sending off his report to Soult, Honoré-Gabriel had
stopped in Antibes to make an official demand for French troops
to garrison Monaco without delay. The return of Napoleon was
obviously going to cause considerable upheaval. And, in fact,
ten days later, on March 13th, troops did arrive in the Principality
—but Allied troops, English and Piedmontese. This intrusion
presaged worse in the near future. The menace that the Grimaldis
had been holding off for centuries—the clutching hand of the
House of Savoy—now loomed nearer. Even the invalid Honoré
IV, so remote from the world, displayed anxiety. His brother
wrote to try and reassure him, on October 17th, 1815: 'It's only
too true, my dear brother, that Monaco will not have a French
garrison any more, but that doesn't affect your rights as sovereign
prince, only that you'll be under the protection of the Sardinian
government instead of the French.' Could Joseph Grimaldi
really have believed there was no more to it than that?

The second Treaty of Paris was signed on November 20th,
1815. By it, without the Prince of Monaco or his subjects having
been consulted, the existing, ancient relationships and agreements
that France had with the Principality of Monaco were transferred
to the Kingdom of Sardinia, to the monarch who ruled over Savoy
and Piedmont. This decision of European statesmen, benefiting
a large State at the expense of a small one, had painful consequences for the Grimaldi family.

To begin with, Honoré-Gabriel had to give up all hope of an
indemnity for the lost revenues of the duchy of Valentinois. A
sum of four and a half million francs had been agreed upon at
the Restoration, but now that the French rights and obligations
had been transferred to the Sardinian government, the French
reckoned that this consequence of its protectorate had been
transferred too. But the King of Sardinia, always ready to take
but not to give, did not subscribe to this point of view.

His Court at Turin revived the formality of homage being
made for Menton and Roquebrune; and on November 30th, 1816,
Louis de Millo gave the oath of loyalty in the name of his Prince

and received the investiture of the two fiefs. This was a first step towards the subordination of the Principality of Monaco, so long aimed at by the House of Savoy.

Then in the autumn of 1817, after months of discussions, the heir to the Principality decided to conclude the negotiations with the Turin Court. He went to see Victor Emmanuel I and agreed to ratify the treaty which the King had signed at Stupinigi on November 8th. This treaty took the place of the Treaty of Péronne, and followed much the same lines. But two days later a commercial agreement established a customs union between the neighbouring territories that imposed heavy sacrifices on the Principality. The Sardinian government obtained the monopoly of tobacco and salt, free entry for its products, and other benefits.

This month of November, 1817, marked the beginning of a period of thirty years in which the Sardinian government applied increasing pressure on Honoré V, and then on Florestan, until it finally succeeded in wrenching away four-fifths of its protégé's territory.

An article of the Stupinigi treaty mentioned that although prevailing circumstances might not allow the Prince of Monaco and his family to maintain with the King of Sardinia the same relations as had existed with the French King, the former believed that the Prince would be eager to do so as soon as possible. The Turin Court promised appointments and favours to the Grimaldi family.

What exactly did these loose expressions signify?—If not that Victor Emmanuel was hoping to see the Princes of Monaco subordinate themselves to the House of Savoy, just as German sovereign princes of the Holy Roman Empire had become subordinate to Prussia or Austria, and had then received appointments at the Court of their sovereign king.

But for Victor Emmanuel or his heirs to succeed, a greater spirit of generosity was needed than the House of Savoy was accustomed to show; though the greatest obstacle was the deep attachment of the Prince of Monaco to France.

Honoré V was also the seventh Duke of Valentinois, which gave him a seat in the French House of Peers. He felt himself to be more French than the French in some ways—as a persecuted Frenchman who was being wrenched from his homeland. Honoré II had freely chosen to turn back to France; Honoré V never gave more than lip-service to the Sardinian government. As soon as an opportunity arose to try and revive the old French protectorate, he seized upon it; in March, 1821, an army revolt forced Victor Emmanuel to abdicate, and Honoré V at once wrote, rather nostalgically, to the Duke of Richelieu, Talleyrand's successor at the Foreign Office:

'The Treaty of Paris, which placed my Principality under the protection of the Sardinian government and removed it from the French, has not been able to break the personal bonds that have always existed between my family and France; it has not lost me the protection of a monarch in whose territory I usually live, and of whom I have the honour to be one of the first subjects, as a peer of France.

'So it is with complete confidence, Monsieur le Duc, that I am asking Your Excellency to support my approach to His Majesty at a time when the disorders near my Principality threaten it with total ruin; before now, your wise counsel and powerful intervention have kept it under the control of its legitimate rulers. . . .

'I am unable to make a precise request in such grave circumstances, and it is not my place to presume the trend of French policy, but I ought to remind Yr. Ex. that Monaco has a harbour useful for war operations, halfway between Marseille and Genoa, and is a safe landing-place with a useful strip of coast; for it to come under a control other than mine would perhaps be dangerous.

'I do not know if the King has sent an ambassador to Turin, but if so, one word from him saying he grants me protection would destroy any new plotting. . . .'

The reply of Richelieu, on April 6th, was merely to say: 'You can be sure that when the time comes the King will certainly grant you the protection that your ancestors have always had from France.'

Considering the age-old attachment of the Monagasques to their princes, the Sardinian government's intrigues would have had little chance of success if circumstances had not combined to help them.

In the first place, a generation had grown up that knew nothing of the Grimaldi family. These young people were no more interested in politics than the rest of the population, but they had been greatly influenced by their contacts with French language and culture over a period of twenty-five years. To people subjected to the effects of the Holy Alliance, especially to Italian people, the return to the conditions prevailing in 1792 and the eradication of the effects of the French Revolution were tantamount to a challenge to their liberty and their unity. Monaco itself was protected from the trends and movements of the times by its isolated position; its only means of access by land was by a rough mule-track that wound down from La Turbie through pine forests and olive plantations. But Menton was more open, and very susceptible to these trends.

Another factor was the poor economic situation of the Principality and the financial difficulties of its ruling family. The winter harvest of 1813 had been bad, and the following year it was no better. Honoré-Gabriel wrote to his father on March 24th, 1815: 'The people are badly hit, frost has ruined their harvest and they are unable to pay their taxes that are in arrears. . . .' And a year later, Joseph Grimaldi reported: 'Your son has had practically no revenue from Monaco because the harvests failed, and therefore the taxes too, and he asks you to make do with 1,500 francs a month, as last year. I can only say his request is a fair one, and you know I'm not on his side when he's not right.'

This letter from Joseph emphasized a new fact. Monaco had always been poor in itself, but ever since that chilly January night in 1297 when the Grimaldis had first set foot on the Rock they had contributed—and very considerably—to the well-being of the population from what the harbour and its fleet of galleys brought in, then from the Spanish or French subsidies for the fortress, and finally—throughout the eighteenth century—from the family possessions in Normandy and the Valentinois. Now all that was finished, the family had been ruined by the French Revolution, and stood in need of some financial help from the Principality. The figure of 1,500 francs a month—18,000 a year—mentioned in Joseph's letter, and that of 42,000 given to Honoré-Gabriel in January, 1815 (a bad year, it is true) as the total product of the year's chief taxes in the Principality, throws sufficient light on the problem. Later, Honoré V fixed the annual quota needed by his administration and his household at around 300,000 francs. This was four times the amount that Honoré III used to draw from the Principality.

Nevertheless, the financial problem could have been solved, for Honoré-Gabriel was generous and had the public good always in view.[1] But this lonely man had a methodical and lofty mind. His theories and principles, though the former were often just[2] and the latter always courageous, never budged when they came up against realities, did not admit the necessary compromises. Greatly in advance of his time, he imposed a directed economy upon the population of the Principality, who were at first incredulous, and later resisted it. He created monopolies, of which the most disliked was the 'exclusive' that covered the supplying of seed and the baking of bread. There were 'nationalizations' too; properties belonging to public authorities were absorbed into the Prince's domains, and he became responsible for their upkeep and expenditure—which greatly exceeded their income; the main products, olives and lemons, came under severe regulations; and State industries were created and heavily protected.

These fiscal and financial measures might appear a very early attempt to establish a 'welfare state,' but to the independent-minded people of the Principality, especially those of Menton, they seemed a heavy yoke and a crushing economic burden. If Honoré V had visited the Principality more often he might have

[1] In April, 1821, when writing to the French Foreign Ministry to explain about his absence from Paris, which had been criticized, Honoré V pointed out that it was not from choice but the consequence of the enormous debts left by his father and the lawsuits that still dragged on; as for the revenues from the Principality, 'the frosts in 1820 destroyed my hopes, and everything had to be sacrificed for my unfortunate subjects. I have given up my town apartment, dismissed my servants, and am reduced to the position of an obscure person stuck in the depths of the country. By making innumerable sacrifices I have saved between four and five hundred people from destitution and despair. . . .'

Although he failed in his struggle against the poverty of Monaco, he did better in Lower Normandy, helped by the fact that the local people were hardier and the land much more fertile; and especially because there he was a mere landowner and not a sovereign prince, and could not apply his own ideas of a directed economy. A book he published in 1838, *Pauperism, and how to Eliminate it*, was possibly a late admission of the mistakes he made by leaving no room for private initiative or freedom of action.

[2] He was thus led, in March, 1815, to annul the edicts made by his uncle Joseph and to re-establish French as the official language of the Principality, and to announce that the Code Napoléon would be applied with suitable modifications.

become aware of their complaints. His officials were scared by his authoritarian ways, and made little attempt to enlighten him.

Nevertheless, when he died—in Paris, on October 2nd, 1841— he was not unaware that the application of his ideas had been a failure. 'Here lies someone who wanted to do good,' was the sad epitaph he had put on his tombstone.

Florestan Grimaldi was still a young boy when he was given entirely into his mother's charge, after her divorce from the sixth Duke of Valentinois. She had little sense but a lively mind. A favourite story of hers was about a revolutionary band who smashed an aviary belonging to a nobleman's town mansion, and liberated the 'unhappy slaves'—who were all caught and eaten by cats. She assured everyone that this was the real account of the Revolution.

She must have been no ordinary educative influence, and it is not surprising that the youngster began to show decided literary tastes. And according to the author of a book published in 1911— *Memoirs of a Paris Doctor*, by P. de la Siboutie—Florestan, when in his 'teens, acted on the stage of several Paris theatres. But that hardly seems likely.

In any case, by 1804 he was a cadet at Fontainebleau. But he did not like military life, which was not surprising for a young man with his tastes, and he soon left the school. Two years later he was conscripted. In poor health, he did garrison duties on the island of Ouessant, at Niort, Bordeaux, and then at Toulon, before being sent to fight in Russia. There he was made prisoner, admitted to hospital at Königsberg, and eventually freed after the fall of Napoleon.

It was on his return from Russia that Florestan first met Caroline Gibert. She was eight years younger than he. Her mother, Henriette Le Gras de Vaubercy, had married again, to Antoine Rouyer, who bought the château at Lametz in 1803. She lived there, and then at St Cyr when her stepfather was appointed administrator of the military college in 1815. Florestan spent the summer of 1815 at the château at Lametz, and there came in contact with the warmth and happiness of a real home, something he had never known. He was then thirty, and had been knocking about Europe for most of his young life. Caroline Gibert was a brunette with strong features and lovely expressive eyes that showed her intelligence and kind nature. Florestan Grimaldi was attracted to her from the start, and she began to have a dominating influence over him that was to last more than forty years. Their story recalls a novel of Balzac's, *A Young Married Couple*, about a weary, shy man who returns from Russia and marries an energetic, comforting woman, and she makes him happy and prosperous.

In the course of that summer of 1815, Florestan wrote to his father from the château at Lametz to say he had asked the Duke d'Aumont to obtain a place for him in the King's household. He did not get one; but the fact that the attempt was made is of interest, as showing the awakening of new ambitions in the young man.

During the next twelve months Florestan kept trying to obtain from his family the means to set up house for himself, and to get his parents' agreement to his marriage with Caroline. Both his father and mother came round to consenting to the union, believing it was for the happiness of the young man, who seemed destined for a quiet, secluded life by his position as a younger son and his personal inclinations and tastes.

The wedding took place quietly on November 27th, 1816. 'There was no wedding-party,' Florestan wrote to his father next day. 'After the civil ceremony we went across to the church for the religious ceremony, and it was terribly cold in there, we fear you would have suffered from it. Monsieur and Madame Rouyer ask you to do them the honour of having luncheon with them and us on Saturday, at ten o'clock. I'm happy now and have everything I could wish for. . . .'

Caroline Gibert did indeed bring happiness into Monaco's ruling family. A year after the signing of the painful treaty of Stupinigi, she gave birth to a son, Honoré-Charles, on December 8th, 1818. As Honoré V was still unmarried, the baby was heir presumptive to the Principality. During the next few years, Caroline patiently and skilfully put her husband's affairs in order, applying deliberation to the long task and displaying an astonishing sense of what could ultimately be achieved; so that she finally succeeded in freeing and retrieving Florestan's fortune. She gave proof of her talents in this direction after the death of Honoré IV; and even more so after the death of Florestan's mother, the Duchesse de Mazarin, when she managed to settle the lawsuits and clear the estate, helped by the lawyer, Eynaud, who continued to advise her throughout her life.

When the financial affairs were in order, the Count and Countess de Grimaldi—the title Florestan had adopted and which he was known by until he succeeded to the Principality—bought the Hôtel de Créqui, in the rue St Guillaume, for 277,000 francs in November, 1827. The mansion had been built by Lemuet in the mid-seventeenth century, and a wing had been added in the eighteenth; it was a huge place and a handsome edifice, but in very poor state of repair. Florestan and his wife had it restored with great care, and took up their residence on the ground and first floors of the main building.

It was usual for these vast town houses to have separate apartments, and one in the eighteenth-century wing was rented by Lamartine in 1830. Many years later, the writer Ernest Renan lived on the second floor of the main building.

Life in the rue St Guillaume was calm and secluded. Florestan Grimaldi indeed had everything he could wish for. . . . He was able to cultivate his literary tastes in peace; his restored fortune made him independent; a loving and devoted wife created a happy home atmosphere. A second child, a daughter christened Florestine, was born on October 22nd, 1833. By then Honoré-Charles was nearly fifteen; he had grown into a hardy youngster with a bold face and an assured manner, brought up by a mother who loved him but did not spoil him. When his uncle died eight years later, still a bachelor, there were great hopes of a brilliant future for Charles.

Such was the family called to govern the Principality by the death of Honoré V in 1841, after a rule of twenty-five years of applied theory that had spread discontent while all the time the growing danger from the Sardinian government had been ignored.

Honoré V had always kept his brother away from the Principality, and when Count and Countess de Grimaldi arrived in November, 1841, to begin the new reign it was the first time either of them had set foot in Monaco. The officials had been so used to blind obedience to Honoré V's authoritarian rule that they were incapable of explaining the existing outlook and feelings of the people to the new Prince, Florestan I, or of pointing out the abuses and suggesting remedies. This was the first handicap, and a heavy one, when time was all important and reforms were needed at once.

Another handicap resulted from the characters and opinions of Florestan I and his wife. He, born into a princely family, held democratic ideas; while she, becoming a princess after twenty-five years of married life, believed in divine right, and whenever a slice of power was wrenched from her in one sphere she tried to win it back in another. Moreover, for twenty-five years she had been used to holding the reins and having matters left to her by a husband disinterested in politics and disliking financial affairs; and so she quite sincerely believed she was doing her duty by him in not ceding an inch of power or authority, not even to their son.

Princess Caroline explained her point of view to him, the eighth Duke of Valentinois, in a long letter written on April 3rd, 1842, just before he went to see the Sardinian government at Turin.

'You've said what you think quite frankly, and I'll reply in the same way. To begin with, you talk about my capability, and I'll tell you this, that only one thing counts for me, the strictness with which I conscientiously carry out the obligations and duties I have taken on, and in my opinion that often serves better than intelligence. My duties, as I understand them, are above the ordinary. I was brought up in a simple and modest position, and was then chosen by your father to enter one of the highest-placed families . . . from that moment my position changed. In spite of my sex, I became head of a family and had to fulfil the obligations attached and get myself forgiven for this preferment. Without false modesty, nor thinking too highly of myself, I can say that after a few years—while keeping to my early habits and even neglecting to launch myself into social circles that would have looked down on me—I had almost reached my goal by carrying out the duties that I had given myself.

'Your father gave me a good name and fortune, in return I must take care to see his position is maintained and his fortune looked after properly. I owe it to my children, as a compensation for not having brought material advantages into the family, to guard those belonging to their father; I owe it to my son especially to see that he receives intact the inheritance that Providence has placed in his father's hands, and I owe him the fruits of my experience and my advice—and I will tell him this, that for six months now he has been in error in several instances, though I admit that the fresh prospects opened before him by the death of his uncle may have confused his mind. . . . In the Principality, he thought that the little aptitude his father has for public affairs meant that he could take charge of them without having received his father's permission to do so; he then took it upon himself to write to some of the officials, and although the letters are no doubt innocuous, he did not take into consideration that they put the people they were addressed to in an embarrassing position . . . he was weakening his father's authority, and thereby giving fresh hopes to Sardinia and increasing the people's uneasiness. . . . You can imagine that in a very small place where people have been used to the strong will of one person they must have been greatly astonished to see a prince letting himself be manœuvred, the wife poking her finger into everything, and a son apparently going his own particular way and often lacking in respect and even consideration where they are due, if only to set an example. . . . I am serving your father's interests here, which will one day be your own, and it's not a game, it concerns a whole family's position. . . . So it is far better that you should have, later on, a solid, well-established authority than to be putting ideas of division or opposition into minds that have been submissive until now, and which you might find yourself up against one day.

'Consider the position you put yourself in if you said at Turin that you're more capable than your father and that you should take his place. I quite believe you don't want to reach that point; what you would be saying in effect is—I love and respect my mother enough to leave her some of the authority she seems to like so much, but only on condition that she leaves me the rest. Oh, no, my young friend, I shall not agree to a deal like that, because my great idea is always to have your father's rights respected and keep those of my children intact. . . . Having no rights myself, I'm under the cover of your father, who thus retains the fullness of his authority. . . .

'I feel in need of a rest after such a long letter, but I've still just enough energy to tell you that ever since you were born you have been most dear to me, and the reason for all my efforts, and that until my dying day you'll be my well-beloved. . . .'

This high-minded letter gives a touching proof of Caroline's noble and spirited character. It also throws some light on how it was that Florestan I, during six years of good intentions in which he made grudging concessions and then largely withdrew them next day, gradually lost the affection and confidence of the people of Menton who had enthusiastically greeted his arrival in the Principality.

The discontented found support all ready for them at Turin. The treaty of 1817 gave the population of the Principality similar rights to those of the people in the Sardinian Kingdom. This opened the way—as Turin must have reckoned—to amalgamation. Quite a number of families in the Principality had some of their members in the Piedmontese army or navy by the mid-1840s. This provided employment or a career which was otherwise lacking; but such people were beginning to think of the Sardinian Kingdom as their main country, the Principality as the lesser, the province they had been born in. . . . It was then an easy stage from discontent to thoughts of integration; even more so, when the proposals made to Florestan I from Turin at the beginning of his reign became known to Menton—the loyalty of Monaco itself was never in doubt. Turin had conveyed to the Prince of Monaco, in very clear terms, its willingness to acquire the sovereignty of the Principality and to pay him a fair indemnity. The simmering inhabitants sighed with relief—the hated 'exclusive' would at last be done away with. . . .

These proposals were renewed to the eighth Duke of Valentinois when he reached Turin in the spring of 1842, and the offer of a fine marriage alliance with a Piedmont family was thrown in. When Princess Caroline heard of this she went at once to complain to the Sardinian ambassador in Paris. 'It's well known that your King covets our little State,' she said to him, 'but we shall defend it with every means in our power, and we do not think we can do better than by reporting the conduct of his agents to the King.'

The offers made by Turin—which were sadly remembered by

the people of Menton—were not repeated. Instead, the encroach-
ments on the rights and powers of the Prince of Monaco were
patiently begun again. The commander of the Sardinian garrison,
for instance, who should have taken his orders from the Prince,
the military governor of Monaco, maintained that as an officer
in the army of the King of Sardinia his obedience was due only
to his sovereign.

On September 28th, 1846, Charles Grimaldi, eighth Duke of
Valentinois, was married to Antoinette de Mérode, in Brussels.
The young couple soon visited the Principality, and the fêtes
and acclamations with which they were greeted, at Menton as
well as at Monaco, showed that the situation was still retrievable.
But action was needed, the handing over of power to the heir,
for instance. Florestan made no move, while another year slipped
by—a respite not to be repeated.

The liberal reforms granted by Pope Pius IX to the Papal
States in October, 1847, set up demands for similar concessions
throughout Italy. The King of Sardinia, Charles Albert, was
quick to take the lead and promulgated his *Statuto Fondamentale*,
making the House of Savoy the champion of the movement for a
united Italy. An agitation at once began in Menton for the
application of identical progressive measures. This insurrectional
movement went on for four months; Florestan granted concessions demanded of him, now that it was much too late, and then
unwisely called in Piedmontese troops. This was letting the cat in
among the pigeons. On March 2nd, 1848, a provisional governing
committee was formed for Menton and Roquebrune, and it
declared these two towns to be free territory, thus opening the
way for union with the Sardinian Kingdom.

Florestan was at Monaco. The population of the Rock remained
loyal, but he was practically besieged in his palace by the Sardinian
garrison. Then Turin renewed its offer, with an insistence almost
amounting to blackmail, to purchase the Principality for six
million francs.

Florestan had never cared for power, and so had easily tired
of it. He was not sorry to come to the opinion—or did his wife
make up his mind for him?—that a younger and more active
person, perhaps closer to the people, would be able to re-establish

order and save the Principality for the Grimaldis. So when his heir arrived from Paris, having witnessed the fall of the July Monarchy, Florestan appointed him administrator of the Principality, on March 10th, 1848, and delegated to him all necessary powers for re-organizing it.

A few days later, Florestan left Monaco with his wife and daughter. Henceforth, the ordinances appeared in the name of the eighth Duke of Valentinois. In fact the reign of Charles III of Monaco had begun.

CHAPTER VIII

A SHREWD RULER: NEW MEANS OF
GETTING MONEY (1848–1889)

ONLY THREE PRINCES RULED AT MONACO during the hundred years from 1848, and all three proved of great importance to their dynasty. The reign of Charles III was constructive; Albert I's was brilliant; and Louis II consolidated the work of his father and grandfather. He was the last of the Grimaldi-Matignons, but passed on the torch to the Grimaldi-Polignacs.

A high sense of duty to one's family and heritage, and a love of power, were necessary to take over the governing of Monaco in March, 1848. Charles Grimaldi was a tall, fine-looking man of thirty; he had a high forehead and small, dark eyes, and wore a moustache and a tuft on his chin, in the fashion of the time. He was ambitious and intelligent, with his mother's poise and balanced outlook, and the authority and courage of the Grimaldis. From both sides of his family he had inherited a doggedness that never slackened.

With these varied and complementary qualities he was able to be diplomatic and audacious by turns, throughout thirteen difficult years, until the day when he concluded a treaty with Napoleon III that left him more a master of his amputated territory than any of his ancestors had been of the whole.

A provisional governing body had been set up at Menton, but Charles took no hasty action; instead, he invited its head, Charles Trenca, to meet him at Carnolès on March 20th, to examine together ways and means of re-organizing the Principality. It was a wise and conciliatory move; but Trenca did not appear, and on the following day Menton and Roquebrune proclaimed their independence. Ten days later, the Sardinian Minister for Foreign Affairs, Count Balbo, announced that his government would continue to 'protect' the two towns.

With events thus set in motion, the end seemed obvious. On April 30th, the governing committee in Menton drew up its *Statuto Fondamentale*; on May 28th, it exiled the Prince of Monaco and his family; and on June 22nd and 26th voted for inclusion in the Kingdom of Sardinia. All that remained was for Charles Albert to accept. But then a sudden halt was called to the turn of events. In Paris, General Cavaignac, the head of the executive government, had just put down the June insurrection. As a restorer of order within the country, he intended that treaties should be respected without; and made this known at Turin. Instead of acceding to the request of the free towns—Roquebrune had followed in the steps of Menton—the King of Sardinia decreed, on September 18th, 1848, that they would be administered according to the prevailing laws until a definite decision was made about them.

Over a year went by before this decision was reached. Instead of invoking the right of people to dispose of themselves— which, coming just after the crushing defeat the Piedmontese had suffered at the hands of the Austrians, at Novare, would have been dangerous—the Lower House of Parliament at Turin recalled the ancient suzerainty of the House of Savoy over Menton and Roquebrune, and on November 10th, 1849, declared the two places to be an integral part of its States. The Upper House, to avoid international complications, did not ratify this vote. Menton and Roquebrune remained 'free towns,' but an indemnity acceptable to the Prince of Monaco would justify their annexation.

Negotiations were begun to determine the amount to be paid, through the intermediary of the French Minister of Foreign Affairs, Drouyn de Lhuys; but these dragged on. The government at Turin was in no hurry, secretly hoping 'little by little to obtain possession by a series of administrative acts,' according to the Duc de Guiche, the French envoy at Turin. Not until December, 1852, was a firm proposition made to Florestan—an annual payment of 75,000 francs, which the Prince of Monaco considered insufficient. His counter-proposal contained a political demand—the abolition of the protectorate and the withdrawal of the Monaco garrison.

Neither side showed any goodwill and the negotiations were

practically at a standstill, when a bold move by the Duke of Valentinois caused them to be revived.

At six o'clock on the morning of April 6th, 1854, he drove into Menton in a six-horse carriage, accompanied by his doctor, Chevalet, and his aide-de-camp, Lucien Bellando. They stopped in front of the Hôtel de Turin, which was the posting-house, on the pretext of changing horses. The Duke was at once surrounded and acclaimed by supporters who had been secretly warned of his coming. They took the horses out of the traces and dragged the carriage to the town hall, waving flags of the Grimaldi colours and shouting 'Long live the Prince!' 'Long live the Grimaldis!'

But, alas, a hostile gathering supported by the local armed police soon broke up the demonstration. The Duke had to be rescued by the Piedmontese *carabinieri* stationed in the town; a bayonet-thrust had already torn his coat, and one of the police was taking aim at him when a sergeant of the *carabinieri* knocked the rifle aside. The *carabinieri* escorted the Duke to their barracks and held him there.

So far, the incident was a purely local one. All that was needed was for the Duke to be escorted back to the Monaco boundary, with much show for his personal safety. But the civil governor of Nice had been informed. He was not a very honourable man, and sought an easy popularity with the public. He hurried to Menton, to claim his prisoner. He made the Duke walk from the barracks to the town hall, thus giving opponents of the Grimaldis an opportunity to insult him. Then, avoiding any responsibility himself, he took the Duke to Villefranche and confined him to the fort there until instructions arrived from Turin.[1]

The Duc de Guiche demanded the release of Charles Grimaldi, and on April 11th orders went out from Turin for him to be set free. That same day, Drouyn de Lhuys sent a note which, although calling the Duke of Valentinois's attempt 'most inopportune,' emphasized the desirability of Turin putting an end to the matter 'by increasing if necessary the amount of the

---

[1] The governor's conduct was called 'dishonourable' in the despatch sent to Paris by the French envoy at Turin, and Drouyn de Lhuys agreed with a firm 'quite true' in the margin.

pecuniary sacrifices.' Political tension was high just then; the Crimean War had begun a fortnight previously, Austria and Prussia were wondering on which side their interests lay, and Victor Emmanuel II was seeking to draw some advantage from the war. The French Foreign Minister's Note concealed a threat that was understood in Turin.

So the talks over figures began again. Victor Emmanuel's Prime Minister, Dabormida, made an effort, and on June 25th, 1854, offered 90,000 francs annually, instead of the 75,000, with perhaps the capital sum as well. This was still considered not enough.

But, now that the Duke of Valentinois had succeeded in reviving this thorny problem, the French Foreign Minister did not allow it to be lost to view again. On September 24th he gave a whole despatch to the subject of the Principality of Monaco.

These few months were very important for the future history of Monaco, for during this period the lines of the vital 1861 agreement between France and the Principality began to emerge; though at the time they referred to an arrangement between Turin and the Principality.

'I should indeed find it difficult to understand,' Drouyn de Lhuys wrote to the Duc de Guiche, 'if Turin does not hasten to put an end to a state of affairs that is, after all, contrary to the treaties and provides a continual motive—an open gap even— for Powers less favourably disposed than we are to meddle in the affairs of Piedmont; for Austria, for instance, and even Prussia. . . . The Turin government would not be showing political foresight if it let this opportunity pass for the sake of some pecuniary sacrifice. . . .'

The Foreign Minister then made reference to rumours of Monaco being ceded to the U.S.A. (which were formally denied by Princess Caroline in an interview with Drouyn de Lhuys a few days later), and went on to sum up the matter: 'It all amounts to this—that Turin should indemnify the Prince of Monaco, fairly and honourably, and remove all occasion for him to open negotiations with any other Power, which would be bound to cause embarrassment to everybody.' The Minister concluded that there were only two possible solutions: either the cession of the whole Principality to Victor Emmanuel; or, if only Menton and Roquebrune were ceded to him, there should be 'a clause explicitly preventing the Prince of Monaco from ceding the remainder of his possessions to any Power but the Kingdom of Sardinia.' Such a clause could constitute a 'special article' in the counter-proposals from Turin.

However, in Turin, Dabormida had been replaced by Cavour, who was busy bringing his country with advantage into the Crimean War, and became less exigent over Monaco. On October 26th, 1854, the French chargé d'affaires in Turin reported a conversation he had had with Hudson, the British Minister. The latter had seen Cavour, who was prepared to pay a fancy price for *all* the Principality, but would be less generous for Menton and Roquebrune alone. Hudson, commenting on this, had said he thought 'four million francs quite a lot for a couple of places that produce nothing but lemons . . . Monaco and its harbour being the commercial and political centre and having the most value.'

In the autumn of 1854, then, the facts of the problem had been stated. But another seven years were to pass and two wars fought before it was finally solved.

During 1855 the Great Powers of Europe were occupied with other matters, but the name of Monaco came up at the Congress of Paris in 1856, when Cavour complained of the Austrian occupation of Lombardy. Hübner, the Austrian ambassador, reminded him of that of Monaco by the Piedmontese, which continued against the wishes of the sovereign prince. Cavour's evasive reply made allusion only to Menton, whereas Hübner had spoken of the whole Principality.

The death of Florestan I on June 20th, 1856, caused no change in the government of the Principality. But Charles III, who had been seen about a great deal in Paris society during the past ten years,[1] and who had established good relations at the Tuileries

---

[1] Count Apponyi, the Austrian diplomat, noted on March 23rd, 1852, when going to attend a theatrical performance at the Castellane town house in the Faubourg St Honoré: 'Before entering the room I stopped to have a word near the stage with the actors and actresses, especially with Mademoiselles Judith, Fix, Maquet, and Rimblot. The Duke of Valentinois was there, pinching the arm of one and the leg of the other.'

—as had his wife too[1]—was now able to make greater use, as a sovereign prince, of his influential connections.

Thus it was that, early in 1857, Napoleon III again intervened to try to settle the question of the two free towns. The Prince of Monaco again repeated his terms—the abolition of the protectorate, and four million francs as an indemnity. Once again Turin refused.

It was a deadlock. And a means of ending it was not found until after Louis Napoleon's successful war against Austria, with Victor Emmanuel as his ally, the freeing of Lombardy, and the subsequent union of Nice and Savoy with France.

The Treaty between Louis Napoleon and Victor Emmanuel in March, 1860, provided for a plebiscite on union with France to be held in Nice and Savoy. Menton and Roquebrune were not mentioned, but on April 15th the electorate of both places was asked to vote on the matter: 833 votes were cast for union with France, and only 54 against. Charles III protested. Paris did not intend to make the same mistakes as Turin, and announced that the voting merely served as an indication and should not justify annexation; upon which, negotiations were begun between Charles III and the French Foreign Office.

In the meantime, Monaco was freed. On July 17th, 1860, the officer commanding the Sardinian garrison, Serra, informed the governor-general that the protection of the Principality had been transferred from the King of Sardinia to the Emperor of the French, and that consequently his troops would be withdrawn next day. There was much satisfaction among the population at the news of the end of an occupation that had lasted forty-five years and been hated all the time. The people prepared to welcome the return of French troops and the renewal of a protectorate that had left good memories behind.

It did in fact seem there would be a return to the Treaty of Péronne, with some adaptation to the contemporary circumstances. But the influence of Charles III at the Tuileries and the friendly relations he had established, together with the confidence given by his loyalty and feelings towards France, all combined to

[1] 'The Emperor was in a lively mood this evening,' wrote Hübner on January 29th, 1856. 'He waltzed with the Marquise Sclafano, the Duchess of Valentinois, and the Marquise Strozzi.'

decide Napoleon III to set aside this survival of the old régime. It is possible, too, that the nephew of the great Bonaparte had little desire to follow the ways of the Bourbons.

The Treaty signed on February 2nd, 1861, therefore only settled the question of Menton and Roquebrune. Its main clauses were: the Prince of Monaco renounced all rights over the two places, and received four million francs in exchange; under Article Five, the French government became responsible for keeping the road joining Monaco to the Grande Corniche in good repair, where it passed through Roquebrune; and agreed to build a carriage-road as soon as possible along the coast from Nice to Monaco. Also, the Prince of Monaco would let the projected railway line between Nice and Genoa pass through the Principality.

The Treaty contained 'special articles,' as Drouyn de Lhuys would have called them, which remained secret until 1918. They revealed reasons for the French protectorate not being renewed. The ideas expressed by Drouyn de Lhuys in 1854 had been taken up; and the Prince of Monaco undertook, for himself and his heirs, not to transfer or cede any of his sovereign rights over the Principality unless it were to France. Only from France would the Prince request or accept a protectorate at any time in the future.

One of Joseph Grimaldi's daughters, the Marquise de la Tour du Pin, protested to Charles III against the cession of Menton and Roquebrune. She reminded him of Claudine's testament forbidding transfer in any manner of any part of the Grimaldi territories. In a few short, abrupt sentences the Prince of Monaco summed up the matter, realistically and with authority, and drew its conclusion better than anyone could have done.

'The treaty I have just concluded with the Emperor leaves the sovereign rights intact and ensures the independence of the Principality. This happy result is due to the courageous struggle that the Prince my father and I maintained for thirteen years, at our risk and peril. Without this persistence, we should no doubt have ceased to be counted among the reigning houses, and so our younger branches would have lost all possibility of succeeding. . . .

'I say further, plainly and frankly, that as head of my house I am not prepared to give any more explanation, and admit no one's right to ask me for it. . . .'[1]

There can be no doubt that Article Five of the 1861 Treaty was an essential point of it in the wise foresight of Charles III and to his no less alert mother, Princess Caroline. They had both realized, several years before, that the remote position of Monaco, which had for so long been a safeguard, might well result in the place becoming a sleepy backwater.

It had been Menton, with its taxes, customs dues, and export trade in lemons, that had chiefly contributed to the public funds of the Princes. With the Principality reduced to Monaco alone, how were the expenses of an administration and a Court to be met? The amount expected in 1852 from land and property-tax was a mere 2,885 francs.

The shrewd management of Princess Caroline had restored the personal fortune of the Grimaldis, certainly; and Antoinette de Mérode had not come empty-handed into the family.[2] Yet what was plenty for a private person was insufficient for a sovereign prince.

What was to be done? While Charles III struggled tenaciously and courageously with the political problem, his mother was applying herself with equal tenacity and courage to the financial problem. It was out of the question to increase the taxes. On the contrary, measures to try and raise the living standard of the Monagasques had to be taken; and in 1852, and again in 1854, the customs duty was lowered. But that was merely the negative

---

[1] The 1861 Treaty between Charles III and France had later effects. Article Six provided for a commercial agreement, which was eventually signed on November 9th, 1865. This established a customs union between France and the Principality, and did away with the salt monopoly in Monaco. As compensation, the Prince was granted an annual payment of 20,000 francs.

This agreement was revised in 1912, when additions were made and it was tightened up in great detail. The annual indemnity was increased to 400,000 francs, with provision for a further 20,000 each time the population of Monaco increased by one thousand over the census of 1908. One of the additions was that foreigners other than French who were expelled from the Principality would not be allowed to reside in the *départements* of the Alpes-Maritimes, Var, or Basses-Alpes.

[2] Charles Grimaldi bought the Marchais estate (the present seat of the family, in the Aisne *département*) with his wife's dowry, in 1854. He had tried to buy back the hôtel de Matignon; and the last of the land in Normandy, together with the house near Bayeux, had gone to Oscar Grimaldi, the natural son of Honoré V.

side of the problem. What was needed was to create new sources of income.

Several ideas were considered—a credit establishment, a discount bank, insurance companies. None came to anything. What was the main advantage of Monaco? A wonderful climate and an enchanting site. In the 1850s, sea-bathing was coming into fashion and seaside resorts were being created. In Germany and Belgium, casinos were in fashion—casinos to shelter gaming-tables—and were making fortunes for small towns and spas that had previously been sleepy, insignificant places.

Princess Caroline sent her faithful adviser, Eynaud, to Baden-Baden, where the Grand Duke had given a Frenchman named Benazet permission to run a casino. Eynaud discovered without much difficulty that the Grand Duke's income had thereby increased by a couple of million francs, and that the benefits on the side came to an even greater amount.

It was essential, though, to have hotels and villas to provide 'comfortable and luxurious' accommodation for the visitors, who were foreigners for the most part and accustomed to a gilded existence. The resorts in Germany and Belgium were pleasant in summer, but far from being so in winter. Monaco, though, was then delightful, with its warmth and gentle sea and blue skies. There was no fear of competition from other places along the French Riviera. In an excess of virtue, the bourgeois France of Louis-Philippe had prohibited public gaming-tables, and the advent of the Second Empire had not brought a change in the law.

With the idea of casinos in the air, when news got around that the Prince of Monaco was prepared to let a *Société des Bains de Mer* —a company to promote sea-bathing facilities—set itself up at Monaco and open public gaming-rooms, there was no lack of applicants all with dazzling propositions.

The first to be granted a concession were a couple of associates, Léon Langlois and Albert Aubert. On April 26th, 1856, they were given a thirty-five-year monopoly in return for a quarter of their profits, and a guarantee of a minimum of 25,000 francs a year. They undertook to create sea-bathing facilities, to build a hotel and villas, and to get a steamer-service and a horse-omnibus service started between Nice and Monaco. They were also supposed to print and publish a weekly paper and to organize fêtes, one of which would be for the financial benefit of the local poor each year. Langlois and Aubert promised to build a casino on the Spélugues plateau, on the other side of the harbour from the Rock; and they bought up a lot of ground there, paying twenty centimes the square yard. . . .

They were in a hurry to open their gaming-rooms, and as Princess Caroline had requested they should not be on the Rock, in Monaco town, they rented the only private house along the Condamine, the harbour front. This house, the 'Bellevue,' had 'a fine view of the harbour, and the gardens of the Rimmel perfumery could be seen stretching from the base of the Rock to the gorge des Gaumates. Behind these gardens, on what is now the rue Florestine, was a profusion of orange and lemon trees and eucalyptus, blending together delightfully and scenting the air.' Unfortunately, the house was poorly furnished, and heaps of rubbish and old plaster still encumbered the drive when, on December 14th, 1856, the roulette wheel was set spinning for the first time.

Having got their gaming-rooms open—their chief interest in the business—Langlois and Aubert went no further. Besides, they lacked the capital to do much more. No transport services were organized. To get to the 'Bellevue' from Nice meant a four-hour journey in the old stage-coach, with ten other passengers, along the difficult Grande Corniche road. Alternatively, there was the old sailing-boat, the *Palmeria*, that went from Nice to Monaco and back once every day, in theory at least. If the sea was rough, the boat stayed in harbour. Moreover, if the captain thought he might get one or two more passengers he gladly waited and delayed sailing. As for accommodation at Monaco . . . there were a few comfortless garrets at the Hôtel de Russie, and that was all. Visitors were obliged to leave the Condamine at sunset.

Not surprisingly, the 'Bellevue' had little clientele and was soon losing money for the couple running it. In November, 1857, they sold out to a person called Frossard de Lilebonne, who only lasted a few months until finding a buyer in Pierre-Auguste Daval. He did no better than his predecessors. Nevertheless, on May 13th, 1858, the foundation-stone of the Casino on the Spélugues was laid by the Prince's ten-year-old son, Albert. But the architect soon became discouraged through lack of money, and left for the United States.

Daval was in debt to the tune of forty million francs a year later, when he gave way to a company whose principal shareholder was the Duke of Valmy and whose managing-director was a man called Lefebvre. Hardly had the deal been concluded than the French armies marched into Lombardy to fight the Austrians; and the gaming-rooms closed down.

During the two months of hostilities Lefebvre transferred his 'Visitors' Club' up to the Rock, and in October, 1859, play began again at the villa Gabarini, in the rue Marie de Lorraine. The minimum stake was two francs. Players who had only a few centimes left could sometimes be seen in the near-by Café du Soleil gambling between themselves to raise the necessary stake.

Lefebvre organized dances and concerts, and advertised more than the others had done; moreover, the Rock was a more attractive place than the Condamine, and there was plenty of money about when the short war ended, as is often the case. So the villa Gabarini began to show a profit; during the last quarter of 1859 its gaming-tables averaged a thousand francs a day on the right side. Though there was one black week when a player won 50,000 francs.

After the gaming-house had been open for eighteen months it gave every prospect of being a nice little business, though with no great future. The ancient *Palmeria* had been replaced by a new boat, the *Charles III*, that could take sixty passengers. Two small hotels had been opened on the Spélugues, the Hôtel d'Angleterre and the Hôtel de Paris. The latter was under the same management as the gaming-house, and was providential for unlucky players; their unpaid bills were included among the company's general losses.

The bank of the villa Gabarini continued to show a profit, though, and the daily average had gone up to 1,200 francs. This was not at all bad for honest croupiers without ambitions; but it was not nearly good enough to enable the company to keep to the terms of the original contract. And that alone was what mattered to the Prince of Monaco—to complete the building of the Casino des Spélugues, to organize better transport facilities, open hotels and villas, in short to provide the means for a tourist influx that would bring prosperity to the Principality, as François Blanc had succeeded in doing at Hombourg.

If Lefebvre had studied Article Five of the 1861 Treaty with as much attention as Charles III did—and as no doubt François Blanc did later—he would have realized its full import; that with the benevolent help of France and at her expense,[1] it was going to enable the main handicap to be overcome in Monaco's attempts to attract tourists: the almost complete lack of public communications. For did it not provide for carriage-roads to Monaco, and was not the railway line intended to pass through the Principality?

But Lefebvre lacked the imagination necessary to become a business magnate. When Charles III told him that unless the Casino des Spélugues was completed and ready to open by January 1st, 1863, his gaming concession would be withdrawn, he lost heart and began to look around for a buyer.

For some years François Blanc had been following the ups and downs of the *Société des Bains de Mer* of Monaco; several of his partisans had been croupiers for Langlois and Aubert, and for Daval. But Blanc had almost gone bankrupt at Hombourg, in the beginning, and had only just been saved by help from the Rothschilds. This hard experience had taught him that the greatest difficulty in making a success of a casino came in its opening months, that unless it could get away to a good start there was no point in opening the doors. So long as Monaco had been under the protectorate of the Sardinian Kingdom, in which gambling was illegal, Blanc had hung back. But now that the Principality was independent, Nice part of France, and the railway line advanced as far as Cagnes, the situation was very different.

However, as a shrewd man of business, Blanc bided his time. It came at the end of 1862, when he was approached by Lefebvre and the Duke of Valmy on one hand, and by Eynaud on the other. In March, 1863, he judged the time was ripe and travelled

[1] During his exile, Louis Napoleon had believed himself to have been swindled while gambling at Crockford's Club, in London. Now he was Emperor he considered a properly managed and lawful gaming-house was a lesser evil than illegal gambling; he also believed that the influx of tourists would be beneficial to Nice and its neighbourhood.

down to Monaco. On March 31st he walked into the office of the *Société des Bains de Mer*, where its attorney, Jagot, was waiting for him.

'You wish to sell your concession,' said Blanc briskly, 'and I'm prepared to buy it. I'll give you 1,700,000 francs, in three instalments. Think it over. I'll be back here at three o'clock, because I have to catch the boat at four, and I want the whole matter to be settled one way or the other before I go aboard.'

He had pulled it off. The next day, Blanc, who had never had any intention of leaving empty-handed, drew up the articles of association; and on April 2nd, 1863, the Prince of Monaco granted him the privilege of operating the *Société des Bains de Mer et du Cercle des Etrangers*,[1] for a term of fifty years.

Two years after the 1861 Treaty that gave political independence to the Principality, the 1863 agreement founded its financial independence. The remainder of Charles III's reign was spent in consolidating this double success.

Already, on March 15th, 1858, he had affirmed his privilege as a sovereign prince by creating the Order of St Charles, of which he was the Grand-Master, and which was conferred for meritorious services to the Principality.

Eight years later, Charles III put a new town on the map. The shrewd management of the *Société des Bains de Mer* was transforming the fields of the Spélugues into a growing suburb of Monaco. It needed a name of its own. The Prince hesitated in his choice. Charleville, perhaps? But that might cause confusion and was not distinctive enough. Eventually he decided, and on June 1st, 1866, Monte Carlo came into being.

An Order and a new town were quite a lot. But to a Catholic family like the Grimaldis, ecclesiastical independence was of great importance. Something was still lacking—a bishop of their own.

In 1861 Charles III had agreed that the Principality should continue to form part of the diocese of Nice. But four years later, on the excuse that his right to nominate the priest-in-charge

---

[1] This part of the name—*Cercle des Etrangers*, or Visitors' Club—expressly emphasized the Prince of Monaco's desire that the Monagasques should not be allowed into the Casino.

The company's capital was increased to fifteen million francs, the number of shares being 30,000. Blanc held 22,000, and the Prince of Monaco received 400.

of St Nicolas of Monaco had not been properly recognized, he revived the idea of ecclesiastical autonomy for the Principality that Honoré III had played with in the past. Charles III was successful in obtaining a consistory decree, on April 30th, 1868, whereby an abbey *nullius* was named for Monaco, having a mitred abbot directly responsible to the Holy See. A few weeks later, the installation of Monsignor Romarico Flughi, the priest in charge of St Nicolas, duly took place; and the ancient church became a cathedral.[1] But two years later, after some dissension in which the ex-tutor of young Albert, Monsignor Theuret, had a hand, Flughi was replaced by a suffragan bishop; the following year, 1871, the Bishop of Ventimiglia was appointed apostolic administrator of the abbey. At his death in July, 1877, he was succeeded by Monsignor Theuret. Fresh negotiations with the Vatican led to the issuing of a Bull creating the diocese of Monaco, on March 15th, 1887. Its first Bishop was, of course, Monsignor Theuret.

In the meantime, Charles III had completed his sovereign prerogatives by issuing, in 1878, the Principality's own currency; this had been provided for in the 1865 commercial agreement with France, and was to be accepted as legal tender there. Finally, in 1885, the first postage stamps of Monaco appeared, bearing the head of Charles III.

These administrative measures underlining the political independence were accompanied by financial measures expressing the material independence. The most important of the latter was indeed a strong indication of the success of Charles III's government.

The railway line between Nice and Menton was opened to the public on October 19th, 1868, and soon brought a great influx of visitors to the Principality. The expectations of Charles III and Princess Caroline were largely fulfilled and then exceeded. The Prince of Monaco could not forget, having been so closely involved in the matter, that the vexed question of taxes had been the prime cause of the amputation of his State, and had almost brought about the end of the Grimaldi dynasty. To his mind,

---

[1] The church of St Nicolas, in which so many of the Grimaldis had been buried, was pulled down a few years later. The present cathedral, which is dedicated to the Immaculate Conception, was begun in 1875 and completed in 1884.

therefore, the suppression of those taxes would crown the economic evolution he had instigated, reward the faithful support of the Monagasques, and perhaps be a revenge over the people of Menton and Roquebrune.

So an edict from the palace, on February 8th, 1869, did away with all rates and taxes. It was a shrewd and intelligent move, as well as a generous one. Although it caused some difficulty for a time in the Principality's finances, it prepared the way for what was to be, with the resulting increase in visitors and in commercial activity, a most prosperous future.

While these later years of the reign were filled with administrative and economic successes, Charles III himself suffered much misfortune; as though in his private life he was called upon to pay for the public triumphs.

His sister, Florestine, had married the Count of Wurtemberg in February, 1863, when she was thirty. He was a widower who had been coming to Monaco for some years, bringing one of his four daughters whose health was being undermined by tuberculosis. The Count was a Lutheran, which ruled out the possibility of marriage into a strict Catholic family like the Grimaldis. But he and Florestine had become very fond of each other, and his conversion in 1862 enabled the excellent alliance to take place. In 1867 he became the Duke of Urach. Their union was a happy one, and two sons were born to them; but it was cut short by the Duke's death in 1869. The Duchess then returned to live with her brother, who by then was a widower himself.

Antoinette de Mérode, who had been so active and shone so brilliantly at the time of the Congress of Paris, continually reminding delegates of the Menton question, had suffered from poor health in the following years and had led a retired life. She spent many months at Marchais, in the north of France, where the grey sweep of country and thick trees reminded her of her native Belgium. She died at Monaco on February 14th, 1864.

That year Charles III, whose sight had always been poor, became completely blind. From then on, while the Principality was enjoying a prosperity it had never known before, the Prince's life was sad and wearisome; though, sharing his time between Marchais and Monaco, this sightless ruler continued until the end to exercise his firm and wise authority over the affairs of the Principality.

'New Year's Day was as sad for me as any other,' he wrote to his son Albert on January 6th, 1877. 'My condition has slightly improved and I can do a few things. But the dizziness, the insomnia, the pains and other sufferings have got no less . . . what discomforts me too, is the effect of odours, especially scent and perfume. They almost make me faint, so that except for people of the household I am unable to receive anyone. . . .'

His life had become increasingly lonely; only a few close friends were occasionally allowed to see him. He let his sister, the Duchess of Urach, take over complete control of the household; but kept his son out of the affairs of the Principality, which was a usual reaction of the Princes of Monaco.

The death, on November 23rd, 1879, of Princess Caroline, his mother who had given him so much affection and help in the early, difficult years, was a further blow to Charles III. He died at the age of seventy-one, on September 10th, 1889. The last twenty-five years of his life had been made hard by infirmities and suffering; but his reign of thirty-three years, though often difficult, had always been courageous and effectual. He had created the Principality anew, and left it compact, rich, and independent, for his successor.

17   The Royal Palace, Monaco.

18   Courtyard and double staircase at the Palace with
the peak of the 'Tête de Chien' rising behind.

19 The Hercule Gallery with frescoes representing the Twelve Labours of Hercules, by the Genoese painter Orazio Ferrari.

20 The Throne Room furnished in scarlet-and-gold brocade with rich velvet hangings round the Throne. Portrait on the left is that of Prince Honoré III, and on the right Prince Louis II, grandfather of Prince Rainier III.

CHAPTER IX

ALBERT THE NAVIGATOR (1889–1922)

IT OFTEN HAPPENS that in the course of time a person of exceptional gifts and character appears in a very old family which has been enriched by the civilization of centuries and many marriage alliances; and that such a person is the very essence of his lineage. In medieval times, he was often a Saint; during the age of classicism, a powerful monarch or a great military leader. By the nineteenth century, it was the scientists who thought they could bring happiness to mankind. And it was then that the ancient tradition of the seigneurs of Monaco reasserted itself and produced a sailor again, but one who was to make his own scientific kingdom out of the sea.

Albert-Honoré-Charles Grimaldi was born in Paris on November 13th, 1848. He was the only child of the family, coddled and fussed over, but was inevitably a lonely lad; and lonely he was to remain throughout his life. His father wisely sent him to boarding school, to the Stanislas college in Paris, but he did not get on well with his classmates and was not very happy there.

He took his First Communion in May, 1861, and was then a bright lad with a brown face and lively, intelligent eyes. The dominant trait in his character already showed, a fierce independence of spirit that led him to argue back—and caused his grandmother, Princess Caroline, to reproach him about it more than once.

He was sent to Orléans, to Father Dupanloup, to finish his studies; and by the time he was seventeen was quite sure what he wanted to be. He spent a few months at a naval school at Lorient, and then in 1866 he joined the Spanish Navy.

At first sight, this seems a surprising choice. The Spain of Isabella II provided little future for an ambitious young man, and it might be thought that Albert would be wasting his time.

But behind the choice was Charles III's great urge to affirm his independence in every way possible, and probably he wanted to make a break with the custom, during the French protectorate, of the Grimaldis serving in the armies of France.

Albert served as a midshipman, then as lieutenant, and a normal naval career seemed to be opening before him. But then came the overthrow of the Spanish monarchy—mainly through the action of the navy, incidentally—and Albert left, not wishing to serve under a Republic. Although he had given up the navy, he had not given up the sea, for in the spring of 1869 he made a cruise aboard a small yacht, the *Isabelle*. His calling was now determined for good—he would follow the sea, be a navigator, if not alone at least sole master of his ship, free of all restrictions except those he imposed upon himself.

This sailor in his twenty-first year, who liked so much to feel free and who had just discovered what he wanted to do with his life—while he was not called to rule—could not have been at all ready for marriage. Until then, his father had shown much understanding and had adopted a liberal attitude towards him, and would have done well to reject the marriage proposal put forward by Napoleon III. But it was a fine alliance; the suggested bride for the heir to Monaco was a daughter of the Duke of Hamilton, Lady Mary Victoria, to whom Napoleon III was slightly related. Through her mother, Princess Marie of Baden, Lady Mary was a grand-daughter of Stéphanie de Beauharnais. She was a lovely girl, with a gentle nature, and very wealthy too; and was eighteen, to his twenty. All the usual requirements were present, and the two seemed suited to each other; only one thing was lacking—love. Neither of them wanted this marriage that was being forced upon them by their parents, and found difficulty in resigning themselves to it.

Still, Albert Grimaldi spent the month of August, 1869, at Baden-Baden, at the Hamilton house there, and the young couple's fears were reduced. They got to know each other, and thought they would be able to come to an understanding, perhaps even to love each other. If she was very pretty, he was most attractive. Neatly built, with a keen and independent look in his pale eyes, which contrasted with his dark hair, he was sensitive, wiry, and had an authoritative bearing. Though distant at times, at others he was full of charm and kindness; like a thoroughbred racehorse, he was both strong and graceful. But, again like a thoroughbred, he liked to be free and had a horror of any constraint. If he needed a wife who was docile and understanding, the couple together needed especially an independent life away from both their families.

Their marriage contract was signed in Louis Napoleon's study at St Cloud on September 18th, 1869. Three days later the wedding took place at Marchais; the civil ceremony was held first, in the main salon of the château, and the religious ceremony in the chapel that had been built for the Dukes of Lorraine. There was a banquet for the guests, and festivities for the villagers which ended at dusk with a grand fireworks display.

After a few weeks spent in Switzerland, and a visit to Baden-Baden, the young married couple went to live at Monaco at the beginning of December. She was starting a difficult pregnancy and was tired and low-spirited, and probably sad at having left her mother and the country she knew. If the atmosphere at the palace had been more welcoming, she might have been less scared by her new life with her husband's family. But a gloom lay over the Court; in addition to the infirmity of Charles III, there was the recent bereavement of his sister. The Duchess of Urach had taken charge of the household and was already beginning to dominate it.

This restricted atmosphere frightened the young wife; it annoyed her husband too;[1] and their loose understanding, which needed many quiet months to consolidate, broke apart. Early in February, 1870, Mary Hamilton left Monaco, and in spite of the affectionate attempts of the grandmother, Princess Caroline, never went back again.[2]

---

[1] Albert wrote to his father on February 20th, 1870, shortly after his wife had left him, to say that he had seen Napoleon III and the Empress, and that the former was against the action his second cousin had taken. Albert went on to say in his letter that 'we should try to meet together, Mary and I, just by ourselves, but that's the difficulty.' Those last words reveal much.

[2] 'My dear Mary,' Princess Caroline wrote on February 5th, 1870. 'My grandson's grief has so saddened me that I'm writing direct to you, to make an appeal to your heart. Can you not forgive Albert for what you reproach him with? The tender love you have aroused in him will give him the strength to change his ways, he has assured me, and to do all he can to make you happy. . . . I'm sure that for your part, my dear Mary, you must feel that a wife is the link of her family. . . .'

The young wife replied from Nice two days later: 'My dear grandmother. I was greatly touched by your letter, and I thank you for all its affection for me. The best memory I have of the recent sad time is the kindness you showed towards me. I am most grateful for this memory, which eases the bitterness of the weeks I spent at Monaco. . . .'

She gave birth to a son at Baden-Baden on July 12th, 1870, who was christened Louis-Honoré-Charles-Antoine.

There can be little doubt that Albert Grimaldi must have had a feeling of relief, of escape, at the break-up of this marriage he had been forced into; and when the Franco-Prussian war began he went off to serve in the French Navy. He was with the North Sea Fleet at first, aboard the *Savoie*, and then with Admiral Fournichon's squadron, on the *Couronne*. After the war, he was awarded the Legion of Honour for his services.

As his father did not admit him into the affairs of the Principality, and the baby, Louis, was being brought up at Baden, Albert went cruising again; this time on a boat of his own, that he bought at Torquay in 1873, the *Pleiades*, which he renamed *L'Hirondelle*. In *The Career of a Navigator* he described with great feeling his impressions when in command of a vessel for the first time.

Two years later he was in Spain, and the new monarch, Alphonso XII, promoted him to naval captain.

In that year, 1875, urged on by his father, Albert Grimaldi tried to resume relations with his wife. He had never written to her during the five years they had been living apart. Now he asked for news of his son, and for photographs of him. She complied, where the boy was concerned; but refused to meet her husband. Application was made to the Vatican for an annulment of the marriage. The proceedings lasted more than four years, but finally the annulment was granted. Six months later, on July 28th, 1880, Charles III published the dissolution of the civil marriage of his heir. Lady Mary had been married again, to a Hungarian Count, a month previously. . . .

During these few years when the loose marriage-knot was being untied, Albert Grimaldi had been studying under Professor Milne-Edwards, who had decided him to specialize in the new science of oceanography. Albert discovered that it lacked the necessary instruments and equipment, and that these had first to be constructed and developed. Then, in 1885, he took *L'Hirondelle* (this one was a vessel of 200 tons and carried a crew of fifteen) on his first research voyage, the first of twenty-seven that were to establish a foremost position for him in the subject of oceanography.

He began by studying the drift of surface currents in the North Atlantic, the Gulf Stream in particular, using specially designed floats. In following years he succeeded in dredging the sea-bed at a depth of nearly 10,000 feet, operating with drag-nets over a considerable area. It took three and a half hours to lower the special equipment, more than nine to raise it again.

On his return from these research voyages he continued his work in the laboratory with eminent colleagues chosen by himself, and published his findings. He was welcomed in scientific circles, where he made many good friends—and on occasion declared that the world had no need of princes, but of men with intelligence and scientific learning. At forty, Albert Grimaldi was set for a great future in the scientific world, when the death of his father brought the responsibilities of the Principality upon him.

For the past fifteen years, the new Prince of Monaco had been accustomed to having sole command of his ship; and he meant to have sole command, after God, of the Rock, the ship of stone anchored in the Mediterranean. But a captain's authority is freely accepted by the crew; and so Albert Grimaldi wished for his accession to be freely accepted by the Monagasques, for a bond to be established between him and his subjects. The heads of the local families were summoned according to ancient custom, and on October 23rd, 1889, they assembled in the main courtyard of the palace and gave the oath of loyalty; this was the first time the ceremony had been held for 165 years, since the fourth Duke of Valentinois had taken the young Honoré III to receive the oath.

Some weeks later, in Paris, Prince Albert married a second time. His bride was Alice Heine, a young American who had been widowed after a short marriage to the Duke of Richelieu. This fresh attempt at matrimony began under the happiest of auspices.[1] Alice Heine was intelligent as well as a pretty blonde, and brought some sparkle and gaiety to a palace where the atmosphere had been dull and sad for many years. As Duchess of Richelieu she had held a brilliant salon at her Paris house, in the Faubourg St Honoré, that was frequented by society people

---

[1] It lasted longer than Albert's first marriage, but was dissolved after twelve years, on May 30th, 1902.

and many connected with the arts. As Princess of Monaco she now drew them to the Principality, which had had a theatre of its own for the past decade.

It had been built at Monte Carlo by Charles Garnier, the architect who carried the responsibility for the new Opera House in Paris. The opening ceremony had taken place on January 25th, 1879, in the presence of Charles III and the Duchess of Urach. Sarah Bernhardt read a prologue written by Jean Aicard about a sleeping beauty in a grotto below the Spélugues; the noises of the building of the theatre had not troubled her dreams, but its orchestra conducted by Romeo Accursi had succeeded in rousing her from a long sleep. . . . Sarah Bernhardt then presented the architect with a large bouquet of flowers, to thank him for having revived the arts of Praxiteles, Apelles, Polygnotes, and Pheidias.

Praxiteles and company might have been rather astonished at this, for neither the greenish, bulbous dome to the building nor the interior decorations recalled Greek simplicity of line. There were florid frescoes along the walls, gilt cherubs on the pillars, and gilded statues of Nubian slaves brandished massive candelabra.

However, the theatre had a great success. The performances were good enough, and as they were only intended to fill in a gap between dinner and the gaming-tables, or to provide a change between sessions with the croupiers, the seats were free.

Ever since the day in May, 1858, when as a boy he had laid the foundation stone of the Casino, Albert Grimaldi had kept his distance from Monte Carlo. But the facts of the situation were obvious. The revenues from the gaming concession had allowed Charles III to put the Principality on its feet again and then to develop and extend the activities of his government. On this solid administrative basis established by his father, Albert I intended to create artistic works and found scientific institutions that would give international renown to the Principality of Monaco.

While still patiently pursuing his scientific career, the Prince agreed with his wife that the theatre ought to have a life of its own, to attract music-lovers and playgoers, and not merely gamblers having a short break from watching the spinning roulette-wheel. And so, in 1892, Princess Alice got Raoul Guns-bourg to come to Monte Carlo. This famous impresario was to manage the theatre for more than fifty years, making it one of the best known and most brilliant in the world. He put on Wagner operas, which previously had been performed only at Bayreuth, and presented the chief works of Massenet for the first time. Plays were given too, and the Comédie Française often sent a company to Monte Carlo. Later, in the twentieth century, there was the glory of Diaghilev and the Russian Ballet. In time, the expenses of the theatre increased to such an extent that charges had to be made for seats. . . .

While the Princess was presiding over the development of the arts, the Prince was governing with a firm hand and continuing his scientific researches with greater means at his disposal. In 1891 he took possession of a three-masted schooner of 600 tons, ordered from Green's shipbuilding yard in London. She was equipped with an auxiliary engine of 350 h.p. and had a small laboratory; a specialist in zoology, Doctor Jules Richard, was appointed to take charge of the laboratory, which remained in his care for the next twenty years. Albert named the schooner the *Princess Alice*; he made several research and survey voyages in her during the years 1892–97,[1] and reached depths of nearly three miles in the ocean south-west of the Azores. These depths were surveyed, and samples taken, and were given the name of Monaco Ditch.

Increasing revenues enabled Prince Albert, from 1898 onwards, to give much aid to the scientific world and to extend his work for peace.

A general meeting of shareholders in the *Société des Bains de Mer* was held on January 11th, 1898, and five days later an agreement was signed by Ritt, the governor-general of the Principality, and Camille Blanc, the son and heir of François Blanc, which extended the gaming concession for fifty years from that date.

---

[1] She was replaced in 1897 by the *Princess Alice II*, a vessel of 1,400 tons, with a 1,000 h.p. engine and a speed of thirteen knots. Her captain until 1906 was an Englishman, H. Carr. The ship's special equipment included a cable enabling depths of 30,000 feet to be reached and loads up to seven tons to be raised. She was succeeded in 1911 by *L'Hirondelle II*, a slightly larger ship, and with her Prince Albert extended his voyages to Spitzbergen and Cape Verde.

In return, the company was to pay ten million francs on the signing of the agreement, and fifteen million in 1913—the year when the 1863 agreement would have expired. Another five million was to be paid for work on improving the harbour.[1] The annual payments were to be: 1,250,000 francs plus three per cent. on the first twenty-five million staked on the gaming-tables, and five per cent. above that figure. In addition, the company became responsible for bringing piped water into the Principality, in sufficient quantity to wash down the streets and drains; for providing gas to light the palace and government buildings, the public buildings, and the streets and avenues; for printing the weekly official gazette and annual directory; for the street-cleaning and refuse-collecting; in short, the company took over most of the cost of the municipal services. Finally, it was to subsidize the theatre by an annual sum of 24,000 francs for each play or opera put on, up to a total of 600,000 francs.

The revenues provided by this agreement were used on public works and social benefits, on art exhibitions, and, especially, on grants to scientific bodies and the founding of scientific institutions. By 1912, the donations made by Prince Albert in the scientific sphere had amounted to nearly fifteen million francs.

He had originally intended to build a museum at Monaco to hold the results of the voyages he had made since 1885; but he enlarged this conception, and planned a museum that would present all aspects of oceanography. The site chosen, in conjunction with his architect, Delefortrie, was a splendid one, on the south side of the Rock itself, at the end of the St Martin gardens; there, on the edge of the cliff, it would look out over the depths of the sea.

The foundation stone of the Oceanic Museum was laid on April 25th, 1899.[2] Representatives of both France and Germany were present at the ceremony, and in his speech Prince Albert showed he had inherited the tactful diplomacy of his predecessors.

---

[1] The work was begun in July, 1901. The harbour was drained and deepened, to receive ships of greater tonnage; two quays were built, one on the south side for commercial use, the other on the north for private yachts and pleasure-boats. The harbour entrance was protected by the building of two converging jetties.

[2] The Museum was opened in 1910. In addition to the aquatic collections of Albert I and those made by the present Prince, it contains equipment used in deep-sea research, a library of scientific works, laboratories for the use of research-workers, and aquariums that are celebrated for the variety and rarity of their contents.

It was a time when Franco-Prussian relations were at their worst since 1870. Albert I spoke of the world-wide influence of French civilization, and recalled that he had served in the French Navy in 1870; he then praised the German Emperor and said how sincere were his efforts for the peace of the world.

The Prince of Monaco believed that the advances being made by science would bring happiness to the world; but for those advances to continue, peace had to be maintained. In the course of a two-months' voyage on the *Princess Alice*, the French physiologist, Professor Charles Richet, easily converted the Prince to his pacifist ideas. As a result, Albert I made a decision that—as usual with him—was soon acted upon. After organizing a Peace Congress that was held at Monaco in the spring of 1902, he founded an International Peace Institute, in February, 1903, and gave it the mission of studying means of settling differences between nations by arbitration; of propagating international understanding, and of eliminating hatred from people's hearts.[1] That was effect given to the theoretical side of his ideas. On the practical side, believing that the deterioration in Franco-Prussian relations constituted a permanent risk of war, he considered that with his French sympathies and education, and being also a sincere friend of the Kaiser, he could serve better than anyone as a link between the two countries and perhaps prevent the spark being struck that would set Europe alight; and so, for twelve years from 1898, he gave himself to this self-imposed and thankless task with courage, skill, and disinterestedness.

The agitation for a retrial in the Dreyfus case had begun in November, 1897, but almost a year passed before fresh revelations led the French government to set the judicial machinery in motion. It was well known—by William II more than anyone— that the foreign Power implicated in the case (on whose behalf Dreyfus was alleged to have been spying) was Germany. But the Emperor could not intervene officially to announce that Dreyfus was innocent. When the retrial began, he seized the opportunity of the Prince of Monaco being in Berlin to ask him to convey to the French President, Félix Faure, the explicit assurances of the German Emperor that Dreyfus was innocent. Albert I saw the

[1] This Institute was transferred from Monaco to Paris in 1912.

President of the French Republic at five in the evening of February 16th, 1899. The interview lasted twenty minutes. At six o'clock the President was dead, from a stroke. Félix Faure had been opposed to the re-opening of the Dreyfus affair, and the story got around that his death had been brought on by the positive statement made by the Prince of Monaco on behalf of the German Emperor. This version of the circumstances of the President's death was kinder than the actual facts; but Albert I said later that he had found Félix Faure so listless and inattentive that he gave up all idea of serious talk.[1]

Some months later, the Prince of Monaco wrote to Madame Dreyfus to invite her acquitted husband to stay at the palace—'I shall be honoured by his visit.'

He again played the part of a semi-official intermediary at the time of the Tangier crisis, brought about by French and German rivalry over Morocco. In Berlin, the Prince patiently put forward the views of the French Prime Minister, Rouvier, and he was able to return to Paris the bearer of satisfying assurances from the Germans. Time seemed to him so important that as soon as he reached Paris he hastened straight to the Foreign Office. There he was told that Rouvier was at the Chamber of Deputies, where a critical debate was taking place. Albert I tried to reach the Prime Minister by telephone, only to learn that the government had just fallen. . . .

This apparent success of the policy of the German militarists led to the International Conference of Algéciras; but France, supported by Britain and Italy, came well out of it.

The fact that the crisis had been created by German policy caused Albert I to have doubts, but he was not yet discouraged. In April, 1907, when the Monte Carlo theatre company was giving

[1] Princess Radziwil wrote in a letter to General de Robilant on June 7th, 1899: 'Bülow dined with us this evening. He broached the subject himself. . . . The Emperor greatly regretted not being able to do anything more to save the two innocent men.

'"What—do nothing *more*? Then it's true, the mission the Emperor gave to the Prince of Monaco?"

'"How do you know about that, and where did you learn about this supposed mission?" '

The Princess explained, and the German Chancellor ended by admitting: 'I believe it's true; I know the Emperor spoke to the Prince of Monaco about the Dreyfus case, and that the Prince's conversation with President Faure was the last the President had before the imprudent incident that caused his sudden death.'

performances in Berlin, he renewed his hopes in the Kaiser, in whom he discerned 'a legitimate pride in the great promise that scientific advances gave for the peace of the world . . . and in the first glimmer of artistic feeling in Berlin.' But a few more years were probably enough for the Prince of Monaco to cease to believe in the usefulness of his self-imposed task. Perhaps he could already see that 'sly expression' on the faces of the men surrounding the Kaiser? In any case, at the time of the Agadir crisis in 1911 the Prince of Monaco kept well out of it.[1]

Meanwhile, since the foundation stone of the Oceanic Museum had been laid, Albert I had continued creating museums and scientific institutions. In 1882 and '83, while preparing for his first sea expeditions, he had become interested in prehistoric archæology and began to explore the caves near Menton, called the 'Roches Rouges,' which were known about but had never been properly examined. In 1895 he completed his diggings and brought to light two examples of the Cro-Magnon period, but of a negroid species new to anthropologists. He also discovered many fossilized remains of animals that were either extinct or no longer native to Europe.

The Prince housed these finds in a museum, which was opened in 1902, together with other prehistoric remains discovered in the grottoes of the St Martin gardens and of the Observatory, and parts of skeletons from the Spélugues grottoes which were evidence of their occupation during the neolithic age; added to these were souvenirs of Roman times, in particular the jewels that constitute the Treasure of Monaco.

But Albert I knew that something more than museums was needed—that the new sciences needed the lecturers and research facilities that would enable succeeding generations to extend the knowledge gained. So, on April 25th, 1906, he founded the

[1] In his *The German War and World Conscience,* that Albert I published in 1919, he sadly recalls the hopes he had placed in Kaiser William, and addresses him thus: 'On several occasions, in agreement with you and Prince Radolin, I spoke to Chancellor Bülow about the relations between France and Germany being deliberately jeopardized by the policy of barbarous militarists or politicians determined to prevent any reconciliation. But the Chancellor always gave me the impression his mind was firmly set.' Albert I concluded: 'Today, I think the German militarists merely allowed you, until about the year 1910, to play upon a general desire for peace, no doubt to mislead world opinion. . . .'

Institute of Oceanography. It included the Museum at Monaco; but the Institute itself was established in Paris. The latter was given a large grant, and was independent of the French State; inaugurated in 1911, it had a French governing board and an international consultative committee of specialists.

The foundation was followed four years later by that of the Institute of Human Palæontology, which was also established in Paris. Courses in geology, palæontology, prehistoric anthropology, and ethnography, were given at the Institute during the winters. It too had a French governing board and an international committee.

While Albert I's beneficence was establishing a work that has brought him world renown, his prosperous Principality was showing signs of discontent.

Back in 1895, the Monagasques had sent a delegation to Marchais to ask Prince Albert that more of the work in the Principality should be given to local-born people. But how could the Prince insist on private companies employing certain people merely because they had been born at Monaco or on the Spélugues? It was not possible, in those days, and nothing had resulted from this self-interested approach. Nevertheless, the more enlightened and active members of the population were pressing for a greater say in the economic policy and the governing of the Principality. It was a difficult problem, for the number of Monagasques by birth or naturalization was greatly exceeded by the number of foreigners residing in the Principality—1,200 as against 16,000, early in the 1900's—and the latter controlled most of the trade and business, and so formed the richest part of the population.[1] Several attempts were made to find a solution. In 1907, a kind of Trade-promotion Board was set up, consisting of twenty-four members chosen by the Prince from a list drawn up by a general commission. It lasted barely two years, and was replaced in May, 1909, by a Chamber of Commerce with twenty-nine members and a few senior civil servants. This only lasted

[1] At the municipal elections in 1910 there were 617 voters—97 being Monagasques by birth, 520 by naturalization.
A census in 1868 had given the population as 3,343. In 1888 it was 9,684, and in 1921, 23,418. It is still around 23,000 at the present day.

until July, when a governing council was formed, but which had an even shorter life.

Public agitation continued, and early in 1910 a committee presented to the Prince the demands of his subjects. Although Albert I was a natural authoritarian, having a sense of discipline and of values, he had a liberal mind and was anxious for the public good. He acceded to the people's demands for universal suffrage, and on June 19th, 1910, a municipal council was duly elected.

The Prince addressed a word of warning to the councillors, in a letter to the mayor on June 29th: 'This small Principality which has earned an honourable place among the peoples of the world, by its worthy history throughout the centuries, must not be allowed to become the victim of the ambitions and speculations that politics arouse. Its princes have given it a prestige that must not be allowed to incur the jeers of outsiders; and the trust they have gained for it must not be weakened. . . .'

On October 16th, 1910, the mayor announced that the Prince had extended his concessions to include the granting of a Constitution. A few days later the heir, Louis, arrived in Monaco as his father's delegate. A month later, in Paris, Albert I greeted the four Monagasque delegates, Reymond, Antoine Marsan, Gastaud, and De Castro, who were to give their views to the three French jurists, Louis Renault, André Weiss, and Jules Roche, charged with the framing of the Constitution.

It was approved by the Prince on January 5th, 1911, and accepted two days later by the upper council of Monaco. Under this Constitution, a public domain came into being, taken from the private domain of the Prince, and the expenditure of the Principality was separated into two lists—a civil and a public. The former covered the Prince's household, the Church and the law courts; while the latter covered public works, schools and fine arts, hospital and health services, and public assistance, these expenditures being voted and controlled by a general council, and finally there was the municipal budget. The Constitution defined the rights of the Monagasques, and set up a governing body composed of a Minister of State and three Counsellors acting under the Prince. Legislative power was vested in the Prince and a general council of twenty-one members elected for four years by universal suffrage; its chairman and vice-chairman to be nominated by the Prince. The Principality was divided into three communes for administrative purposes—Monaco, Conda-mine, and Monte Carlo—each to have a municipal council of eleven members elected for a three-year term, who nominated its mayor and deputy mayor.

On February 10th, Albert I arrived by train at Monaco—'The silence was broken only by the booming of the gun, firing its salute at regular intervals. Cheering and clapping at last broke out. . . . A car came along the two solid ranks of spectators. In it were the Prince and his son, and a couple of officials. Cheers sounded from left and right as the car passed by at a moderate speed. . . . The Prince acknowledged them with a motion of his head and his hand, very calmly and much at ease.'

So the sovereign prince renewed contact with his people after many months of absence on his part, of agitation on theirs. The population showed by its welcome that it was not forgetting the Grimaldis remained the only real guarantee of the independence and prosperity of the Rock of Monaco.

But men are never satisfied. Calm did not return to Monaco; and the agitation only died down when the Great War began, and the Prince took the opportunity to suspend the Constitution, on October 8th, 1914.

Nearly every year Albert I went to Kiel, and he was there for the Regatta in June, 1914. On Sunday, the 28th, he was with the Kaiser on board the *Meteor* when they noticed a launch coming towards them. Standing up near the helmsman was Admiral Müller, waving a piece of paper. The launch came alongside, the Admiral put the paper into his cigarette-case and threw it up to the deck of the *Meteor*. When the Kaiser opened it he found a telegram inside announcing the assassination of the Archduke Ferdinand at Sarajevo. The Kaiser went white, let the telegram flutter to the deck, and said, 'Now I must begin all over again!' Was he alluding to some agreement he had made with the Arch-duke of Austria a few days previously? Probably. The exclamation was above all a foreboding that the Kaiser was to be overridden by those who wanted a war.

The Prince of Monaco returned to Paris, and was still there

when general mobilization was proclaimed. 'What stupidity! The best of both nations is going to be sacrificed,' he cried in despair. 'The manager of a stud who acted like this would be dismissed!'

He went to Monaco and lived aboard the *Hirondelle II*, moored in the harbour; while his son rejoined the French Army. Albert I proclaimed the neutrality of the Principality, but willingly allowed hospitals and convalescent homes for Allied soldiers to be set up there.

The shattering of one of the dearest dreams of this great European saddened him deeply, and the war with its trail of death and destruction tormented this sincere pacifist. The entry of the United States into the war, whose soldiers he considered were 'coming to help Europe in a final fight against oppression,' revived his hopes in the future of mankind. Later, he had faith in President Wilson and his ideal of a League of Nations.

In spite of his anguish of mind, Albert I had not neglected his tasks as a ruler. On November 17th, 1917, the Constitution was re-established, but with important modifications. Administrative and judiciary powers were separated; a department for external relations was created, under the direction of the Prince; the general council was reduced to twelve members; the three communes and their councils disappeared and were replaced by a single municipal council to consist of fifteen members with a mayor and three deputy mayors.

Only Monagasques could be elected to the general and municipal councils, which meant only a small minority of the population. But it would have been both dangerous and unfair not to give the majority opportunities to express opinion, and so on June 19th, 1920, a consultative Chamber of Commerce came into being, representing trade and business and professional interests of foreigners living in the Principality. Two years later, Albert I studied the Constitution again, and instituted a Finance Committee responsible for the preparation of the Budget.

Previously, the Prince had negotiated a new Treaty with France, replacing the 1861 Treaty. It was signed on July 17th, 1918. France guaranteed to defend the independence and sovereignty of the Principality, and the Prince undertook in return to exercise his rights in conformity with the political, military, and economic interests of France. From this main principle developed other Articles: agreement over the international relations of the Principality, and over the regency or succession, which must go only to a Monagasque or a French subject; the ceding of all or part of the Principality was possible only to France; should there be no heir or heiress and the line become extinct,[1] Monaco was to be formed into an autonomous State and become a French Protectorate; military and naval forces were allowed into the Principality if its security and that of France were threatened.

As though to reward a life so largely devoted to the advances of science and humanity, the year 1920 brought Albert I much private satisfaction and world acclaim.

On March 20th, Princess Charlotte, the daughter of Louis, was married to Count Pierre de Polignac; and at the end of the year a daughter, Antoinette, was born to them. And so a new branch, the Grimaldi-Polignac, burgeoned on the old tree of the Grimaldis. This assurance of the continuance of his line, through his grand-daughter, a brunette with light blue eyes who resembled him, must have sweetened the last years of this old man in his lonely grandeur.

The French President, Paul Deschanel, paid an official visit to Monaco, as predecessors of his had done in 1896 and in 1909, and thus gave proof of the close interest of France in the Principality.

Then the American Academy of Science awarded Albert I its gold medal for the year, and he went to Washington to receive it.

The year before, at an international conference on hydrography held in London, the setting up of an international centre had been decided on and the delegates had unanimously voted for it to be at Monaco, 'because of the renown given to the Principality by the Prince's fine work on the subject of oceanography.' This tribute gave much pleasure to the Prince, as much as his election ten years previously to the Royal Society, as a foreign member.

His long and noble life, so usefully employed for the benefit

---

[1] At this time, there was only one person in the line of succession at each generation—Albert I, Louis, and Louis's daughter, Charlotte. If she had no children, the heirs were the descendants of Florestine, Duchess of Urach, and her husband. But the French government would not accept a German as the ruler of Monaco.

of mankind, came to an end on June 26th, 1922, in Paris. He had been not only a great patron of science but also a most eminent member of that world which knows no frontiers. His father had brought prosperity to Monaco; he had brought it renown and made of it a place where international talents flourished.

CHAPTER X

MODERN TIMES (1922–1961)

IT WAS A DIFFICULT TASK to succeed Albert I; it would be still more difficult to find anyone more unlike him than his son. If this dissimilarity had sometimes prevented understanding between father and son, nevertheless it was to give the dynasty a fresh opportunity. Louis II, a stable and sensible man, knew how much he differed from his sad but brilliant father. He therefore made no attempt to follow in the footsteps of Albert I, but wisely and realistically set his own course. This eventually enabled him to meet and overcome the difficult times between the two World Wars, and so to prepare the way for a new prosperity in a world greatly changed.

Louis Grimaldi had grown up at Baden-Baden, a much-loved child and rather spoilt by those around him; but he had 'an even, good-tempered and docile nature,' as his mother wrote in October, 1876. Prince Albert could have claimed his son as soon as he reached the age of seven, and it was perhaps on the sensible advice of Princess Caroline that he did not do so. This sailor, still passionately pursuing a life of independence, would have been a somewhat absent-minded and distant supervisor of studies, and the little boy would have been very lonely at Monaco or Marchais, surrounded by aged and ailing relatives.

But after Mary Hamilton had married again, she divided her time between Vienna and her husband's estate in Hungary. This changed the situation. Moreover, it was time for the heir to the Principality to receive a French education and visit Monaco. During the summer of 1880 father and son became acquainted.

'I am much affected by all that Your Highness has written about Louis, and am glad to hear of the good impression received during the meeting with this dear child, so beloved by all of us,'

242

wrote Louis's mother, on September 4th, 1880. 'Your Highness must have seen that our aim during these ten years has been to surround Louis not only with the deep and tender affection he arouses in us, but also to shelter him from anything which might shock or hurt him. He was very pleased to see you, Sir; he often speaks about the meeting, but never makes any reference to the past. He takes everything so naturally, and we should thank God for it, and try to keep this delightful frankness intact as long as possible.'

There is no doubt that Louis owed his gay nature and his direct approach to the realities of life to this happy childhood at Baden.

Albert I's love of the sea had shown itself at an early age; his son's love for the army was equally strong and equally quick to affirm itself. He became a cadet at St Cyr, and then went into the cavalry. He was a good-looking young man of twenty, still gay and easy-going; but the change from his early environment, and the passage of the years, had turned his childhood docility into dogged patience and serene independence. He was an excellent horseman and a first-class shot; he enjoyed amateur acting, at which he was extremely good, and was a lively companion.

As Prince Albert followed his father's policy of not allowing his son any part in state affairs, Louis considered himself free to live a man's life—which for him meant a soldier's life. At his own request he was posted to the army in North Africa, to the Foreign Legion, and as second-lieutenant he accompanied two reconnaissance groups penetrating southern Algeria. In 1895 he was awarded the Legion of Honour for gallantry in the field. As his father had received the same high award, when a naval lieutenant, another tradition was beginning in the Grimaldi family.

Louis always had very happy memories of the ten years he spent with the army in North Africa—the tune he most often asked the orchestra of the Hôtel de Paris to play was 'The March of the Foreign Legion.' In the hard, rough military life, Louis acquired a knowledge of men that is uncommon among princes; he made staunch friends, for in addition to being a fine soldier he was an unassuming and trustworthy comrade.

But in order to equip himself for his rôle of heir to the Principality he was obliged to give up his military career. His first statesman-like act, it will be remembered, was at the difficult moment in October, 1910, when he arrived in Monaco as his father's delegate.

On general mobilization in August, 1914, Louis Grimaldi rejoined the French Army. He was on the staff of the First Army, then of the Fifth, and was several times mentioned in despatches. The first, on December 2nd, 1915, was for his active initiative as a liaison officer: 'Showed outstanding courage and coolness while undertaking various missions at the front.' The second mentioned several dangerous missions, and added: 'Insisted on helping the inhabitants of a village recaptured from the enemy which he was the first to enter, while still under heavy bombardment.' A third, in April, 1919, read: 'An energetic officer who, on April 16th, 1917, and following days showed great resource at the Chemin des Dames. As liaison officer between Army Headquarters and the divisions engaged, he crossed ground under heavy fire, with complete disregard for his own safety, to get information needed by the high command, and everywhere sustained morale with his good humour, complete coolness, and unshakable faith in ultimate success.'

He ended the War as a colonel, and in 1920 became a Grand Officer of the Legion of Honour. He remained in uniform, and was on the staff of General Le Rond, supervising the plebiscite in Upper Silesia, when the news of his father's death caused him to return to Monaco.[1]

The Principality was still prosperous; however, the War had brought its flourishing activities to a halt, and had considerably reduced the resources of the *Société des Bains de Mer*. In 1918 Camille Blanc had had to ask Prince Albert to accept a reduction in the annual payments. The Prince would not agree to this, and had called in Basil Zaharof, who bought out Camille Blanc and appointed his own managing-directors.[2] This change, coming at a time when world conditions were unstable and a new clientèle was coming to Monte Carlo, created feelings of uncertainty in

[1] Louis II was later promoted to brigadier and then to major-general; and on October 12th, 1929, he was awarded the *Médaille Militaire*, the highest French distinction for staff officers.

[2] In 1925, Zaharof sold his interests in the Casino to a group of Paris bankers, who in 1953 sold out to the Greek shipowner, Onassis.

the Principality which for the past two generations had enjoyed a solid prosperity.

Louis II faced the future undismayed and with the quiet courage which characterized him. He undertook to complete his father's work, and at the same time to ensure the inheritance for his grandson, Rainier, who was born on May 31st, 1923.

The improvements being made to the harbour, begun by Albert I in 1901, were completed. A tunnel was driven under the Rock, to allow merchandise to be transported direct from the harbour to the land on the west of the Rock which had been reclaimed from the sea. There, the industrial suburb of Fontvieille was growing up, with its brewery, its electric power-station, and its flour-mill. In 1931, Albert I's last foundation, the International Hydrographic Centre, was opened. And finally, the choir-school that Monseigneur Perruchot had started in 1904 was given increased support by Louis II. On his initiative, a Society of Friends of the Choir-school to aid it socially and financially was founded in 1935.[1]

After some political disagreement that resulted in the dissolution of the Councils in 1930, the following year was a turning point in the reign of Louis II. The President of the French Republic, Gaston Doumergue, paid an official visit to Monaco; and the Prince went to North Africa to preside with Marshal Franchet d'Espèrey and the Governor-General of Algeria at the centenary celebrations of the Foreign Legion, which were held at Sidi-bel-Abbès. Even at the age of sixty, and after ten years' rule, it was easy to see in Louis II the young lieutenant who had gone so gaily into battle in southern Algeria. After this farewell to his youth, he devoted himself entirely to his task as sovereign prince, which became increasingly burdensome owing to the world economic crisis.

The depression had spread from the United States to Britain. People still holidayed and gambled at Monte Carlo, but there was not the prosperity of former times. Then came a severe blow; in 1933 the French government allowed roulette and *trente et quarante* to be played in French casinos. Italy followed suit, not only at the Venice Lido but also at San Remo. Monte Carlo had

[1] Rainier III has since appointed Nadia Boulanger, the international concert-pianist, to be its precentor.

lost its monopoly. Two years later, for the first time since it was established, the *Société des Bains de Mer* showed a deficit. The managing-director resigned, the staff accepted a cut in salaries, and a loan of nine million francs was obtained to help the company over a difficult period.

This occurrence was no surprise to the Prince of Monaco, with his knowledge of the world. But he had been following with great interest the growing importance of tourism and sport in the modern world; and he turned to these to help the Casino provide prosperity for the Principality.

Visitors who stayed for long periods had almost vanished; in their place were tourists who came for a few days, and who usually wanted some small souvenir to take away with them. It was a time, too, when the hobby of stamp-collecting was on the increase, and some of the early series of Monaco stamps—dating back to Charles III—had already acquired real value. In 1936, Louis II set up a department for the issuing of postage stamps, which supplied finely engraved series for souvenir hunters as well as for philatelists all over the world. By the late 1940s, there were more than 25,000 buyers of each new set.

In 1911 the International Car Rally of Monte Carlo had been inaugurated, and soon became a world tourist championship. The Rally was started again after the War. The competitors set out from distant points in Europe to reach Monte Carlo by routes devised so that they cover the same number of miles, facing ice, snow, gales, and fog on the way.

Prince Louis could see a great future for the motor-car, and was aware of the spirit of competition and love of risk in the youth of the period; and so in 1929 he encouraged the Automobile Club of Monaco to found the Grand Prix of Monte Carlo. This is also known as 'The Race of a Thousand Turns.' A hundred circuits are made around the town, and because of the twists and turns the competitors have to change gear more than 2,000 times in a race of some 200 miles. Only twenty drivers, chosen from among the best in the world, are invited to take part in this gruelling test, which each year attracts more than 100,000 spectators.

But motor-car racing was the sport of only a few. Louis II wanted to provide the means for his subjects and visitors to participate in athletics in greater numbers. For that a stadium was needed—and therefore vacant land, which was rare in the Principality. However, the Grimaldis had given proof of dogged-ness and ingenuity for over six centuries. The Prince engaged the necessary technicians, and by 1939 sufficient land had been reclaimed from the sea; at the foot of the Rock the Louis II Stadium was moored for all time.

Albert I had dreamed of world peace; Louis II, more realistically, did not expect an end could be put to conflicts, but he wanted to try to make them more humane. An international conference took place in 1934 at the palace of Monaco, at which the Prince proposed that certain towns should be declared 'open' in the event of war. He was also interested in a project for an international status for doctors; this received the name of the Monaco Project. These were noble but vain attempts to stem the rising tide of barbarism. . . .

September, 1939, saw the exodus of foreigners from Monaco, but soon the 'phoney war' took charge in the little State, as it did in France and Britain. There was a further exodus after the German break-through in May, 1940; but it was the entry of Italy into the war that was fatal for Monaco. A fortnight later, Italian troops entered the Principality, violating its neutrality. They remained until 1943, when the Germans took over. There was no real Resistance Movement in the Principality, but two Mona-gasques were executed in August, 1944, for having become members of a group. Mrs Tranchard, who kept the Scotch Tea-Rooms at Monte Carlo, several times helped British and American pilots, in addition to refugees arriving via La Turbie.

On August 15th, 1944, the Franco-American landings began in southern France, and the Allied forces quickly advanced up the Rhône valley towards Lyon. Rainier Grimaldi enlisted in the First French Army. In the meantime, Monaco had been liberated. On September 3rd a taxi with two American soldiers in it arrived on the Place d'Armes in front of the palace; they had lost their way, and were not followed by other troops. The American command respected the neutrality of the Principality.

Louis II died on May 9th, 1949, after several months of illness courageously borne. Just before, at the end of April, he had delegated his powers to his grandson, Rainier.

By his patient perseverance, Louis II had been able to consolidate the work of his predecessors sufficiently for it to survive the Second World War, and the Italian and German occupations. He, the last of the Grimaldi-Matignons, was the first Prince to die at Monaco since Antoine I, the last of the Grimaldi male line. An ancient tradition was thus restored. So, too, was the old custom whereby the Prince's coffin was carried by representatives of old Monagasque families dressed in the black-and-white robes of penitents.

The man who succeeded him as Rainier III had been a bonny, fair baby when his godmother, the Duchess of Vendôme, had held him to be christened. When three years old he had dressed up in the uniform of a little *carabinier*, being almost hidden under a helmet like a London policeman's. Later, he was a sturdy, open-faced lad playing with boys of his own age; and then an athletic schoolboy, the champion boxer at his weight at Summerfields school at St Leonards-on-sea, in Sussex.

At the beginning of September, 1939, he arrived at Rosey College, near Geneva. 'This solidly built, smiling youngster, though rather shy, looked round rather uncertainly at his new surroundings,' the Headmaster, Henri Carnal, wrote later. Prince Rainier soon found his feet and took his place in the life at Rosey; he had been well prepared for it by his English education, which had naturally developed his character as well as his mind. Being cheerful and unaffected, he was popular with both his fellow-pupils and his teachers. He had plenty of energy, and was the life and soul of school dramatics, especially when plays of Labiche or Courteline were performed. Perhaps he had inherited his grandfather's natural aptitude for acting.

Switzerland was a haven of peace, and also a meeting-place for all nationalities and all shades of opinion. Rosey was a Switzerland in miniature—peaceful and international, and it had a great influence on the adolescent Prince. In those tranquil surroundings he was able to develop a sound sense of balance; and the contact with children of many races in a friendly and neutral country gave him an international outlook when still young. Rainier Grimaldi, devoted to Monaco and with decided leanings towards France, grew up to be quite at home in the vast modern world.

On leaving school he went to the University of Montpellier, and from there to study political science at Paris. When he was almost twenty-one, Princess Charlotte decided, in full agreement with Louis II, to renounce her rights to the succession in favour of her son. An edict issued on June 2nd, 1944, made Rainier Grimaldi the next heir. Less than three months later, the Allies landed in southern France; and before long the heir to Monaco had become Second Lieutenant Grimaldi in the First Algerian Infantry Regiment of the First French Army. He went through the hard winter campaign in Alsace, and on February 12th, 1945, General de Monsabert decorated him with the Croix de Guerre with Bronze Star. 'Second Lieutenant Grimaldi, having volunteered for the French Army, ably fulfilled the duties of an officer on active service. Gallantly carried out liaison duties in areas under enemy fire.' Two years later he was awarded the Legion of Honour for his military services.

The funeral ceremonies of Louis II took place on May 17th, 1949, and for six months the Grimaldi standard was flown at half-mast. But on November 18th it once again fluttered high above the old palace; and Monaco began to prepare to celebrate the accession of Rainier III.

On Easter Monday, 1950, the whole Principality seemed to be picked out in red and white. In the evening a long banner of twinkling lights spread from Monte Carlo, along the harbour front, and up to the Rock, itself deep in shadow but with the palace and the fronts of the surrounding houses floodlit and standing out brilliantly at the top. The next day, April 11th, a religious ceremony was held at the cathedral; and for the first time Rainier III wore the royal-blue uniform of a reigning Prince, with the red-and-white sash of the Order of St Charles. During the afternoon, after reviewing the guard on the Place d'Armes, Rainier III presented them with his standard; and that of Louis II, still with its bow of black crepe, was deposited in the museum. The new reign had begun, amid the rejoicings of the 2,000 Monagasques and the 25,000 other inhabitants of the Principality.

Rainier III soon proved that he intended to continue the work of his predecessors, but as a patron of letters instead of science. He founded an annual literary prize, with a selection committee of eminent French writers under the chairmanship of his father, Prince Pierre. The aim of this committee was to bring to the notice of the sovereign prince an author writing in the French language worthy of receiving the Rainier III Prize, which is awarded for the writer's complete works. Over a period of ten years this committee has shown careful judgment, for its prize-winners—Julien Green, Henri Troyat, Jean Giono, Jules Roy, Louise de Vilmorin, Marcel Brion, Jacques Perret, Hervé Bazin, Joseph Kessel, and in 1960, Alexis Curvers—are among the established authors in French literature today.

Rainier III applied himself diligently to his task as ruler, whether it concerned a commercial agreement with France, the work of the Medico-juridical committee of Monaco, the proposals made by delegates of the Principality at meetings of the World Health Organization, or the setting up of an International Academy of Tourism or the Monte Carlo T.V. station. In spite of these affairs of state, he still retained much of the unassuming, athletic youngster he had been at Rosey; he played tennis and golf well, but above all—like a true Grimaldi—he had a love of the sea. Like Albert I, he was interested in underwater research, and he too made his own equipment.

Albert I had often made difficult, and sometimes dangerous, voyages; but Rainier III's underwater exploits were even more daring. The Monagasques were proud of the champion diver who was their Prince, but they were anxious too; especially when they heard he had taken part incognito in a motor-race. The future of the dynasty, and with it the Principality, resided in one person. They asked themselves whether there would not soon be a Princess to brighten the ancient palace, and children to carry on the line.

May, 1955. The Cannes Festival was at its height and the carnival procession was making its way along the Corso. On one of the floats was a tall girl, strikingly fair and pretty, in a simple dark dress lightened by a large white bow. As she smiled gaily back at the cheering crowds, a bunch of lilies thrown towards her got caught in her silken hair and brushed against her eye. Half-closing her blue eyes, Grace Kelly laughed still more. . . .

Everyone had looked forward to seeing her at Cannes. She was renowned for her beauty and her talent, and had won the 1955 Oscar for the best performance by an actress. But there was more to her than that: behind the charming smile was a person with real character. Was she not already a legend in Hollywood?

The daughter of a wealthy building-contractor in Philadelphia, of Irish descent, she had chosen a career in the theatre and cinema, and had perseveringly worked her way to the top. She had just caused a great surprise in the film world by her triumph as a young heroine over the vamp. She always dressed with a quiet, distinguished elegance, and had been voted one of the ten best-dressed women in the world; this film-star was a young lady, a great lady. . . .

Before leaving the French Riviera, Grace Kelly took a fancy to visit the Principality of Monaco. Not Monte Carlo—but the Rock and its palace. On May 6th, wearing a flowered dress and with her fair hair severely drawn back into a chignon covered with little white flowers, she entered the palace grounds saluted by the sentry. The sky was deep blue, and the old stone walls were glowing yellow in the strong sunlight; the ancient fortress suddenly took on a festive air. Grace Kelly briskly crossed the main courtyard and went up the horseshoe steps into the palace, to reach the gallery named after Hercule Grimaldi and the state apartments. On the right of the ante-room, through artfully placed mirrors, could be seen the red drawing-room, the York bedroom, the yellow drawing-room and, right at the end, a charming Louis Quinze bedroom hung with Alsatian flowered prints and containing Pompadour rose-coloured furniture. Near the window was a large double mirror with the initials of Marie de Lorraine; in front of it stood a small chair of tooled leather. Grace Kelly sat down; with the mirror reflecting her elegance, she gazed out at the beautiful but deserted private gardens.

To the left of the ante-room with its mirrors was the Salle des Gardes, then the blue drawing-room. Grace Kelly was con-templating the portrait of Marie Leczinska when the doors opened and a man's step was heard. Rainier III came forward, his eyes smiling behind his sunglasses. She gave an American bob, and they shook hands. Together they strolled through the rooms and out into the open, a young couple who already seemed happy and confident.

Grace Kelly had gone up the steps of the palace alone, she came down them accompanied by the Prince. Together they visited the gardens and walked round the ramparts, which give a view of the whole Principality. The walk ended in the Tropical Gardens. They had both suddenly become serious and rather thoughtful.

On December 8th of that year, Rainier III embarked at Le Havre for a private visit to the United States. It was known that he wanted to go fishing for barracuda off Florida, but the fact of his chaplain, Father Francis Tucker, an American, being with him indicated some other motive for his journey. At the age of thirty-two, the descendant of the Grimaldis was crossing the element which had always served them so well; Albert I had renewed alliance with it, Rainier III was setting out on it not to seek fresh worlds but to seek happiness.

Since that brief day in May, the Prince had been more aware of his solitary state and had gone more often to spend the evening with his chaplain and confidant. The latter had encouraged him in his inclination to give to the Principality a beautiful Princess who was a devout Roman Catholic, and in all probability fine children too, in whom would be combined Latin and Celtic blood, tradition and progress. In an age of radio, secrets are soon broadcast; and when Rainier III landed at New York, the newspapers greeted him as the last absolute ruler in Europe and gave a visit to Philadelphia as one of the reasons for his journey.

It was well known at Monaco that the palace Christmas Tree was a tradition dear to the Prince's heart. So when it was learnt that he would be away from the Principality for Christmas, the Monagasques expected some special news from him. At nine-thirty on the evening of December 24th, Radio Monte Carlo re-transmitted Rainier III's Christmas message from the United States. He spoke of his delight in visiting America and his pleasure at finding that the Principality was 'known and loved here.' He ended: 'May this Christmas festival, which is the festival of hope, have for you—as it has for me—a message of firm confidence in the future of the Principality. May the Principality grow more beautiful and prosperous in an atmosphere of peace and concord. May the coming year wipe out past errors and may God continue to show us His favours in guiding and protecting us in 1956 as He has in the past.'

Pleased at having heard their Prince's voice but nevertheless rather disappointed, the Monagasques switched off their sets. Still, Rainier III was prolonging his stay in the United States, and he and Grace Kelly were always seen about together in New York.

On the evening of January 4th they were at the Stork Club. When they left they were surrounded by reporters. Grace Kelly smilingly replied to their questions: 'Nothing to say—yet.' This was a skilful evasion to protect their last precious hours of privacy. The following evening, the American public and the Principality learnt that the engagement of the Prince and the film-star had just been celebrated at a family lunch at Philadelphia.

Monaco was in a ferment on April 12th, 1956, for the beginning of a triumphal week; a ferment greatly increased by the presence of 1,800 reporters and Press photographers. Grace Kelly was to arrive that morning on the liner *Constitution*, on which she had embarked eight days previously, giving a dazzling smile as the cameras flashed around her.

The *Constitution* put in at Cannes and landed the future Princess's luggage—two whole lorry-loads. Meanwhile, Rainier III was pacing nervously up and down the bridge of the *Deo Juvante*, his white yacht with a red funnel, the Grimaldi colours. At ten o'clock, the yacht set sail to meet the big steamer. Among the waiting crowds along the quaysides there were perhaps some Monagasques thinking of an earlier Prince of Monaco who, two centuries ago, had waited eight days until a bridge was made for his fair young bride from Genoa to disembark.

Rain and strong winds had been forecast the evening before; but now the *mistral* had dropped, though there was still a swell on the Mediterranean which made it difficult for the yacht to come alongside the ship. For half an hour the two vessels dipped and rolled, surrounded by gaily beflagged boats and launches, while three helicopters circled around and three aeroplanes zoomed overhead. At last, Grace Kelly came down the flower-carpeted gangway, while thousands of red carnations thrown from the decks of the *Constitution* fluttered down to the waves; and then the sun broke through the clouds.

Along the quaysides, the crowds had been waiting patiently for hours. Suddenly there came the booming of the palace guns and the hooting of sirens—the *Deo Juvante* was entering the harbour. The Onassis yacht sent up a fireworks display that spread the Grimaldi blazon across the sky, over the engaged couple. Moving slowly through a throng of beflagged boats, the *Deo Juvante* moored at the foot of the Rock.

At noon Grace Kelly descended the gangway which still separated her from her future realm. A large white organdie hat concealed the emotion on her face; she was wearing a simple navy dress, to which was pinned a spray of mauve orchids, and was carrying Olive, her poodle, in her left arm. At the foot of the gangway two nervous children, a little fisher-boy and a young lemon-picker, held out to her bunches of lilies of the valley—the lilies that bring good fortune.

Blessed the bride that the rain falls on, says a French proverb. It started to rain on April 13th and kept on for three days and nights. It was raining when Grace Kelly fulfilled her first official engagement and presented Marcel Brion, the winner of the Rainier III Literary Prize for 1956, with his cheque for a million francs. It rained on the press photographers waiting for the engaged couple to come out of the Sporting Club on the night of the 15th. But on the 17th the sun made its appearance for the beginning of the ceremonies. The whole world was interested in the happy ending to the most picturesque romance of the half-century; Providence itself seemed thus to mark approval of this union of a Prince and a film-star, which was even more that of a Christian couple.

There were great public rejoicings and a fireworks display in the clear night sky. While up on the Rock, the old yellow houses pressed tightly together were like the fingers of a ghostly hand. In the harbour, the outlines of the many yachts and launches were defined by the bluish floodlighting. From the palace ramparts,

Grace Kelly looked down again upon her realm. Perhaps her mind went back to that spring afternoon, just a year ago. . . .

The civil marriage ceremony was held in the throne room, at eleven in the morning of April 18th. Two young people stood rather nervously opposite the high stone chimney-piece on which winged figures support the Grimaldi coat of arms.

'Have I the permission of Your Highness to proceed?' asked Monsieur Marcel Portanier, the President of the Council of State.

The Prince gave his assent.

Grace Kelly then murmured her willingness in a barely audible voice. Rainier III nervously touched his neck with his right hand, then he too made his vow. She turned and looked with emotion at the man who in the eyes of the law had just become her husband.

At ten-thirty-five the next morning, a beautiful young woman, whose serious face was half-hidden by a light tulle veil, walked up the nave of the cathedral on the arm of her father. Then, to the sounds of Purcell's 'Alleluia,' and preceded by Father Tucker and the Bishop of Monaco, Rainier III, in full-dress uniform, came and took his place beside her in front of the altar.

Bossuet, in his day, had reminded Louis XIV and the Court of the vanities of human glory. Monseigneur Barthe, the Bishop of Monaco, also delivered this warning, but added that there was no need to emphasize it to the Prince. Father Carton, a Catholic priest from Philadelphia, spoke in praise of his parishioner; and the Papal Legate, Monseigneur Marella, the Papal Nuncio in Paris, read the letter from the Pope in French and English. Then followed the actual wedding ceremony. For all the microphones and amplifiers, no one heard Princess Grace say 'Yes.' But T.V. viewers just saw her lips move.

Rainier III placed the ring on his wife's finger, and she started to put his on for him. But it stuck, and the Prince pushed it down himself; but not entirely. He held out his hand to the Princess who smilingly pushed it the rest of the way. The couple sat down and looked at each other. He clasped his hands, while tears welled up in her eyes. This was their moment. Two human beings, far removed from pomp and ceremony, gave their promise for better or for worse, facing their lot together.

A few hours later, a white yacht with a red funnel sailed out of the harbour amidst the din of sirens; while two rockets with parachutes linked the American flag and the Monagasque standard high in the sky. Standing in the bows of the vessel, Rainier III and Princess Grace of Monaco were facing the open sea and happiness.

Two years later to the very day, the Monagasques assembled in the main courtyard of the palace, the courtyard which had held so many general assemblies, and where at grave moments in the past the very heart of Monaco had seemed to beat, stressing the close link between Prince and people. In that courtyard there have been solemn scenes, and anguished ones on occasion; but on this glorious spring day there was a happy, glad sight—a new shoot had appeared on the ancient tree of the Grimaldis.

A man and a woman, each holding a child, appeared beneath the Hercule gallery and stood at the head of the steps. Rainier III held the year-old Caroline close to him; Princess Grace presented to the crowd a placid month-old baby, Albert-Alexandre-Louis-Pierre Grimaldi, Marquis des Baux, the tiny heir to the oldest reigning dynasty in Europe.

Caroline, named after the wise Princess who, in the previous century, had made a happy family of the Grimaldis; Albert, named after the learned Prince who had traced such a brilliant path for his heirs to follow. The choice of these names is both a witness and a promise.

Deo Juvante

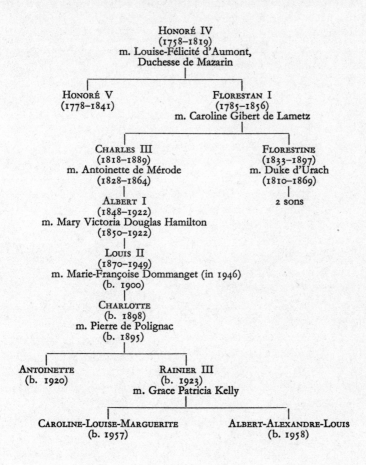

HONORÉ IV
(1758–1819)
m. Louise-Félicité d'Aumont,
Duchesse de Mazarin

HONORÉ V
(1778–1841)

FLORESTAN I
(1785–1856)
m. Caroline Gibert de Lametz

CHARLES III
(1818–1889)
m. Antoinette de Mérode
(1828–1864)

FLORESTINE
(1833–1897)
m. Duke d'Urach
(1810–1869)

ALBERT I
(1848–1922)
m. Mary Victoria Douglas Hamilton
(1850–1922)

2 sons

LOUIS II
(1870–1949)
m. Marie-Françoise Dommanget (in 1946)
(b. 1900)

CHARLOTTE
(b. 1898)
m. Pierre de Polignac
(b. 1895)

ANTOINETTE
(b. 1920)

RAINIER III
(b. 1923)
m. Grace Patricia Kelly

CAROLINE-LOUISE-MARGUERITE
(b. 1957)

ALBERT-ALEXANDRE-LOUIS
(b. 1958)

MAIN EVENTS IN THE HISTORY OF THE
PRINCES OF MONACO

1297 Capture of the fortress of Monaco by François Grimaldi the Spiteful.

1301 Monaco abandoned by the Grimaldi family and the Genoese Guelphs.

1304 Rainier I, commanding French land and sea forces, inflicts a crushing defeat on the Flemings at Zierikzee. He is made a Grand Admiral of France.

1331 Charles I recovers Monaco.

1357 His son, Rainier II, loses Monaco.

1419 Jean I and his brothers Ambroise and Antoine successfully petition Queen Yolande of Aragón for the return of the Rock and fortress to the Grimaldis.

1427 Jean I becomes sole ruler of Monaco.

1428 He sells out to Philippe-Marie Visconti, Duke of Milan.

1431 Commanding a Milanese river-fleet, Jean I defeats the Venetians near Cremona.

1436 Jean I recovers Monaco.

1448 He cedes the suzerainty of Menton and Roquebrune to Savoy.

1462 Louis XI of France recognizes Monaco's right to sea-tribute.

1465 Lambert Grimaldi marries Claudine Grimaldi.

1477 Treaty of Alliance with Milan.

1489   Charles VIII of France grants letters of safe-conduct and protection to Lambert Grimaldi.

1500   Jean II nominated Governor of Ventimiglia.

1505   He is assassinated by his brother Lucien.

1506–1507   Genoese forces besiege Monaco.

1509   Treaty of Alliance and perpetual friendship signed with France.

1514   Claudine Grimaldi's Will and Testament establishes the rights and conditions of succession.

1516   Proclamation of the Statutes of Menton by Lucien Grimaldi.

1523   Barthélemy Doria assassinates his uncle Lucien.

1524   By the Treaties of Burgos and Tordesillas, Monaco becomes a Spanish protectorate.

1529   The Emperor Charles V visits Monaco.

1534   Etienne Grimaldi, the Gubernant, becomes the adopted father of Honoré I.

1561   Death of the Gubernant.

1605   A new agreement extends the scope of Spain's protectorate over Monaco.

1612   Honoré II assumes the title of Prince.

1631   The plague appears in Monaco and wipes out a third of the population.

1641   By the Treaty of Péronne, Monaco becomes a French protectorate again.

1642   The Prince of Monaco is received by Louis XIII at Perpignan and is created Duke of Valentinois.

1663   Louis I and his wife, Catherine-Charlotte de Gramont, found the Convent of the Visitation at Monaco.

1666   Louis I distinguishes himself in a naval battle against the English off Dunkirk.

1678   Promulgation of the Statutes of Monaco, known as the *Code Louis*.

1688   Antoine Grimaldi marries Marie de Lorraine, and the hereditary rank of foreign prince is conferred upon him by Louis XIV.

1692   Antoine Grimaldi wounded at the battle of Namur.

1697   Birth of Louise-Hippolyte, and of the Chevalier de Grimaldi.

1698   Louis XIV appoints Louis Grimaldi his Ambassador-Extraordinary to the Holy See.

1699   Louis Grimaldi arrives in Rome to take up his appointment.

1701   Louis Grimaldi dies in Rome. Antoine I succeeds him and begins an almost continuous residence of thirty years in Monaco.

1707–1714   Antoine I improves and strengthens the fortifications of the Rock.

1715   Louise-Hippolyte is married to Jacques de Matignon.

1731   Death of Antoine I, followed by that of his daughter, Louise-Hippolyte. Jacques de Matignon becomes Jacques I of Monaco.

1732   The Chevalier de Grimaldi, a natural son of Antoine I, is appointed governor-general of Monaco by Jacques I and begins fifty years of administrative rule.

1733   Jacques I abdicates in favour of his son.

1734   Honoré III receives oath of loyalty from his subjects. He leaves Monaco, and remains absent until 1749.

1750   Honoré III meets the Marquise de Brignole-Sale.

1757   He marries her daughter, Marie-Catherine.

1767   The Duke of York, brother of George III, dies at Monaco.

1770–1771   Proceedings for legal separation of Honoré III and Marie-Catherine de Brignole.

1793   France annexes the Principality of Monaco.

1798   Honoré-Gabriel, the future Honoré V, enlists in a cavalry regiment.

1800   He is wounded at the battle of Hohenlinden.

1804   The Grimaldi family sell the Matignon mansion in Paris.

1806   Thorigny estate sold.

1814   The Principality is returned to the Grimaldis.

1815   In March, Honoré-Gabriel reaches Monaco and takes possession.
       In November, by the second Treaty of Paris, Monaco becomes a Protectorate of the Kingdom of Sardinia.

1816   Homage made to the House of Savoy for Menton and Roquebrune.
       Florestan Grimaldi marries Caroline Gibert.

1817   The Treaty of Stupinigi determines the form of the Protectorate.

1846   Florestan's son, the future Charles III, marries Antoinette de Mérode. They visit the Principality and receive a warm welcome at Menton.

1847   Pope Pius IX institutes liberal reforms, and the King of Sardinia follows suit. The people of Menton demand similar reforms.

1848   Leading citizens of Menton and Roquebrune set up a provisional governing body and declare their towns to be free territory. Florestan I delegates his powers to his son Charles.

1849   The Sardinian government proclaims Menton and Roquebrune part of the Kingdom of Sardinia.

1854   Charles III visits Menton.
       Purchase of the Marchais estate.

1856   The first gaming concession is signed.

1858   Charles III's son, Albert, lays the foundation stone of the Casino des Spélugues.
       The Order of St Charles is created.

1860   Savoy and the county of Nice are united to France, and as a result Menton and Roquebrune are too.

1861 France renounces the protectorate over Monaco, and agrees to pay an indemnity of four million francs for the Principality's loss of Menton and Roquebrune.

1863 François Blanc acquires the gaming concession.

1864 Death of Antoinette de Mérode.

1865 A commercial treaty establishes a customs union between the Principality and France.

1866 Charles III names Monte Carlo.
      Albert Grimaldi joins the Spanish Navy.

1868 Charles III obtains ecclesiastical autonomy for Monaco.
      Opening of the railway line between Nice and Menton.

1869 Rates and taxes suppressed in the Principality.

1879 Opening of the theatre built by Charles Garnier at Monte Carlo.
      Death of Princess Caroline.

1885 First postage stamps issued, bearing the head of Charles III.
      Albert sets off on the first of his scientific voyages.

1887 A Papal Bull creates the diocese of Monaco.

1898 An agreement signed with Camille Blanc extends the gaming concession for fifty years.

1899 The foundation stone of the Oceanic Museum is laid.

1901 Work begun on improving the harbour.

1902 The Museum of Human Palæontology is opened.

1903 Albert I founds an International Peace Institute.

1906 The Institute of Oceanography is founded.

1909 Election of Albert I to the Royal Society.

1910 The Institute of Human Palæontology is founded.
      Universal suffrage granted to the people of Monaco, and a Constitution is promised them.

1911 Constitution proclaimed

1914   Constitution suspended on outbreak of World War I.

1917   Constitution re-established.

1918   A new Treaty is concluded with France.

1921   Building of International Hydrographic Centre is begun.

1929   Monte Carlo Grand Prix first held.

1935   Company running the Casino in difficulties.

1936   Department for the issuing of postage stamps is set up by Louis II.

1944   Princess Caroline renounces her rights to the succession in favour of her son, Rainier.

1950   Rainier III founds an annual Literary Prize.

1956   Wedding of Rainier III to Grace Patricia Kelly.

1958   Birth of Albert Grimaldi, Marquis des Baux.

BIBLIOGRAPHY

MANUSCRIPT SOURCES

Archives at the Palace of Monaco.
Archives of the Foreign Ministry, Paris.
Archives of the War Ministry, Paris.
Condé Archives, Château de Chantilly.
National Archives, Paris.

PUBLISHED WORKS

Historical documents published by command of the Princes of Monaco
Historical documents on the rulers of Monaco and the House of
 Grimaldi before the fifteenth century. (*Monaco, 1905*)
Historical documents on the Principality of Monaco (1412–1641), 3
 volumes. (*Monaco, 1888–1891*)
Letters from Marshal de Tessé to Prince Antoine I of Monaco. (*Monaco
 and Paris, 1911*)

Works of Prince Albert I of Monaco
La guerre allemande et la conscience universelle. (*Paris, 1919*)

Memoirs and letters
Apponyi: Journal du Comte Rodolphe Apponyi, 4 volumes. (*Paris,
 1913–1926*)
Baroche, Mme Jules: Second Empire, Notes et souvenirs. (*Paris, 1921*)
Bülow: Mémoires du chancelier prince de Bülow (1894–1919), 4
 volumes. (*Paris, 1930*)
Bussy-Rabutin: Mémoires, 2 volumes (*Paris, 1857*), correspondence
 (1666–1693), 6 volumes. (*Paris, 1858–1859*)
Dangeau, Marquis de: Journal, 19 volumes. (*Paris, 1854–1860*)
Feuilles d'histoire (1913 – IX).
Gramont: Mémoires du Comte de Gramont. (*Paris, 1866*)
Hübner, Comte de: Neuf ans de souvenirs d'un ambassadeur d'Autriche
 à Paris, 2 volumes. (*Paris, 1908*)
La Fare: Mémoires. (*Paris, 1839*)
La Fayette, Mme de: Mémoires. (*Paris, 1839*)
Lennox, Lady Sarah: Life and letters of Sarah Lennox (1745–1826),
 2 volumes. (*London, 1901*)
Marchand: Mémoires de Marchand premier valet de chambre et
 exécuteur testamentaire de l'Empereur, tome I. (*Paris, 1930*)

Motteville, Mme de: Mémoires, 4 volumes. (*Paris, 1855*)

Northumberland: Diaries of a Duchess (1716–1776), edited by James Grieg. (*London, 1926*)

Orléans: Correspondence complète de Madame, duchesse d'Orléans, 2 volumes. (*Paris, 1857*)

Radziwill: Lettres de la princesse Radziwill au général de Robilant (1889–1914), 4 volumes. (*Paris, 1934*)

Saint-Evremond: Oeuvres (Correspondence tome III), 3 volumes. (*Paris, 1863*)

Saint-Simon: Mémoires.

Sévigné, Mme de: Lettres, 14 volumes. (*Paris, 1862–1866*)

Other works on the Grimaldi Family and Monaco

Chevalier, Jules: Mémoires pour servir à l'histoire des comtes de Valentinois tome II. (*Paris, 1906*)

Graves, Charles: Gros jeu. Histoire secrète de Monte Carlo. (*Paris, 1953*)

Labande, Leon-Honoré: Histoire de la principauté de Monaco. (*Paris, 1934.*) Expedition de Jean Ier Grimaldi, seigneur de Monaco a Constantinople (1437). (*Monaco, 1908.*) Inventaires de Palais de Monaco (1604–1731). (*Monaco, 1918*)

Lacoste, Roger: La politique à Monaco. (*Paris, 1911*)

Lamboglio, Nino: Le rôle historique de la principauté de Monaco. (*Bordighera, 1918*)

Mantero de Suiramay: Monaco de 1909 à 1915. (*Nice, 1916*)

Monaco, ses princes et ses princesses. (*Paris, 1956*)

Monaco, dans sa splendeur. (*1956*)

Ollivier, Gabriel: Portus Herculis Monoeci. (*Monaco, s.d.*)

Saige, Gustave: La seigneurie de Monaco au milieu du XVI° siècle et jusqu' au milieu du siècle suivant. (*Monaco, 1892.*) Monaco, ses origins et son histoire. (*Monaco, 1897.*) Glanes d'archives: les Grimaldi chez eux et en voyage. (*Monaco, 1906*)

Smith, Adolphe: Monaco and Monte Carlo.

Miscellaneous sources of reference

Astraudo, duc de: Les petits Etâts de l'Europe. (*Nice, 1942*)

Fitzgerald, Percy: The Royal Dukes and Princesses of the Family of George III, 2 volumes.

Jesse, J. Heneage: Memoirs of the life and reign of King George III, 3 volumes. (*London, 1867*)

La Force, duc de: Lauzun un courtisan du grand roi. (*Paris, 1946*)

La Roncière: Histoire de la marine française, 5 volumes. (*Paris, 1899–1920*)

Saint-René Tallandier, Mme: La princesse des Ursins. (*Paris, 1926*)

Segur, Marquis Pierre de: La dernière des Condé. (*Paris, 1899*)

INDEX